Dutch Translation in Pra<

Dutch Translation in Practice provides an accessible and engaging course in modern Dutch translation. Taking a highly practical approach, it introduces students to the essential concepts of translation studies, heightens their awareness of the problems posed in Dutch translation, and teaches them how to tackle these difficulties successfully. Featured texts have been carefully chosen for their thematic and technical relevance, and a wide range of discursive and grammatical issues are covered throughout.

Features include:

- nine chapters reflecting different areas of contemporary life and culture in Belgium and the Netherlands such as people and places, Dutch language and culture, literature, employment, finance and economics, media and communications, art history and exhibitions, fashion and design, and the Earth, energy and the environment
- authentic extracts drawn from up-to-date Dutch texts used throughout to illustrate and practise various topical and translation issues, with many supporting exercises and open translation activities to encourage active engagement with the material, the development of strong translation skills and vocabulary acquisition
- chapters structured to provide progressive learning, moving from an introductory section explaining the context for the texts to be translated to information on translation techniques, and detailed close readings and analyses of words, phrases, style, register and tone
- a strong focus throughout on addressing issues relevant to contemporary Dutch translation, with practical tips offered for translating websites, dealing with names, and handling statistics and numbers in translation
- attention to language areas of particular difficulty, including translating 'er', passive constructions, punctuation, conjunctions and separable verbs
- helpful list of grammatical terms, information on useful resources for translators and sample translations of texts available at the back of the book.

Written by experienced instructors and extensively trialled at University College London, *Dutch Translation in Practice* will be an essential resource for students on upper-level undergraduate, postgraduate or professional courses in Dutch and Translation Studies.

Jane Fenoulhet is Professor of Dutch Studies at University College London.

Alison E. Martin is Lecturer in German Studies at the University of Reading, UK.

Dutch Translation in Practice

Jane Fenoulhet and Alison E. Martin

LONDON AND NEW YORK

First published 2015
by Routledge
2 Park Square, Milton Park, Abingdon, Oxon OX14 4RN

Simultaneously published in the USA and Canada
by Routledge
711 Third Avenue, New York, NY 10017

Routledge is an imprint of the Taylor & Francis Group, an informa business

© 2015 Jane Fenoulhet and Alison E. Martin

The right of Jane Fenoulhet and Alison E. Martin to be identified as authors of this work has been asserted by them in accordance with sections 77 and 78 of the Copyright, Designs and Patents Act 1988.

All rights reserved. No part of this book may be reprinted or reproduced or utilised in any form or by any electronic, mechanical, or other means, now known or hereafter invented, including photocopying and recording, or in any information storage or retrieval system, without permission in writing from the publishers.

Trademark notice: Product or corporate names may be trademarks or registered trademarks, and are used only for identification and explanation without intent to infringe.

British Library Cataloguing in Publication Data
A catalogue record for this book is available from the British Library

Library of Congress Cataloging in Publication Data
A catalog record for this book has been requested

ISBN: 978-0-415-67237-5 (hbk)
ISBN: 978-0-415-67238-2 (pbk)
ISBN: 978-1-315-74553-4 (ebk)

Typeset in Times New Roman
by Swales & Willis Ltd, Exeter, Devon, UK

Printed and bound in Great Britain by
TJ International Ltd, Padstow, Cornwall

Contents

	Acknowledgements	vi
	Introduction: getting started	1
1	People and places *Practical tips: translating for websites*	8
2	Dutch language and culture *Practical tips: dealing with names in translation*	24
3	Literature *Practical tips: translating* er	43
4	Employment *Practical tips: translating the indefinite pronouns* men, je *and* ze	59
5	Finance and economics *Practical tips: dealing with statistics and numbers in translation*	78
6	Media and communications *Practical tips: translating separable verbs*	96
7	Art history and exhibitions *Practical tips: passive constructions*	112
8	Fashion and design *Practical tips: punctuation*	131
9	The Earth, energy and the environment *Practical tips: conjunctions*	150
	Conclusion: revising your translation	169
	List of grammatical terms	176
	Useful resources for translators	179
	Sample translations of third texts	181
	Index	188

Acknowledgements

The questions that we address in this book derive from our teaching of translation in a variety of different contexts over a number of years. We wish to thank our students for their insightful questions and observations, which have enabled us to refine the ways in which we reflect on the translation process and on teaching translation at undergraduate and postgraduate level.

In the process of putting this book together, we have received help from a variety of different people, whose assistance we are most happy to acknowledge here. Our two anonymous reviewers for Routledge provided swift and detailed feedback which offered a fresh perspective on the book as a whole and enabled us to refine some aspects of the project. Our Senior Editorial Assistant at Routledge, Isabelle Cheng, has provided sound advice throughout and dealt enthusiastically with even the most trivial of queries. In the final stages our Production Editor, Geraldine Martin, and Caroline Watson, who oversaw the copy-editing, typesetting and proofreading, ensured that the project headed smoothly towards completion. Alison E. Martin would like to thank Kris Steyaert for his expert help with queries that arose in the course of the chapters she wrote. The authors wish to thank each other for the most congenial of collaborations. Finally, both authors would like to thank Elisabeth Salverda most warmly for her extremely careful, thorough and professional proof-reading of a first draft of the book and for producing the index to *Dutch Translation in Practice*.

JF and AEM

The authors and publishers would like to thank the rights holders for permission to include extracts from the following sources.

Onno Kosters, *Alles en niets*, citybooks Utrecht, 2010. citybooks is an initiative of the Vlaams-Nederlands Huis deBuren. citybooks are multimedia city portraits by international authors and artists. The stories, essays and poems are available in Dutch, English and French as web text, e-book and audiobook free of charge from www.citybooks.eu.

http://www.antwerpen.be/eCache/ABE/4/762.Y29udGV4dD04MDM0MDMQ4.html

Bobby Roeplall, GFC Nieuws, Paramaribo. Linked from Nederlandse Taalunie website (accessed 13 July 2013) by GFC Nieuws, http://www.gfcnieuws.com/?p=176410.

Abedelkader Benali, *Laat het morgen mooi weer zijn* (Amsterdam/Antwerp: Arbeiderspers, 2005), p. 153.

Margot Vanderstraeten, *Mise en Place* (Amsterdam/Antwerp: Atlas, 2009), p. 33.

Abdelkader Benali, *De stem van mijn moeder* (Amsterdam/Antwerp: Arbeiderspers, 2009) pp. 13–14.

L. Lembrechts, 'Discriminatie op de werkvloer: een onderzoek naar de ervaringen van zwangere werkneemsters in België', *Over.Werk. Tijdschrift van het Steunpunt WSE*, 22(1) (Leuven: Steunpunt Werk en Sociale Economie/Uitgeverij Acco, 2012), pp. 30–35, p. 30.

Stichting Nederland Maritiem Land, Monitor Maritieme Arbeidsmarkt 2006 (Amsterdam: IOS Press BV, 2007), p. 16.

Federaal Planbureau, Brussels, http://www.plan.be/press/communique-837-nl-64-67-regionale+economische+vooruitzichten+2008+2014 (accessed 29 November 2013).

Stichting Nederland Maritiem Land, Monitor Maritieme Arbeidsmarkt 2006 (Amsterdam: IOS Press BV, 2007), p. 18.

Vivien Waszink and Marc van Oostendorp, 'Veranderen nieuwe media de taal?', in *Taalcanon*, 2012, http://www.taalcanon.nl/themas/maken (accessed 15 April 2014).

While every effort has been made to contact copyright holders, we would be grateful to hear from any we were unable to reach.

Introduction
Getting started

A TEXTBOOK FOR LEARNER-TRANSLATORS FROM DUTCH INTO ENGLISH
Mobile texts: the inspiration for this textbook

This textbook takes as its basis a course in advanced translation from Dutch into English that has run for many years and in different guises at University College London. It is the case that in recent years the ways of teaching translation have changed in response to a number of important shifts that are being felt throughout the field of Dutch Studies as taught at universities around the world. In fact, the *Nederlandse Taalunie* (Dutch Language Union in English), the intergovernmental treaty organisation overseeing all matters to do with the Dutch language, is in the process of implementing a policy that aims to internationalise Dutch Studies and encourage transnational and intercultural approaches. Furthermore, the *Nederlandse Taalunie* (NTU) supports a centre of expertise in literary translation – the *Expertisecentrum Literair Vertalen* (http://literairvertalen.org/) – which was originally established to professionalise translators of literature into Dutch, but which is now seeking links with universities outside the Netherlands who translate in the other direction. In short, there is a new climate of interest in translators and translation.

Three important processes underlie this revolution: globalisation; EU enlargement and the European Commission's *New Framework Strategy for Multilingualism* (2005); and student mobility and multilingualism. It is these three processes that also brought about a rethink of the advanced translation course. Cutting across all three of these processes is the recent profile of Dutch as the native language of 23 million people around the globe. In fact, Dutch is an official language not only in the Netherlands and Belgium but also in Suriname, Aruba, Curaçao and Sint Maarten, while its daughter language, Afrikaans, is spoken by around 6 million in South Africa and Namibia (Willemyns, 2013).

In the field of translation, the development of global English has led us to reflect on the importance of the local (Fenoulhet and Ros i Solé, 2010) while accepting the role of global English. Linked to this is the importance of digital technologies and social media, which are not just instruments for the promulgation of a global variety of English, since they also actively assist in its fragmentation as well. For translators into English, a hyperawareness of the audience for and purpose of a translation is essential, along with a willingness to entertain multiple new versions of a target text.

In the context of Europe, it is not too far-fetched to view the Dutch language as a local language as well as one that has its own global reach. It is important for the standing of Dutch-language culture in an enlarged Europe that its writers are read in the other European countries. Not only the English-speaking countries of the Republic of Ireland and the UK benefit from literary translation into English: it has the added advantage of making Dutch writers more widely available to publishing houses in any language. All the indications are that literary translation is gaining in importance in the European context, and that literary translators are becoming better organised, as the recent PETRA recommendations demonstrate (Buekenhout and Vonck, 2012). This is one of the reasons why translating literature forms part of this textbook.

From this brief sketch of significant changes in the learning context, it is clear that teaching and learning take place in an environment in which borders are now there to be crossed and intercultural skills are highly valued, and it is important that the field of Dutch Studies responds with new teaching and learning materials that take into account new attitudes to languages and to the role of translation in our complex world.

Who is translating what, and how?

The student population in London – as in other major cities and universities around the world – has changed dramatically in the last decade so that there is no longer a 'standard' student profile. Once, that profile was a native speaker of English learning Dutch, usually from scratch, with an occasional Dutch speaker long resident in the UK. We can no longer assume that students are native English speakers, though they will be highly competent academic users of the language, and their linguistic backgrounds tend to be EU languages, Russian or one of the home languages spoken in the UK. It could be said, therefore, that the paradigm of translation from the foreign language into the mother tongue is no longer useful, and needs to be replaced by one based on knowledge of, competence in and affinity for the two languages and cultures involved in an act of translation. Although our course involves translation in one direction only, from Dutch into English, the techniques and processes are transferable to other languages. And it is clear that the changes we have experienced in London are happening in most cities in the UK and beyond. In order to make this textbook relevant for the coming years, we adopt this new model of the language learner.

Such a fundamental shift brings with it a number of accompanying shifts of emphasis – for example, towards viewing the act of translation as a form of close reading, or towards translating as (re)writing in English. We do not work on the basis of an imagined perfect translation compared to which all attempts at translation fall short, but on the understanding that texts will need different versions for different media and audiences, and we welcome multiple versions because new translations highlight new aspects of a source text. That is why we have chosen to end each chapter with an open translation exercise. This is not to say that anything goes. Far from it: our students learn to explain and document their strategy for a particular piece and must always be able to justify the decisions they take. This book also encourages good habits with the open translation exercise by prompting application of the strategies explained in the book, accompanied by reflection on decisions and choices. At the back of the book, students will find an example of an English translation of each open exercise text. This is for the purpose of comparison and further reflection, and should not be taken as *the* correct version.

To learner-translators and their teachers

When planning this textbook, we have taken the new world of translation into account, but have not attempted to reproduce the course as taught at UCL. The chapters do not represent classroom sessions. Instead, we have tried to construct a series of engagements with different types of text that can either be used in class or that you, the student, can work through on your own, perhaps preparing for a translation course at a higher level. At the same time, it is possible to base a translation class on one of our translation passages, which have been tried and tested in the classroom during the process of writing this book.

First of all, then, how can we best describe the level of this book, and which learner-translators does it have in mind? Broadly speaking, we are thinking of a student in higher education who has been studying Dutch for at least two years – that is, who has reached the final year of a bachelor's degree, or is working at a similar level on a master's course. In terms of the Common European Framework of Reference for Languages, this book is suitable for all those at level C, and there may always be some of you at the upper end of level B who can benefit from using it, too. You will need to be highly proficient in English or have near-native competence. However, this can only be a general guide, because a student who is already an experienced language learner when taking up Dutch might well find the book useful at an earlier stage. If your purpose is self-study, then a 'try it and see' approach is a good way of deciding when to start with translation practice at this advanced level.

How the book is structured

The nine chapters each reflect a different area of contemporary life and culture in Flanders (Belgium) and the Netherlands where there is a need for translation into English. Our list is not exhaustive, and the picture is constantly changing. We chose these topics because of what we know from former students now working in the field, and from our own experiences and contacts. It is important to note that we use authentic texts for translation and have not adapted them. This is because we see translation partly as a problem-solving activity and start from the idea that there are always ways of making a Dutch text accessible to an English readership. You may find that the texts vary in difficulty; this is partly to do with how they are written, and partly to do with students' own linguistic and cultural background.

Because of this, it has not been possible to build in a smooth progression towards greater complexity in the texts for translation. However, in the earlier chapters, we provide a commentary on the text for translation, which contains more help and explanations, and also refers you to relevant topics elsewhere in the book.

One question you might ask is whether it is possible to dip in and out of the different chapters or whether it is advisable to work through the chapters in order. We have tried to arrange the book so that both ways will produce a satisfactory learning experience. However, we advise all students to start with Chapter 1. To assist those who wish to dip in and out, we have included at the back of the book a list of grammatical terms found throughout the text. You will also find certain topics explained in more detail in the Practical Tips sections present in each chapter – these are listed in the table of contents, so you can consult them as needed. Also, a list of useful resources and an index are included at the end of the book.

Each chapter has the same format so that you will know what to expect. This removes the uncertainty that might otherwise distract you from the main focus, which is on particular aspects of translation from Dutch into English selected for that chapter, and on the sample texts for translation. We start each chapter with an introduction explaining the contexts for the two texts to be translated, and linking them to particular translation issues and sources of information. Following each Dutch text, we explore all the aspects of translation relevant for that particular text under the following headings: translation strategies and techniques; text and language (divided into a section on words and phrases, and a section on sentence analysis); style, register and tone. In addition, Chapter 1 includes a discussion of the first draft and how to improve it. Once we have highlighted selected aspects of the translation we show you how they feature in the text and explain how to deal with them when translating. Only after we have repeated this process with all the chosen key points do we expect you to translate the whole text.

Each chapter contains three Dutch texts on related topics: two are presented in the manner just described, while the third is simply for students to put into practice what they have learned in the chapter. We know that translators work in many different ways depending on their personal attributes, such as learning style, so as you progress through the book, try to become aware of what suits you best. Do you prefer to plunge in and produce a very rough translation, almost as a way of reading the text closely? Or do you like to analyse the text, look up and research vocabulary you don't know? There is no right or wrong way as long as you proceed with awareness. Each chapter contains sample translations of the two main texts for translation. Except where we indicate that a translation is not by us, these sample translations are by the authors of this textbook and are included so that you can compare your solutions to translation problems with our own. Remember that your solution may be just as good as ours, if not better!

Located in between the treatment of Texts 1 and 2 in each chapter you can find the Practical Tips section. This is independent of the discussion of particular texts and deals with a topic in the translation process that we consider particularly important. Some of these topics deal with grammatical questions, particularly where Dutch and English do not have similar structures; others deal with more practical considerations, such as how to approach the translation of names or how to translate texts for websites. Sometimes the emphasis is on source text comprehension, sometimes on target text production. The selection of topics was made in accordance with our experiences as translators and teachers of translation, and aims to provide more in-depth explanations than is possible in the discussion of a specific text. Such is the nature of translation that you are bound to encounter problems we have not tackled, which is why we have included a list of resources for you at the back of the book.

Introducing some basic translation principles and key terms

We have already given a general idea of how we see translation, but to enable you to get started on your first translation here are some important concepts explained.

Translation is much more than the transfer of words from one language into another language. It is a process rather than a specific action, and so embodies a range of operations and a great deal of movement backwards and forwards between two languages and cultures. The **goal of translation** in this book is to produce a text in English that functions effectively for the purpose for which it is required. There are many **translation techniques** that can assist the process of translation, and we suggest these throughout the book, at the points where they are most relevant.

For ease of reference, we use the terms **source text (abbreviated to ST)** to refer to the text that is to be translated, and **target text (TT)** for the resulting text. In our case, the ST is always in Dutch and the TT is always in English.

Whatever your personal translating style, **ST analysis** is a vital component of the **translation process**. You will need to use it to find out what kind of specialist vocabulary the ST contains, and what **research** might need to be undertaken – an important component of the translation process.

If the ST is a **literary text**, this analysis could be more complex since the whole **mode** or **style of writing** is part of the writer's artistry that you will need to reproduce in the TT.

If the ST is a mainly **functional text**, an analysis of its function, layout and **register** (the text's degree of formality, and specialism) will tell you how it functioned in the **source culture**, i.e. in the Netherlands or Flanders. However, it will not necessarily tell you how the text is expected to function in the **target culture**. For example, a policy document designed to guide public spending in the Netherlands will most likely be translated into English purely for information.

The **translation brief** specifies the purpose of a translation in the target culture. In the absence of a translation brief, it is best to invent one for yourself – this has the advantage of ensuring you take a **consistent approach** to the translation task. This book will teach you to develop a **translation strategy** to guide your decision making during the translation process.

As we have just seen, source text analysis involves assessment of the purpose, type and style of a text. A vital part of the process of analysis is **grammatical analysis**. It is not enough to look up words you do not know when trying to work out what a source text is saying: grammatical analysis is the key to understanding how these words relate to one another – that is, to pinpointing precise meaning. To assist you with grammatical analysis, all grammatical terms used in the chapters are listed together with a short explanation at the back of the book.

The question that students most frequently asked is: **How closely should I stick to the source text?** The answer differs depending on whether it is a literary text or a more functional text, and on the use to which the TT will be put, as well as on the target audience. Always aim for accurate comprehension of the ST – you need to know exactly what the ST says and reproduce that in the TT. As a general rule, try also to reproduce the stylistic effects, character portrayal, mood and tone of a literary text. With a functional text, ask yourself how it can best fulfil its purpose in the target culture – e.g. if it is to appear on the web, do you need to break it up into small units? Or, if it contains information about places, have you given the information in language that will enable your readers to google the places or find them on maps?

While you are learning to translate, our recommended approach is that you start by producing a version of the TT that sticks quite closely to the ST – one that is fairly 'faithful', to use traditional terminology – and then revise it. **Revision** is a key part of the translation process: it is only by repeatedly revising and improving your work that you learn to produce good and effective translations. The topic of revision is also dealt with in the conclusion to the book.

Resources

There are so many of these now, and virtually all of them are available via the internet. As a student in higher education, you will probably have access to important dictionaries free of charge via your university library website. There are several Dutch–English translation dictionaries, but remember that if you want to understand the finer points of meaning, the monolingual Dutch dictionary is best. Van Dale is the best-known Dutch publisher of dictionaries and its online resources give access to all the dictionaries a Dutch–English translator needs, including the *Oxford English Dictionary*. Go to http//www.vandale.nl for more information. The main reference dictionary for the Dutch language is the *Groot woordenboek van de Nederlandse taal*, generally known as the *grote Van Dale* or 'big Van Dale'.

The other indispensable resource you will need access to is some kind of grammar book, ideally both a learner's grammar and a reference grammar. *Dutch. An Essential Grammar* by William Z. Shetter and Esther Ham is designed for learners and is also available as an e-book. For reference, there is *Dutch. A Comprehensive Grammar* by Bruce Donaldson or *A Reference Grammar of Dutch* by Carol Fehringer. The largest reference grammar, aimed at a Dutch-speaking audience, is the *Algemene Nederlandse Spraakkunst*, which is now available online. We provide a fuller list of resources at the back of the book.

Bibliography

Bellos, D. (2011) *Is That a Fish in Your Ear? The Amazing Adventure of Translation*. London: Penguin.

Buekenhout, P. and Vonck, B. (eds) (2012) *Towards New Conditions for Literary Translation in Europe. The PETRA Recommendations*. Brussels: EU. Available online at: http://www.petra2011.eu/sites/default/files/the_petra_recommendations_1.pdf (accessed 1 January 2014).

den Boon, T. and Geeraerts, D. (eds) (2005) *Groot woordenboek van de Nederlandse taal*, 14th edn. Utrecht: Van Dale Lexicografie.

Donaldson, B. (2008) *Dutch. A Comprehensive Grammar*, 2nd edn. London: Routledge.

Fehringer, C. (1999) *A Reference Grammar of Dutch*. Cambridge: Cambridge University Press.

Fenoulhet, J. and Ros i Solé, C. (eds) (2010) *Mobility and Localisation in Language Learning. A View from Languages of the Wider World*. Oxford/Bern: Peter Lang.

Haeseryn, W., Romijn, K., Geerts, G., de Rooij, J. and van den Toorn, M.C. (1997) *Algemene Nederlandse Spraakkunst*, 2nd edn. Groningen/Deurne: Nijhoff/Wolters Plantyn. Available online at: http://ans.ruhosting.nl/e-ans/ (accessed 1 January 2014).

Shetter, W.Z. and Ham, E. (2007) *Dutch. An Essential Grammar*, 9th edn. New York and London: Routledge.

Willemyns, R. (2013) *Dutch: Biography of a Language*. Oxford: Oxford University Press.

1 People and places

Introduction: texts and contexts

In this chapter we will be working with the theme of identifiable people and places. The most important area of work for translators that involves specific geographical locations is tourism. These locations will frequently be significant cities, and the museums, galleries and historical buildings in them. The texts chosen for translation in this chapter represent different approaches: one that aims to capture the atmosphere and history of a city and another that aims to use very few words to convey all that is on offer in a new museum. Audiences for tourist material translated into English are many and varied. Those being targeted via the internet may well not be native speakers of English, and you are translating with a screen display in mind. Paper brochures and information sheets may be aimed at more specific audiences: visitors to museums can often choose between materials in a number of languages. Translators of tourist materials require different kinds of knowledge: topographical information will enable them to navigate a place; architectural and historical information will enable them to understand what it is they are seeing; cultural information will help to give them a sense of the rich visual, written and musical culture of Flanders and the Netherlands.

The first text is web-based and was written to introduce a poem about the Dutch city of Utrecht composed by Onno Kosters for the website www.citybooks.eu/. It is a contemporary text, though it also looks back to the history of Utrecht. In a similar way, the second text, which is also taken from a website, introduces the new Museum aan de Stroom in Antwerp, which presents the history of the city. Since both texts deal with real places, it is very important that translators do some preliminary research using the internet. Web-based resources are too numerous to list, and should be approached critically unless they are official websites of institutions. Information should always be cross-checked using more than one source before you include it in your translation. In the case of Utrecht and Antwerp, you should use the municipalities' own websites first: http://www.utrecht.nl/smartsite.dws?id=13353 and http://www.antwerpen.be/. As in the case of Antwerp, not all cities have information available in English, so you can add the official tourist site to see how they refer to themselves in English, for example: http://www.visitantwerpen.be/bze.net?id=1470. Maps are also an important tool of the trade available to all through the internet, so a good translator will make sure that s/he uses names and terms that English-speaking readers will be able to find on a map. In the case of the second text, the actual website of the museum can be used to give you a good sense of the surroundings that are referred to in the text, e.g. *de stad, de stroom, en de haven* – the website makes it clear that we are dealing with a large river and port. Such knowledge subtly informs the way you translate.

As this is the opening chapter, and as all the chapters follow the same model, here is our approach in outline: we break up the translation of our texts in stages. Once you have gained more experience, you may want to develop your own set of actions, which may well be differently structured. The steps we use are as follows.

1   The first stage combines an initial read-through of the text with research and reflection on your target audience.
2   The next stage involves analysis of linguistic features of the text, or word and sentence meaning.
3   The final stage involves an assessment of the style of writing, and the importance of style for the target text and its audience.
4   Produce your first draft of the translation.
5   Read through and revise.

Text 1: *Alles en niets*

The first text in this chapter is best understood in the context of the project of which it is part. It aims to provide web-based literary pieces that are mainly about European cities by a number of European writers, each writing in his or her own language with a translation in English or French. The stories are presented both for listening and reading. The extract below is actually the introduction to a collection of poems inspired by the city of Utrecht.

Alles en niets
To sympathise with the pains of love, you must share in its feelings.
Belle van Zuylen aan James Boswell, 15 juni 1764

'Herinnert ge u dien laatsten avond niet'
sprak ze 'toen ik uw tranen heb ontzien
en zonder meer de wereld achterliet?'
Martinus Nijhoff, *Awater*
                  ('Bij helder weer is de toren vanaf een afstand
                  van vijftig kilometer zichtbaar.')

Alles en niets bestaat uit negen met elkaar verweven gedichten, die zelf telkens uit twee 'hoofdstukken' bestaan: een verhalend gedeelte en een reflectie.
   Rode draad is het ontstaan van het landschap waaruit Utrecht zou verrijzen, en de stichting en ontwikkeling van de stad en haar omgeving. We

(continued)

> *(continued)*
>
> volgen Utrecht vanaf de Romeinse tijd via de storm in de 17e, de liefde in de 18e en de stadsuitbreidingen van 19e eeuw naar het heden. In een visioen wordt ons ook een blik gegund in de toekomst, meer precies het jaar 2108, als de wijk Ondiep een paradijs is geworden en de hoogste wolkenkrabber van Nederland, de Belle van Zuylen, toch gebouwd blijkt te zijn.
>
> Personages in *Alles en niets* zijn de stad zelf en Martinus Nijhoffs Utrechtse held Awater uit het gelijknamige gedicht, gepubliceerd in 1934. Hoofdrollen zijn evenwel weggelegd voor de schrijfster Belle van Zuylen en de Schotse biograaf James Boswell, die elkaar in 1764 in Utrecht leerden kennen. Er ontstond een relatie, waarvan de precieze aard onbekend is gebleven. Uit de correspondentie tussen de twee is evenwel af te leiden dat er in elk geval van Boswells kant van verliefdheid sprake was. Deze werd door Belle van Zuylen (door Boswell ook 'Zélide' genoemd) nooit helemaal beantwoord. *Alles en niets* citeert onder meer uit de briefwisseling tussen de twee en brengt hen in heden, verleden en toekomst tot leven.
>
> Source: Onno Kosters, *Alles en niets*. citybooks 2010. Online at: http://www.citybooks.eu/nl/steden/citybooks/p/detail/alles-en-niets (accessed 18 November 2013).

1. Translation strategies and techniques

Before you start, here is a simple technique you might like to use: if you have access to a scanner or photocopier, make a copy of the text so that you can highlight things, colour code or simply write notes. It helps to engage actively like this with the text you are about to translate. Below are two key questions to help you make a first analysis. The first concerns background knowledge relevant for understanding the text, while the second involves reflection on your target audience.

i. What are the first things that you notice about the text?

- *It looks varied, with a quote, a poem, a line between brackets, and two paragraphs.*
  This suggests that the translation will need to adopt different voices and modes of writing. NB: In this case, we do not expect you to translate the poem, though we have included a previously published translation in the sample translation on page 15.

- *It is describing a poem on the website as well as the city of Utrecht.*
  Research is needed both on Utrecht, depending on how much you already know, and into the rest of the website from which the passage is taken.

- *It mentions three names – Martinus Nijhoff, Belle van Zuylen and James Boswell – as well as the more mysterious Awater.*

People and places 11

Background research improves the confidence with which you approach a translation, so do a search for the names to find out whether they refer to real historical people. Taking the example of Martinus Nijhoff, googling this name produces two rather different results, one of which is the name of a Dutch publishing house and the other of a Dutch poet. The text provides two different kinds of information, which makes it clear that we are dealing with the poet – first of all, his name appears underneath the poetry quotation at the top of the document and, second, in the main part of the text the figure 'Awater' is described as Martinus Nijhoff's *held* ('hero') in the *gedicht* ('poem') of the same name.

ii. What do you know about the target audience for your translation and how will it affect your translation?

Here is another simple technique to help you decide how to pitch your translation – that is, what adjustments to make for your target audience: if you do not have a specific translation brief, e.g. from an agency, it is best to give yourself one. This will guide many of your translation decisions and ensure consistency.

The brief for this particular text is to translate it for a non-Dutch-speaking European audience who have found the citybooks online and would like access to them. In this case, it is worth noting that English will not be everyone's first language. What are the important differences between the source text (ST) audience and the target text (TT) audience? There is one big difference: that the ST audience can be expected to be familiar with Dutch culture and know something about Utrecht, which is an important city in the Low Countries. This means that you must try to imagine yourself in the new reader's position, with the result that you may have to provide additional information for readers less familiar with the source culture. Take the example of *de wijk Ondiep*: your research should have told you that this is a part of the city where there have been riots. This knowledge helps to explain why the writer of the piece might want to imagine that it *een paradijs is geworden*. You could consider adding some background information, perhaps by inserting an adjective to give 'the troubled district of Ondiep' rather than the more neutral 'district of Ondiep'.

2. Text and language

This step is crucial since it determines the accuracy of your translation. You will find a bibliography of reference works, including grammars, at the back of the book.

i. Words and expressions

Go through the text and highlight all the unfamiliar words and all those you recognise but are uncertain about. Here are some examples of tricky words, together with suggestions for approaching them.

Verweven: in the translation dictionary you will find this word given as the infinitive of a verb meaning 'interweave'. However, it behaves more like an adjective in the sense that it appears before *gedichten*. If you look up *verweven* in a Dutch-only dictionary, it should tell you that the past participle has the same form as the infinitive. In other words, *verweven* can also mean 'interwoven'. Remember that there are inseparable prefixes in Dutch that do not form their past participle according to the rule of adding the prefix *ge-*. You can look this up in any reference grammar of Dutch. For example, Fehringer (1999), section 32, or try the link http://ans.ruhosting.nl/e-ans/ to see example 1b in the online Dutch Grammar, *Algemene Nederlandse Spraakkunst*.

Stadsuitbreidingen: this noun looks more alarming than it is. Break it down into its constituent parts and you may not even need to look it up. *Stad+s+uitbreiding+en*. The two lexical elements are *stad*/city and *uitbreiding*/expansion, with the linking element -*s*- and the plural ending -*en*.

Utrechtse: The word occurs in front of the noun *held*, or 'hero', so we can assume it is an adjective, especially since it has the adjectival ending -*e*. The name Utrecht is also visible. What is missing from the analysis so far is the grammatical information which specifies that a place name + -*s* forms an adjective denoting 'from or of the place in question'. Again, you can look this up in a reference grammar, e.g. Fehringer (1999), section 3.1 (d).

ii. Sentences

This brings us to a larger 'unit' of translation: the sentence. Below we analyse a grammatically complex sentence with the aim of helping you to unravel it prior to translating it. Moreover, this will also help to give you a simple technique for dealing with such sentences more generally.

> *In een visioen wordt ons ook een blik gegund in de toekomst, meer precies het jaar 2108, als de wijk Ondiep een paradijs is geworden en de hoogste wolkenkrabber van Nederland, de Belle van Zuylen, toch gebouwd blijkt te zijn.*

This is one example of a long, complex sentence – there are several in this short text. Using brackets is a quick way to identify the components of this kind of sentence. As there are three active verbs, indicated below in underlined type, we would expect to be able to bracket three components.

> (*In een visioen wordt ons ook een blik gegund in de toekomst, meer precies het jaar 2108,*) (*als de wijk Ondiep een paradijs is geworden*) (*en de hoogste wolkenkrabber van Nederland, de Belle van Zuylen, toch gebouwd blijkt te zijn.*)

Component 1 contains a passive verb, i.e. one that is formed from *worden* + past participle of the verb *gunnen*, which translates as 'is granted'. The only possible subject of this verb is the phrase *een blik*, which can be translated as 'a look' or 'a glimpse'. So, translating very closely and literally: 'a look is granted to us' – *ons* – into the future – *in de toekomst*. This still leaves the opening phrase 'in a vision' – *in een visioen* – and the closing phrase 'more precisely the year 2108' – *meer precies het jaar 2108*. As with most complex sentences, the challenge is to rearrange these elements into a sentence that flows well in English while keeping the underlying meaning. One possibility is: 'In a vision we are granted a look into the future, more precisely the year 2108.'

Component 2 is a subclause introduced by *als*, which can be translated as 'if' or 'when'. Since the emphasis here is clearly on time, 'when' is preferable. The verb is *is geworden*: since we are speaking of the distant future 'will have become', and the subject of the sentence is *de wijk Ondiep* – 'the district of Ondiep'. Putting these elements together gives 'when the district of Ondiep will have become', which is completed with 'a paradise' – *een paradijs*: 'when the troubled district of Ondiep has become a paradise'.

There is one word that is implied in Component 3 – that is, it is not explicitly repeated: *als*. We know this because this component also has the subclause word order with the verb at the end: 'and when [. . .] turns out – *blijkt* – to have been built – *gebouwd te zijn*. The middle part of this component, indicated here by [. . .] simply supplies the missing subject: 'the tallest skyscraper in the Netherlands, the Belle van Zuylen'. So the third component can be translated as: 'and when the tallest skyscraper in the Netherlands, the Belle van Zuylen, turns out to have been built'.

Putting it all together gives the following sentence (which could still be improved!):

> *In a vision we are granted a look into the future, more precisely the year 2108 when the troubled district of Ondiep has become a paradise and the tallest skyscraper in the Netherlands, the Belle van Zuylen, turns out to have been built.*

3. Style, register and tone

i. Stylistic analysis of the source text

The use of language tells us that this is a form of literary writing. The text uses sophisticated lexis and situates itself in relation to other writers and a particular literary text from the canon of Dutch literature, the poem 'Awater' by Martinus Nijhoff. Preliminary researches will have shown that the citybooks project, of which this text by Onno Kosters forms part, is a literary project. The text also uses complex sentences and refers to an imagined future as well as the past. Its register is quite formal in addition to literary.

14   *People and places*

ii. Assessment of the style of writing appropriate to the target text

The formal and literary features of the ST do suggest that the translator should ensure that s/he creates a literary text in English. Given the context of the city-books project, which is to present writers in Dutch to a wider audience via the web, translators have a responsibility to represent the author to the outside world via their translation.

   At the same time, there are some target audience considerations, especially the need to make the content of the text accessible to someone unfamiliar with the city of Utrecht or with Dutch writers. This may mean including small amounts of additional information. We have already discussed the example of the Ondiep district of Utrecht above. The literary dimension provides other examples, such as the name Belle van Zuylen, which occurs twice before the text explains who she is. You could consider bringing in the information that she is an eighteenth-century Dutch writer earlier, or you may decide that it is clear from the first quotation. In the case of the Dutch poet Nijhoff, too, this information can only be inferred. As this is a demanding text, you might decide it will be in keeping with the feel of the text for your target reader to have to do some work, or you can choose to help them a little.

   Judging the right style and tone for your translation is a matter of balancing these different considerations in order to decide on the orientation of your translation: close to the source text, or moving in the direction of the target audience? In the case of a literary text, it is advisable to recreate the 'feel' of the source text – audiences with no knowledge of Dutch look to a translator to provide a representation of the writer through his text.

4. The first draft of the translation

This can be done at any point when you feel ready to start translating. Some translators start after the first read-through and stop when they encounter lexical and grammatical difficulties. If you use this method, you may need to revise your translation more than once, as it is likely to be more uneven than a well-prepared first draft. Use the above analyses to help you translate and keep a note of the sources you find useful.

5. Revising and improving the first draft

The most useful technique is to leave enough time to do nothing for a few hours. When you come back to the translation after a break, you will be in a much better position to judge it. In later chapters, we will explain techniques for improving a translation, but for now, simply try to read it as a piece of English with no reference to the Dutch text. Mark any passages that your intuition tells you are not right. Now check against the ST to see whether you have omitted something or misunderstood the ST. When you have finished, turn to the sample translation below and compare your version with ours.

People and places 15

Sample translation of Text 1: *Alles en niets*

All and nothing
'Have you forgotten our last night,' she sighed,
'when I allowed your tears to censor me
and slipped out of the world so silently?'
Martinus Nijhoff, *Awater*, translated by David Colmer
(On a clear day the tower can be seen from a
distance of 50 kilometres.)

All and nothing consists of nine interlinked poems each with two 'chapters': a narrative part and a reflective part.

The theme linking them is the origin of the landscape in which the city of Utrecht was to come into being, and the founding and growth of the city and its environs. We will follow Utrecht from Roman times via the great storm in the seventeenth century, love in the eighteenth century, and the urban expansion from the nineteenth century to the present day. In a vision, we will look into the future, the year 2018 to be precise, when the troubled district of Ondiep has become a paradise and the tallest skyscraper in the Netherlands, the Belle van Zuylen building, has been built after all.

The characters in *All and nothing* are the city itself and the Dutch poet Martinus Nijhoff's hero Awater from the poem of the same name, published in 1934 and set in Utrecht. Other leading parts are played by the writer Belle van Zuylen and the Scottish biographer James Boswell, who got to know each other in Utrecht in 1764. Some kind of relationship grew between them, though its exact nature is not known. From the correspondence between them, we can deduce that at least on Boswell's side, there was some romantic involvement which Belle van Zuylen (or 'Zélide' as Boswell sometimes called her) never fully reciprocated. Using quotations from the exchange of letters, *All and nothing* brings the two to life in the present, past and future.

PRACTICAL TIPS: TRANSLATING FOR WEBSITES

Web texts

Before discussing how to translate texts for use on websites, we need to understand their particular characteristics. Not surprisingly, these are the characteristics you should be aiming to recreate when you translate from Dutch into English for the web. Web texts are sometimes even seen as a

(continued)

(continued)

'genre' – that is, a particular form with predictable features; at the same time we also need to take into account special features connected with the digital medium in which they are published. Normally a website is translated as a whole to ensure that the different components all connect to one another. This is related to the use of technical tools by professional translators and will not be discussed here. However, you can read about it in *Web Translation as a Genre* (3/2009) published by the EC and available as a free download from the European Commission website (http://bookshop.europa.eu/en/web-translation-as-a-genre-pbHC8009160/).

Here we will discuss the **format**, **style** and **content** of web texts. As can be seen from the two texts in this chapter, pieces of writing composed for the web are normally short, as are the individual paragraphs that make them up. This is because reading on screen is thought to be slower and also because users tend to read differently, scanning the web page for key terms, for example. One general rule is that a web page should be able to stand alone – in other words, it should be written or translated in such a way that the reader does not need to move between pages of the same site. Headings are particularly important in web texts, as these will be picked up by search engines. Most users of websites visit them for a few minutes, normally to search for specific information or carry out a transaction, and clear, unambiguous headings make this possible.

There is general agreement that the style of web texts is clearer and more straightforward than that of texts in print (see also EC publication 3/2009) and that the personality of the writer should not show through. The content, too, is concise, with a definite focus and no extraneous information. You should aim to reproduce these features, but at the same time you will need to take your target audience into account.

Translating for the web

Web translations are normally more reader-oriented than translations generally. When translating from Dutch into English, the questions are: Who is the audience, given that the web is a global medium? Do translators into English need to take localisation into account at all? To answer these questions, you will need to know something about the target audience and about the purpose of the website or web page that you are translating. If you are translating marketing materials, for instance, you can ask the person commissioning the translation where the primary market is located, but most of the time you can assume a very broad target audience that includes speakers of languages other than English. One exception to this is the EU with its policy of multilingualism: here you can assume that official information is intended primarily for a UK audience, and may well need adapting accordingly.

Even where you are translating across a cultural boundary and assuming the role of cultural mediator, make sure that you do not overload the translated web text with unnecessary cultural information. For example, footnotes are out of the question. Furthermore, you may find that you need to leave some elements of meaning implicit in the translation, rather than spell everything out. You should also eliminate repetition and redundant elements.

Trediting

'Some of the actions which [translators] called localising could also be considered as editing: they adapt the text lightly, in order to improve its structure, to adjust the level of detail given to the reader, or to match the style with what the reader would expect' (EC publication 3/2009). The kind of editing described in the quote is also known as 'trediting' among translators in the European Commission. In other words they have to make adjustments as they translate in order to make sure that the resulting translation both fits the description of a suitable web text and does not come across in unintended ways when a new audience reads it.

Text 2: *Het MAS. Dat moet je gezien hebben*

This text is taken from the front page of the website of Antwerp's newest museum: Museum aan de Stroom, or MAS. Since websites are dynamic and constantly changing, it is unlikely that it will still be the first page for very long, so what we have here represents a snapshot of how the museum wanted to present itself in 2013. Because the text is from the front page, its function is to introduce the entire museum so that viewers can then follow their own interests by clicking through to different aspects of what the museum has to offer visitors. When approaching this kind of web-based visitor information, it is not possible to fully separate text and context – in other words, the layout and general presentation of the website itself works hand in hand with the actual text to create an overall impression.

Het MAS. Dat moet je gezien hebben

Het MAS vertelt in een indrukwekkend gebouw een vernieuwend verhaal over Antwerpen in de wereld. En over de wereld in Antwerpen. Onder meer. Want het is ook het kijkdepot, het museumplein, de wandelboulevard, het dakpanorama ... Het MAS is een totaalbelevenis.

(continued)

18 *People and places*

> *(continued)*
>
> De kern van het verhaal is de lange geschiedenis van uitwisseling tussen de stad en de wereld. Met de sporen van die uitwisseling vertelt het MAS nieuwe verhalen. Over de stad, de stroom en de haven. Over de wereld in al zijn verscheidenheid. Over de eeuwenlange verbondenheid van Antwerpen met de wereld. Dat is de unieke combinatie van het MAS: het is Antwerps én het is mondiaal.
>
> Het MAS vertelt dit verhaal aan de hand van een tijdelijke tentoonstelling een kijkdepot en vier thema's waarin iedereen zich kan terugvinden. De thema's zijn verdeeld over vijf verdiepingen. Machtsvertoon | Over prestige en symbolen Wereldstad | Over hier en elders Wereldhaven | Over handel en scheepvaart Leven en dood | Over mensen en goden + Over boven- en onderwereld.
>
> De objecten worden niet naast elkaar tentoongesteld. De stukken worden met elkaar verbonden in een dynamische scenografie. Ze doen veel meer dan informeren. Ze vertellen verhalen, ze beklijven, ze zijn de acteurs in een alsmaar wisselend theaterstuk.
>
> Elke verdieping is een nieuwe wondere wereld. Niet alleen kijken is de boodschap. De bezoeker wordt ook gestimuleerd door de muziek van huiscomponist Erich Sleichim. Of hij ervaart de andere hedendaagse kunstenaars van het MAS. Of hij kan ruiken in de geurboxen van het thema Wereldhaven.
>
> Het MAS verenigt de collecties van een aantal Antwerpse musea. Het toont ook de collectie precolumbiaanse kunst van Paul en Dora Janssen-Arts. Maar het heeft ook oog voor de stad en de wereld buiten zijn muren. Het bezit de grootste collectie havenkranen ter wereld en het ondersteunt en werkt samen met vele grote en kleine (erfgoed) gemeenschappen verspreid over de hele stad.
>
> Source: http://www.antwerpen.be/eCache/ABE/4/762.Y29udGV4dD04MDM0MDQ4.html (accessed 18 November 2013).

1. Translation strategies and techniques

As with the first text, we begin with two key questions to help you make a first analysis. The first question concerns background knowledge relevant for understanding the text, while the second involves reflection on your target audience.

i. What are the first things that you notice about the text?

- *It consists of several very short paragraphs or sections, roughly equal in length.*
   This suggests that the visual appearance of the text is important and should be viewed in relation to the organisation of the web page.

- *The third paragraph does not consist of full sentences but contains words and phrases separated by a vertical stroke. Also, it is not clear which words belong together.*

  On first reading the passage through, it is clear that these are key themes describing what the museum is displaying to the public. Although it may go against the grain to produce this kind of disjointed text, it does have a clear function and fits with the general context of providing a brief overview so that users of the website can choose which themes they want to explore further. The grouping of words is more difficult, but the use of capital letters can help, as well as a better understanding of the contents of the museum – so this is where research comes in.

- *There are a couple of unfamiliar proper names.*

  No general principle can be applied here, unless it is that each one should be looked at separately. So, 'Erich Sleichim' is merely mentioned in passing and the translation can do the same. One word of warning, though: make sure you transcribe the name correctly. It is all too easy to make mistakes and this kind of error is notoriously difficult to spot later on. 'Paul en Dora Janssen-Arts' is a little trickier since it is not clear whether 'Arts' is an English term somehow applied to this Antwerp art collection or something else. Again a warning: when you see a familiar term like 'arts', which seems to fit the context, it is easy to jump to conclusions. Research shows, however, that the collectors' names are actually Paul Janssen and Dora Janssen-Arts, which is how married women form their family names in the Netherlands and Flanders, 'Arts' being Dora's maiden name. What we conclude from this is that the hyphen is an integral part of the name.

ii. What do you know about the target audience for your translation and how will it influence your choices and decisions?

The audience for this text is potentially a global one – anyone who reads English and is thinking of visiting Antwerp, or who has heard about the new museum and would like to know more. This suggests that you should try to make the translation as accessible and informative as possible. In other words, you should focus on your target audience rather than on the source text and, while aiming to convey the information content, you may decide to make some changes – for example, to the sentence structure.

2. Text and language

This step is crucial since it determines the accuracy of your translation.

i. Words and expressions

There are some unusual words and expressions in this translation that are connected with the innovative nature of the new museum, and others connected with the fact that Antwerp is an important port. In the case of the city's name *Antwerpen*, this is one of the clear-cut cases where there is an English equivalent: Antwerp.

Here are some examples of particular lexical challenges and some suggestions for tackling them. In the case of specialist museum terminology such as *het kijkdepot* and *een dynamische scenografie*, you will probably not find these in a dictionary or in the EU database, IATE. The process for finding an English equivalent involves several steps: first, check the MAS website so that you understand what the terms are referring to – in the case of *kijkdepot*, for example, you will find that this is a space where objects are displayed in a particular way; next try googling some possible translations such as 'art depot' to see if the phrase exists in English; then check the websites of similar contemporary museums and galleries in the English-speaking world to see if the concept is used anywhere. This research will provide you with a few examples of the use of 'depot' in English for displays of art. Another possibility would be to explore the terms 'storage' and 'store' as all museums have objects and works of art that are not displayed in their public viewing spaces. You can undertake similar research for the phrase *een dynamische scenografie*: in this case, simply typing the word *scenografie* into the search box on the MAS website will provide you with a clear description so that you can then experiment with a few possible equivalents.

> *Geurboxen* is another innovation which can be approached by linguistic analysis: *geur* (smell, scent) + *box* (box, container), while the context makes it clear that visitors can experience certain smells by sniffing the boxes.

> *Wereldhaven* appears straightforward, but beware of translation dictionaries here. Many give 'harbour' as the first English equivalent, also mentioning 'port'. This is a case where some knowledge about Antwerp and also the contrasting meanings of the two English terms is needed. Because of its size and commercial significance, Antwerp can be described only as a 'port'. A related term is *havenkranen*, and as a semi-technical term, it can be found in the IATE term base. As it is a plural form, it is advisable to look up the singular form: *havenkraan*.

> The expression *boven- en onderwereld* needs to be approached with caution. First, the specific Dutch use of the hyphen means that, in full, the phrase reads: *bovenwereld en onderwereld*. The fact that these form part of the theme of *Leven en dood* (Life and death) helps with the interpretation of the terms. Because the museum emphasises the global nature of Antwerp, it is worth considering translating these terms in a general way rather than giving them a specifically Christian translation like 'heaven and hell'. It is also worth noting that this pair of terms is also used to refer to the law-abiding world and the criminal underworld.

ii. Sentences

At sentence level, this is a straightforward piece to translate since the sentences are short and fairly uncomplicated. There is only one, more complex sentence:

Het MAS vertelt dit verhaal aan de hand van een tijdelijke tentoonstelling een kijkdepot en vier thema's waarin iedereen zich kan terugvinden.

Using the bracketing technique introduced in the discussion of the first text gives us:

(Het MAS vertelt dit verhaal)(aan de hand van een tijdelijke tentoonstelling een kijkdepot en vier thema's) (waarin iedereen zich kan terugvinden).

The sentence is broken up into three component parts and, in what follows, we analyse the function of each component. The first bracket contains the basic idea of the museum's story-telling function – make sure you try out different possibilities for translating *dit*, such as 'that' and 'the' rather than 'this', since these can sometimes make a text more easily readable in English. The second bracket contains the part of the sentence that explains what means the museum uses to tell its story, and the third set of brackets goes into more detail about the four themes.

Although the sentences are relatively easy to translate, you may find it difficult to make them sound right in English. The opening sentence is a case in point: you should consider rearranging some of the elements of the sentence until you achieve an acceptable word order in English. The main problem is the separation of the verb *vertelt* from its object, *een vernieuwend verhaal*.

Finally, there is the question of incomplete sentences and what to do about them. This is a matter of style and register, so see below.

3. Style, register and tone

i. Stylistic analysis of the source text

This text uses what we can best describe as a 'web register', a special kind of language that uses layout and images to reinforce its message and is neither too formal nor informal. The style is informative, conveying its message in short, punchy sentences.

ii. Assessment of the style of writing appropriate to the target text

The web register in English is very similar to that in Dutch, simply because it is associated with the medium. Within this register, there is room for stylistic choices – in this case these should be guided by the way in which the museum seeks to profile itself to the outside world as innovative. The ways of doing this are to keep the innovative-sounding terms, the short, striking sentences, and to aim for a tone that is upbeat and bright.

Remember that there is no place in this register for notes and explanations because the computer screen and associated layout do not provide enough space. This means that you have to be decisive in selecting terms, placing these in a context that is rich in meaning.

22 *People and places*

> **Sample translation of Text 2:** *Het MAS. Dat moet je gezien hebben*
>
> *The MAS. A must-see museum*
>
> **With its impressive building on the river Schelde, the MAS has found new ways to tell the story of Antwerp in the world. And of the world in Antwerp. And much more besides. Because it is art depot, museum square, boulevard, rooftop panorama ... The MAS is a total experience.**
>
> At the heart of the story is the long history of exchange between the city and the world. The MAS uses the traces of these exchanges to tell new stories. About the city, the river and the port. About the world in all its variety. About Antwerp's centuries-old connections with the world. This is what is unique about the MAS: it combines the local and the global.
>
> The MAS tells this story using a temporary exhibition, the art depot and four themes which everyone can recognise. The themes are displayed over five floors: Power | Learn about prestige and symbols || World city | Learn about here and elsewhere || World port | Learn about trade and shipping || Life and death | Learn about people and gods + underworld and other worlds.
>
> Objects are not displayed side by side but linked in a dynamic scenography. They do much more than inform. They tell stories, they make a lasting impression, they are actors in a constantly changing theatre.
>
> Each floor is a new world of wonders. The message is: it's not enough to look. Visitors' senses are stimulated by the music of resident composer Erich Sleichim or by the other MAS contemporary artists. Or they can inhale the aroma boxes in the World Port section.
>
> The MAS brings together the collections of a number of Antwerp museums, and it is home to the Paul and Dora Janssen-Arts collection of pre-Columbian art. But it is also alive to the city and the world outside its walls. It owns the largest collection of dock cranes in the world and it supports and collaborates with many large and small (heritage) communities spread across the entire city.

Dutch translation in practice

To round off the chapter, we have selected a passage from the same website as Text 2 for you to translate on your own. Try to follow the steps mapped out for you in the discussion of the first text. This time you will have to do your own research and analysis. We list the steps again in the order in which we used them, but you could keep a note of how you approach the process to start working out what kind of translator you are.

1 Translation strategies and techniques – reading, researching and reflecting on the target audience.
2 Text and language – word and sentence meaning.
3 Style, register and tone.
4 Make the first draft of your translation.
5 Look critically at the first draft and improve it where you can.

For a sample translation of this passage, see p. 181.

Text 3: | *Machtsvertoon* | *Over prestige en symbolen*

De vierde verdieping concentreert zich op het thema 'Machtsvertoon', met collecties over prestige en symbolen.

Macht is verleidelijk, overal. Belangrijke leidersfiguren, maar ook mensen in hun dagelijks leven, overtuigen anderen ervan dat zij macht verdienen door te verleiden en ontzag te wekken.

In alle culturen spelen mooie, vaak sacrale statussymbolen een belangrijke rol bij machtsvertoon. En als macht onder druk komt te staan, worden deze symbolen het eerst vernietigd, ontheiligd of ontvreemd.

De MAS-collectie herbergt duizenden van deze statusobjecten, uit de hele wereld. Dat moet niet verwonderen. Door de exclusiviteit van dit erfgoed werd het gemakkelijk het voorwerp van internationale kunsthandel en van museale verzamelingen.

Fascinerende verhalen

Het thema *Machtsvertoon* confronteert bezoekers met de fascinerende verhalen achter deze exclusieve voorwerpen. Verhalen over macht dichtbij en verder af, vroeger en nu.

- Van macht en imago van de wisselende machthebbers in Antwerpen tijdens de Opstand (1568–1648), tot Japan, waar het besef van rangorde steeds opduikt in de geschiedenis en verhoudingen tussen 'hoog' en 'laag' ook in de opvoeding duidelijk aanwezig zijn.
- Van het prestige van Afrikaanse leiders van de 16de tot de 19de eeuw tot een collectie Indonesische wapens uit de koloniale tijd en de visie van Maori kunstenaar George Nuku op Polynesisch erfgoed in Westerse musea.

Source: http://www.antwerpen.be/eCache/ABE/4/762.Y29udGV4dD04MDM0MDQ4.html (accessed 18 November 2013).

2 Dutch language and culture

Introduction: texts and contexts

The broad context for this second chapter is the Dutch language and culture in what is often called the 'Dutch language area', or *Nederlands taalgebied* in Dutch. This term provides a way of grouping all those territories where Dutch is the official language. While we normally only mention the Netherlands and Flanders – the Dutch-speaking part of Belgium – in this context, the Dutch language area actually also covers the following: Suriname in South America, where Dutch is the official language; the Dutch Antilles islands of Aruba, Curaçao and Sint Maarten in the Caribbean, which form part of the Kingdom of the Netherlands and where Dutch is an official language; the islands of Bonaire, Sint Eustatius and Saba, also part of the Netherlands Antilles, where Dutch is an official language.

The Dutch Language Union, or *Nederlandse Taalunie* (NTU) in Dutch, is an intergovernmental treaty organisation originally set up in 1989 by the Netherlands and Belgium to promote and manage the Dutch language across both countries. It now includes the countries listed above in its activities, and also has a special relationship with South Africa where Afrikaans, which is closely related to Dutch, is one of that country's official languages. The Dutch Language Union draws up language policies for Dutch, including the official spelling rules, and funds useful publications such as dictionaries and language-learning materials. It also supports the network of lecturers teaching Dutch at universities around the world. *Taalunieversum* is the name of the Dutch Language Union's website, which offers all kinds of useful information, including the section *Taalhulp*, which you can find at http://taalunieversum.org/sectie/taalhulp. From here you can follow links to lists of translation dictionaries, lists of specialist terms and the reference grammar of Dutch *e-ANS*, which we introduced in Chapter 1.

As you can see from the description of the Dutch language area given above, it is possible to describe Dutch as a world language, with 23 million people who have Dutch as their first language. For more facts and figures, see the Dutch Language Union's website: http://taalunieversum.org/inhoud/feiten-en-cijfers. The Dutch language comes into contact with many different languages and is thus part of the multilingual globalised world. Of course it is also one of the official languages of the European Union, which today also promotes multilingualism.

For more on this topic, see the Introduction to *Dutch Translation in Practice*. Those students considering a career as a translator involving translation out of Dutch will find that Europe and its institutions offer many opportunities.

In the context of globalisation, it is important to reflect on where the local fits in. When it comes to culture in the Netherlands and Flanders, there is an enormous variety of cultural institutions, and culture itself ranges across all the art forms. While the visual arts, fashion, and design lend themselves readily to international exchange, literature written in Dutch is not immediately accessible, dependent as it is on translators to make it available. Even so, Dutch and Flemish writers have always been in touch with wider literary trends. So to speak of Dutch culture, the focus of this chapter, is really to leave open a whole range of possibilities. A painter like Vermeer, who remained in the Dutch town of Delft throughout his life and painted scenes that are iconically Dutch, can have global significance while other artists, poets, novelists and musicians remain known only within their national circle.

For this chapter we have chosen texts that cover two extremes: Brussels as a cultural centre and the Dutch language in the Caribbean. The city of Brussels brings with it an additional complexity: the fact that it is itself a bilingual city where Dutch and French are both official languages.

Text 1: *Politieke reus, culturele dwerg*

This short extract comes from a book on cities as centres of cultural life. The article from which it is taken argues that Brussels is missing out on one and a half billion (*miljard*) euros because of a lack of co-ordination among cultural organisations and the need for a distinctive profile. It further argues that the main cultural asset of Brussels is the fact that it is *the* place for *art nouveau* and surrealism.

Politieke reus, culturele dwerg

Brussel is een stad met verschillende politieke functies. Sedert 1831 is het de hoofdstad van België en in de laatste decennia van de vorige eeuw verwierf het ook de status van hoofdstad van de Vlaamse en de Franse Gemeenschap van dit land, maar bovenal ook de titel van hoofdstad van de Europese Unie. De administratieve rol van Brussel staat dus niet ter discussie. Toch is Brussel ook een stad met veel culturele troeven. Denken we maar aan de overweldigende schoonheid van de Grote Markt, aan instellingen als het Théâtre National, de Koninklijke Vlaamse Schouwburg (KVS), le Théâtre du Parc, het Kaaitheater, de BOZAR, Rosas, de Koninklijke Muntschouwburg, het Instituut voor Natuurwetenschappen,

(continued)

> *(continued)*
>
> Flagey, of aan het Stripmuseum en de stripmuren, aan Le Botanique of de Ancienne Belgique, de Zinnekeparade en de Ommegang, aan het Kunstenfestival des Arts, aan de dynamiek op de Kunstberg, enzovoort. Intrinsiek hoeft Brussel zich op kunst- en cultuurvlak dus nergens voor te schamen, alleen is het zo dat op een groep ingewijden na, weinigen dit weten. De stad wordt onvoldoende met cultuur geassocieerd, terwijl het potentieel er toch overduidelijk wel is.
>
> Source: Gatz, S. and Mennekens, H. (2011) 'Brussel, cultuurstad tussen Barcelona en Berlijn', in De Backer, M. and Stouthuysen, P. (eds) *Cultuur en/in de stad. Stadslucht maakt vrij 4.* Brussels: VUB Press, p. 213.

1. Translation strategies and techniques

The purpose of this section is to guide you through a preliminary analysis of the source text.

i. What are the first things you notice about the text?

It contains a large number of proper names.

The first step is to group them: most are cultural institutions in Brussels, but there are two that refer to the political and social structure of Belgium: *de Franse Gemeenschap* and *de Vlaamse Gemeenschap*.

Next identify likely sources of information on the first group – the cultural institutions. The individual websites of each organisation are the best place to start, since this is where they establish the names by which they wish to be known. This is important in the case of Brussels as a bilingual city. Taking the first four cultural institutions – all theatres – as an example, two of them are given in Dutch in the ST and two of them are in French. As a general rule, those theatres that perform in French use a French name and those that perform in Dutch use a Dutch name. In other words, the language of the theatre's name serves a particular function of alerting audiences to the language used in that particular theatre. So the 'Théâtre National' is the French-speaking equivalent of a national theatre, and the *Koninklijke Vlaamse Schouwburg* is the main Dutch-speaking theatre. In the case of theatres in Brussels, translators need to bear in mind this special bilingual context and devise a strategy that takes it into account, and also provides English readers with some additional information where needed. For example, *Koninklijke Vlaamse Schouwburg* will not be readily understood by English readers. You could consider giving it the word-for-word translation 'Royal Flemish Theatre', but note that its own website uses the name 'The Brussels City Theatre' in English. There are many sensitivities in the

Brussels context, and this necessitates a mixed strategy that takes into account the preferences of the institutions themselves. The sample translation below uses just such a mixed approach.

An additional feature of the list of names is that some of them refer to cultural practices rather than institutions – for instance, *de Zinnekeparade* and *de Ommegang*. Both are well known and easy to find through an internet search. Since they are part of the tourist scene in Brussels, their English equivalents are well established.

For the official Belgian terms *Franse/Vlaamse Gemeenschap*, it is best to turn directly to IATE, the European translation database (http://iate.europa.eu/SearchByQueryLoad.do?method=load). Looking at the opening screen, type in a search term, in this case *de Franse Gemeenschap*, select Dutch as your source language, and tick the box labelled 'en' for English as your target language. It is best to leave the optional criteria set at 'any domain'. Now click 'search' in the top right-hand corner and if the translation is contained in the database, it will appear below.

ii. What do you know about the target audience for your translation and how will it affect your translation?

The brief for this translation is to transfer it into English for information, and the target users are people working in the cultural industries, such as agencies that promote cultural enterprise between Belgium, the Netherlands and the UK. This means that your readers can be expected to have a certain amount of knowledge about cultural institutions in Brussels and are likely to be interested in the politics of the text. This suggests a general orientation of the translation towards the target audience and a reasonably communicative approach, rather than one that seeks to accurately convey the structure and language of the source text.

2. Text and language

This stage in your preparation is best done before you start translating since it helps you to gain an accurate understanding of the text by checking the meanings of key words and by analysing complex sentences.

i. Words and expressions

Highlight all the words in the text you are unfamiliar with or are uncertain about. It is best not to guess because a wrong guess can lead to unnecessary errors as you try to make the rest of the sentence fit in with the guessed word.

> *Sedert*: this alternative to *sinds* is more frequently used in Flanders than in the Netherlands.

Verwierf: in order to look up this past tense of a verb in a dictionary, you first need to know its infinitive form, i.e. the form that ends in *-en*. The spelling rule on *f/v* alternation (see, for example, section 2.2 of *Dutch. An Essential Grammar*) tells you that *f* is used at the end of a word and *v* is used in between two vowels, so it is likely you are looking for a verb that ends in *-ven*. Finally, you should also consider the possibility that this is a strong verb, i.e. one that changes its vowel sound. You probably know the verb *helpen*, which forms its past tense by changing the vowel sound to *ie*, giving *hielp*. This is a common alternation, which also applies in the case of *verwierf*, so its infinitive form looks like this: *verwerven*.

Troeven: in order to look up this plural noun in the dictionary you need to know its singular form. As with the previous word, the *f/v* alternation is in play here: *v* between two vowels and *f* at the end of the word to give *troef*.

Op . . . na: a feature of the Dutch language is that words that belong together do not have to be next to each other in a sentence. In grammars they are sometimes described as 'discontinuous' elements. *Op . . .na* is a two-part preposition meaning 'except for', but the two elements are separated by the noun phrase to which they apply. Here: **op** *een groep ingewijden* **na**.

Ingewijden: the important thing here is to recognise that you are dealing with a plural noun ending in *-en*. Nouns designating a particular group of people are frequently derived from adjectives. You may have come across *de blinde* (the blind person) and *de blinden* (the blind people). *Ingewijd* means 'initiated', so *de ingewijde* is 'the initiated person' and *de ingewijden* are 'the initiated people'. (See, for example, *A Reference Grammar of Dutch*, section 4.) The passage uses the phrase *een groep ingewijden*, which can be translated as 'a group of the initiated' or a group of initiated people'.

Toch . . .wel is another example of a phrase consisting of discontinuous elements that wrap around *overduidelijk*. *Toch* and *wel* are known as 'particles'. These are small words that are used more often in Dutch than in English. They supply emphasis and nuance, but not the kind of meaning that can readily be translated, so that *toch* and *wel* are frequently omitted from the English translation. Here they reinforce each other and are used to emphasise that it really is the case that Brussels has the potential to be seen as a city of culture.

Staat niet ter discussie: the phrase *niet ter discussie staan* is used to indicate that something is not being questioned, is not in any doubt. You may not find this phrase in a small translation dictionary or monolingual Dutch dictionary. If you have access to the main Dutch dictionary, known as the *grote Van Dale*, you can find it there.

ii. Sentences

In this section, we lay bare the process that experienced translators run through when they encounter a difficult and complex sentence whose meaning they cannot altogether establish on a simple reading. It may seem hard to believe for those learning the craft of translation, but with practice, this process becomes almost automatic – something a translator does as a matter of course.

> *Intrinsiek hoeft Brussel zich op kunst- en cultuurvlak dus nergens voor te schamen, alleen is het zo dat op een groep ingewijden na, weinigen dit weten.*

This is the most complex sentence in the Brussels text. As we did in Chapter 1, we will again use bracketing to break up the sentence into its components. This technique helps you to gain control of a sentence that you find impenetrable. And just as we noted above that it can be counter-productive to guess the meaning of a word, in the case of sentence structure, it can lead to seriously erroneous translations. Any technique that makes you stop and think how different parts of a sentence relate to one another, is useful when you are not sure what a particular sentence means. Try colour-coding if you don't like bracketing! There are three clauses: three verbs with three subjects. The underlined words are the verbs.

> (*Intrinsiek hoeft Brussel zich op kunst- en cultuurvlak dus nergens voor te schamen*), (*alleen is het zo*) (*dat op een groep ingewijden na, weinigen dit weten*).

The first set of brackets contains the main clause (a) and the other two contain the dependent clauses (b) and (c). Starting with the main clause (a) (*Intrinsiek hoeft Brussel zich op kunst- en cultuurvlak dus nergens voor te schamen*), Brussels is the subject and the verb *hoeft + te* is completed by the verb *zich schamen*. Notice the discontinuous elements again – if you can remember to look out for these, you will find that source text comprehension becomes much easier! *Zich schamen voor* is a reflexive verb meaning 'to be ashamed of' and *hoeven + te* is an auxiliary verb meaning 'ought to' or 'should'. So the phrase *hoeft zich nergens voor te schamen* means 'should not be ashamed of anything'. The phrase *nergens voor* is what we call an '*er* construction'. This kind of pronominal construction will be discussed in more detail in Chapter 3 in the Practical Tips section, which is devoted to analysing and translating *er* and related words such as *nergens*. The remaining phrase in the main clause (a) is: *op kunst- en cultuurvlak*. It uses the dash after *kunst-* to replace the word *-vlak* so as to avoid using *-vlak* twice (see also Chapter 1, Text 2). The easiest way to translate this phrase is to move the English word for *vlak* to the front of the phrase, to give the expression 'in the area of art and culture'.

Having established that 'Intrinsically, Brussels has nothing to be ashamed of in the area of art and culture', the sentence goes on to qualify this statement with clause (b) (*alleen is het zo*), 'although it is the case', which is followed by clause (c) in bold type containing the explanation of this reservation: (***dat*** (*op een groep ingewijden na*), ***weinigen dit weten***) – 'that few people know this'. All that remains now is to insert the remaining embedded phrase *op een groep ingewijden na*, which we analysed in the previous section as meaning 'except for a group of the initiated'. Putting all this together gives the rather long sentence: 'Intrinsically, Brussels has nothing to be ashamed of in the area of art and culture although it is the case that few people know this except for a group of the initiated.'

3. Style, register and tone

i. Stylistic analysis of the source text

The source text is written in an academic style, probably for an academic audience, which means that readability is less important than the inclusion of detailed information and commentary. The register of the text is quite formal and its tone is neutral.

ii. Assessment of the style of writing appropriate to the target text

Given that the target audience is not primarily an academic one, and that the translation brief suggests a more accessible text is desirable, the style of the target text may be simplified slightly, for example by dividing up long sentences. The register and tone can be maintained as long as this does not affect the accessibility of the resulting text.

4. The first draft of the translation

With this kind of text, use the first draft to produce an accurate translation. Given that the transfer of information is the main aim of the translation, it is best to concentrate on the correct analysis of the meaning and structures of the source text. At this stage your version may sound a bit literal or like a translation.

5. Revising and improving your first draft

Read through the first draft and mark any passages that seem awkward or less than clear. One technique is to make changes to the English of these marked passages to make them more fluent and communicative, then check them against the source text to make sure that you haven't accidentally lost or deleted any words, or changed the message of the text. Finally read through the whole translation, checking punctuation, spelling and coherence. Now compare your version with the sample translation below.

Sample translation of Text 1: *Politieke reus, culturele dwerg*

Political giant, cultural dwarf

Brussels is a city with several political functions. Since 1831 it has been the capital of Belgium, and in the last decades of the last century it also gained the status of capital of both the Flemish and the French Communities in this country, but above all, it acquired the title of capital of the European Union. The administrative role of Brussels is therefore not in any doubt. And yet Brussels is also a city that has a great deal to offer when it comes to culture. We need only think of the overwhelming beauty of the central market place – the Grote Markt, or Grand Place. Then there are such institutions as the Théâtre National, the Koninklijke Vlaams Theater (which uses the name Brussels City Theatre in English), the Théâtre du Parc, the Kaaitheater, BOZAR (Centre for Fine Arts in English), the dance centre Rosas, De Munt/La Monnaie opera house, the Royal Belgian Institute of Natural Sciences, and the music and film venue Flagey; or the Belgian Comic Strip Center and frescoes, Botanique, the Ancienne Belgique music venue, the Zinneke Parade and Ommegang pageant, or the Kunstenfestival des Arts, the dynamism of the Mont des Arts and so on. So Brussels has everything to be proud of in the area of art and culture. The trouble is that, apart from a group of insiders, very few people know this. The city is not associated with culture as much as it should be, while it most definitely has the potential.

PRACTICAL TIPS: DEALING WITH NAMES IN TRANSLATION

It is widely recognised that the translation of proper names poses problems for translators, and many commentators have divided such names into categories in order to propose particular translation methods. The most commonly identified categories are personal names, geographical names and institutional names. Before addressing each of these in turn, we would like to suggest that the old problem of the translation of names may have become less challenging. At the very least, the picture is changing thanks to two things: the ubiquity of the internet and the use of English as a global means of communication. For example, we now have immediate access to what organisations call themselves in English. The choices they make on their websites have been subjected to scrutiny, often for marketing and branding considerations, and when we think of the way in which most users of websites search for trustworthy information, we see that they would normally visit the website of the organisation they are interested in. This gives both translators and their audiences access to very precise information. In the case of bilingual Brussels, for example, it tells us which language is primary, French or Dutch; whether the institution is monolingual, bilingual, or even trilingual with English added. Many institutions have carefully chosen their English name to reflect an international outlook and distinguish themselves from more parochial local organisations.

(continued)

(continued)

The case of the intergovernmental treaty organisation, the *Nederlandse Taalunie*, is particularly interesting here. According to its website, including its pages in English, it is the *Nederlandse Taalunie* (NTU). Its logo is based on these three letters, but notice that Text 2 uses NT, an abbreviation to be avoided in English because of its associations with such UK institutions as the National Trust and National Theatre. We could conclude from the *Nederlandse Taalunie*'s use of its Dutch name that as an organisation responsible for Dutch as a world language, it has taken a decision to give more prominence to the Dutch language and to get audiences used to its name in Dutch. However, it is also the case that some target audiences will need additional information, perhaps in the form of a gloss between brackets. Since this is an important institution in the context of Europe, we would expect to find an authoritative translation in the IATE database, which is the case: Dutch Language Union.

Names of people

In a certain sense, we are our names! They are our personal identifiers, so why change them, unless an individual requests this? In our multilingual Europe and in a world where movement across borders has become the norm, English speakers have had to adjust to the wide variety of names that are found in multicultural cities, for example. This means that they are more tolerant of foreignness, and the basic principle for translating personal names should be to keep them and not adapt them to the target culture, even if this means that people will not always know how to pronounce them. The Dutch writer Cees Nooteboom, for instance, is used to the different and slightly amusing way in which the English pronounce the vowel sounds in his family name.

Names of places

This is the most difficult category of names to translate as there are different approaches, and it is not always possible even to be consistent within a particular translation. It is helpful to identify a number of subcategories: countries, cities and towns, rivers and lakes.

Countries

Starting with the countries where Dutch is spoken, *Nederland* has traditionally posed a problem for translators. The country is frequently referred to as Holland, even though its recognised and official name is 'the Netherlands'. This name can easily be confirmed by checking the Dutch embassy's website in London, or the Dutch government website: www.government.nl. The IATE database similarly gives 'the Netherlands'. There is one particular sphere, however, where 'Holland' is the norm: tourism. Even the Netherlands Tourist Board uses 'Holland' on its website and more widely in publicity. Where there are alternative English translations of a country's name, the translation you choose will depend on the domain you are working in. Generally speaking, if it relates to popular culture, you use 'Holland' and if it relates to official spheres you use 'the Netherlands'.

België may be straightforward with one English equivalent – 'Belgium' – but its federal political structures are more complex. However, there are accepted translations that can be obtained from either the IATE database or the English portal of the Belgian government website: http://www.belgium.be/en/about_belgium/government/. As a translator you should consider yourself as having a responsibility to promote the correct terminology for the names of official structures and entities. This is in any case expected of professional translators working in the areas of government and policy.

Cities

It is not possible to give a hard-and-fast rule for how to translate the names of cities and towns, although generally speaking, the better known the city, the more likely it is to have acquired an established translation in English. If this is the case, then this is what should be used. Here are the main examples:

Antwerpen	Antwerp
Brugge	Bruges
Brussel	Brussels
Den Haag (also known as *'s Gravenhage*)	The Hague
Gent	Ghent
Hoek van Holland	Hook of Holland
Oostende	Ostend

The Flemish university town of *Leuven* is sometimes known as 'Louvain' in English, but this translation is not recommended as this is a Dutch-speaking town in Flanders, the Dutch-speaking part of Belgium, and the Flemish name is the one currently in use.

Rivers and lakes

The two large rivers separating what are traditionally described as the northern Netherlands from the southern Netherlands, are a good place to start. The *Maas* flows through France, Belgium and the Netherlands. This means that it has a

(continued)

(continued)

French name as well as a Dutch name, e.g. *le Meuse* (French) /*de Maas* (Dutch). As there is no separate English name, a translator has to choose between the two. As a general rule, if you are translating a Dutch text that is referring to the river as it flows through the southern part of the Netherlands, you should use the Dutch term 'Maas'. This is because it links up with other names, such as the *Maasvlakte*, which is part of the Europoort complex near Rotterdam.

The second largest river is the *Waal*, which is referred to in English as either the 'river Waal' or the 'Waal river'. The same applies to the river in Amsterdam, the *IJ*. One point to note, though, is that the two letters actually spell one sound and the correct written form uses two capital letters: the 'river IJ' or 'IJ river'. Similarly the *IJsselmeer*, the large inland lake to the north of Amsterdam, is written 'IJsselmeer' in English. It is sometimes also called 'Lake IJssel'.

Institutions and organisations

The translation of names of institutions and organisations has been dealt with in great detail already, so, taking universities in Flanders and the Netherlands as an example, the best approach is never to make a guess and always check the institution's website to see how it wishes to be known in English. As you will notice from the examples below, there is no agreed format for the name of a university in Flanders or the Netherlands – in this respect it is a strictly local affair.

Universiteit Antwerpen	University of Antwerp
Universiteit Gent	Ghent University
Universiteit van Amsterdam	University of Amsterdam
Rijksuniversiteit Groningen	University of Groningen
Universiteit Utrecht	Utrecht University

The *Vrije Universiteit Brussel* is an interesting case because it has chosen to use its Dutch name even on its English web pages. This suggests that, like the *Nederlandse Taalunie*, it is keen to stress the importance of the Dutch language to it as an institution.

Text 2: *Meer aandacht voor de Nederlandse taal in Suriname*

This text is taken from the Dutch-language daily newspaper, *GFC Nieuws*, in Paramaribo, the capital city of Suriname. If you need to research the immediate context for the article, you should first try the newspaper's website: http://www.gfcnieuws.com. For example, in assessing the type of language used in the source text, you might want to compare it with other articles in the paper, to see if it is written in a style that is typical for this type of publication. The text that we focus on here is an extract from a longer article that, in addition to appearing in *GFC Nieuws*, has been displayed on the website of the Dutch Language Union because the organisation wanted to stimulate debate about the use of Dutch in Suriname. The article points out that more could be done to raise the quality of Dutch in Suriname and that there is funding available to help with this.

Meer aandacht voor de Nederlandse taal in Suriname

Hoewel Suriname lid is van de Nederlandse Taalunie (NT) waar de samenwerking op het gebied van de Nederlandse taal centraal staat, wordt het beleid betreffende de taal heel verschillend uitgevoerd. De samenwerking op de belangrijkste werkterreinen zijn: taal en taalhulpmiddelen, technologie, onderwijs in en van het Nederlands, literatuur en lezen, de positie van het Nederlands in Europa en in de wereld en digitalisering van het Nederlandstalig erfgoed. In de NT werken Aruba, Curaçao, Nederland, Sint-Maarten, Suriname en Vlaanderen op enkele afgesproken gebieden samen.

Nederland en Vlaanderen zijn westerse "hooggeïndustrialiseerde" landen terwijl Suriname tot een zogenaamde Derde Wereld land gerekend wordt. Bij het adequaat vormgeven van een goed taalbeleid heeft Suriname daarom veel hulp nodig. Deze bijstand wordt maar zeer matig aangeboden door de andere rijkere landen in de NT. Van de subsidieregelingen wordt door Suriname ternauwernood gebruik gemaakt, en van Surinaamse neerlandici en taalkundigen wordt er door bijdragen te leveren in de media infrequent geprofiteerd om bijvoorbeeld voorlichting te geven. Het taalniveau in ons land is mede hierdoor bar slecht. Dit valt niet alleen op bij het geschreven woord maar ook het mondeling taalgebruik. Ook digitalisering van ons erfgoed bevindt zich nog in de kinderschoenen.

Source: Bobby Roeplall, *GFC Nieuws*, Paramaribo. Linked from Nederlandse Taalunie website (accessed 13 July 2013) by GFC Nieuws. Online at: http://www.gfcnieuws.com/?p=176410.

1. Translation strategies and techniques

The features of a text that strike you when you first read it through are most likely the ones that will inform your overall approach or strategy.

i. What are the first things you notice about this text?

- *The Dutch used is slightly different from the Dutch in the Netherlands or Flanders.*
  The article is written in standard Dutch, but there are some differences in usage from the Dutch used in the Flemish daily newspaper *De Standaard* or *De Volkskrant* in the Netherlands, for example. However, these small variations do

not affect comprehension and are part of the rich variety of Dutch as a world language. Although this shouldn't interfere with your understanding of the passage, you may wish to reflect on whether it is necessary to capture the linguistic variation in your translation. The choice is between a strategy that reproduces a 'local' flavour in English or one that removes the Surinamese 'feel'.

- *The passage assumes a background knowledge of language policies regarding Dutch.*

    We have tried to fill this gap for you in the introduction to this chapter, though further research will help you to write confidently about the topic in English. The website of the Nederlandse Taalunie is the obvious place to start.

- *The article refers to Suriname as a 'zogenaamde Derde Wereld land'.*

    You may be surprised that the author refers to Suriname as a Third World country, or feel uneasy about the term, which is no longer heard in Europe and has been superseded by a phrase like 'developing country'. How you deal with this depends on whether you decide to stick closely to the Dutch text or orient your translation more in the direction of an English audience. Put differently, as a translator, you must decide on the orientation of your translation – either towards the source text or towards the target text.

ii. What do you know about the target audience for the translation, and how will it affect your decisions?

The audience who would take an interest in this text would probably be involved in the world of languages; they might well be researching language policies, or languages in Caribbean countries. If we assume an academic audience for the text, this does not necessarily mean that we need to translate the text in an academic style. In this case, it would clearly not be appropriate because the article is an authentic example of how the Surinamese themselves think and write about their language. For this reason a translation strategy that keeps some of the original flavour would be a sound choice.

2. Text and language

Whatever translation strategy you employ, your starting point must always be an accurate and precise understanding of the source text. This is achieved through analysis of word and sentence meaning.

i. Words and expressions

   Werkterreinen is the plural form of *werkterrein*. This word is an example of a noun that can be translated in a number of different ways, depending on the context in which it is used. If, for instance, we type it into the EU terminology database IATE, which we discussed earlier in this chapter in the Text 1 section on translation strategy, translations are listed under nine different headings ranging across contexts such as transport, law, finance and business. Sample translations are 'business area' and 'line of action' under the business heading, 'range of operations' under finance, or 'scope' under communications policy. None of the nine topics exactly matches ours, which is language policy. Nevertheless, the IATE translations are authoritative and relate to similar institutions and areas of business, so are worth still bearing in mind. The *Van Dale* online gives 'working space' and 'work area' as English translations of *werkterrein*. One technique to try in this situation is to type out your translation of the sentence with a gap, and copy and paste it a few times so that you can try out several of the possibilities to judge which works best.

Nederlandstalig erfgoed: this specialist term is found in the context of libraries and museums. *Erfgoed* in the meaning of heritage is not particularly problematic, but it is combined in this text with the adjective *Nederlandstalig* to indicate cultural heritage involving the Dutch language, for example books and manuscripts. Also, the final sentence of the text refers to *digitalisering van ons erfgoed* – the preservation of this heritage using digital means.

Hooggeïndustrialiseerde landen: the challenge here is to break down the long word into its constituent parts – *hoog/geïndustrialiseerd/e*. At the heart of the word is the past participle of the verb *industrialiseren*, meaning 'to industrialise', which has the ending *-e* because it has the function of an adjective describing *landen*, or 'countries' in English as 'industrialised'. The prefix *hoog-* supplies additional information about the nature of this industrialisation. In contrast to Dutch, English gives this kind of information by means of an adverb, here: 'highly', rather than by adding another prefix to the adjective. This results in 'highly industrialised'.

Neerlandici: this unusual-looking word is actually the plural form of the noun *neerlandicus*, the term used to denote an academic working in the field of Dutch Studies – the study of Dutch language, literature and culture.

Hierdoor: this word forms part of a complex area of Dutch grammar related to the word *er*, which will be dealt with in more detail in Chapter 3. For the time being, we will draw your attention to different occurrences of this grammatical feature. It was also mentioned above in the discussion of the complex sentence in Text 1. Here it consists of the preposition *door* preceded by *hier*, which is actually translated into English as 'this' to give *hierdoor* = 'through this'.

Bevindt zich in de kinderschoenen: this is an idiomatic phrase consisting of the verb *zich bevinden*, literally 'to find oneself', 'to be located', and *in de kinderschoenen* – again literally meaning 'in the shoes of a child'. It should be clear from the nonsensical literal translation, which simply does not fit with the idea of digitalisation, that the translator's job is to look for a different kind of meaning here. In this case we are dealing with a set expression in Dutch meaning 'at a very early stage' or 'only just beginning' in English. If you decide to try and keep some of the flavour of the ST, you can search for a similar expression in English: 'is in its infancy'.

ii. Sentences

There are several long sentences in Text 2, so you will need to make use of the bracketing technique if you are at all unsure about how the different parts of the sentence relate to one another. We have selected two sentences for analysis here.

> *Hoewel Suriname lid is van de Nederlandse Taalunie (NT) waar de samenwerking op het gebied van de Nederlandse taal centraal staat, wordt het beleid betreffende de taal heel verschillend uitgevoerd.*

This time, we will start by identifying the verbs by underlining them:

> *Hoewel Suriname lid <u>is</u> van de Nederlandse Taalunie (NT) waar de samenwerking op het gebied van de Nederlandse taal centraal <u>staat</u>, <u>wordt</u> het beleid betreffende de taal heel verschillend <u>uitgevoerd</u>.*

It is the third of the verbs that requires explanation here before we look at the meaning of the different clauses. *Wordt + uitgevoerd* is what is known as a passive verb construction. You can revise the formation of passives in any learner's or reference grammar, such as *Dutch. An Essential Grammar*, Chapter 23, and *A Reference Grammar of Dutch*, section 46. In this book we discuss how to translate passive verbs in greater detail in Chapter 7. The principal verb in the passive construction *wordt uitgevoerd* is the separable verb *uitvoeren*, 'to carry out', 'put into practice'. When the past participle *uitgevoerd* is used with the present tense of *worden* to give *wordt uitgevoerd* this can be translated as 'is put into practice'.

The problem posed by the whole sentence is that it does not begin with the main idea, main verb or main clause. Again bracketing is helpful:

> (*Hoewel Suriname lid <u>is</u> van de Nederlandse Taalunie* (*waar de samenwerking op het gebied van de Nederlandse taal centraal <u>staat</u>,*)) (<u>wordt</u> *het beleid betreffende de taal heel verschillend <u>uitgevoerd</u>*).

Taking the clauses in the order in which they occur, we first encounter a subclause (a) introduced by *hoewel*, or 'although'. Notice first that the verb *is* is not found at the end of the clause. This is because Dutch grammar allows phrases introduced by a preposition like *van de Nederlandse Taalunie (NT)* to override the basic rule that the verb is placed at the end of a subclause. Notice, second, that there is another clause (b) that is actually embedded inside (a): (*waar de samenwerking op het gebied van de Nederlandse taal centraal <u>staat</u>,*). This is because it is adding information about the organisation *de Nederlandse Taalunie*. Our still fairly literal translation of the sentence at this point might look like this: 'Although Suriname is a member of the Dutch Language Union where co-operation in the area of the Dutch language is central'.

The most important thing when analysing the whole sentence is to understand that clauses (a) and (b) together constitute the first element of the sentence as a whole. This explains why clause (c) (<u>wordt</u> *het beleid betreffende de taal heel verschillend uitgevoerd*), the main clause, starts with the verb *wordt*. The subject of this verb is the noun that follows it: *het beleid betreffende de taal*, literally 'policy concerning language'. Rearranging the sentence elements to suit English word order gives us: 'policy concerning language is put into practice'. Finally, *heel verschillend* tells us how: 'very differently'. Let us now assemble all these clauses and phrases to produce a sentence in English containing all the information that was in the ST sentence. 'Although Suriname is a member of the Dutch Language Union where co-operation in the area of the Dutch language is central, policy concerning language is put into practice very differently.' Of course, this may not be the final form of the sentence in your translation since it will have to be revised to fit in with the rest of the piece to ensure it is clear and readable.

The second sentence is:

> *Van de subsidieregelingen* wordt door Suriname ternauwernood gebruik gemaakt, en *van Surinaamse neerlandici en taalkundigen* wordt er door bijdragen te leveren in de media infrequent geprofiteerd om bijvoorbeeld voorlichting te geven.

This is probably the most tricky sentence in the entire piece because of a stylistic choice made by the author to use a more expressive word order in which he twice moves preposition phrases beginning with *van* to the beginning of a clause. These are the underlined phrases. The technique we advocate here is to rearrange the Dutch sentence to make grammatical relationships clear and to leave out phrases containing supplementary information: *Er wordt ternauwernood gebruikt gemaakt van de subsidieregelingen // en er wordt infrequent geprofiteerd van Surinaamse neerlandici en taalkundigen.* Thus the basic idea of the sentence is that 'There is scarcely any use made of subsidy arrangements // there is infrequently advantage taken of Surinamese experts in Dutch language and culture.' Clearly this second phrase is not yet formulated in acceptable English, but at least now we can see that the basis of the sentence is the use of two constructions that mirror each other. Finally, this sentence again uses passive constructions – this is part of a more formal style of written Dutch, one that uses an impersonal register.

3. Style, register and tone

As we saw in the grammatical analysis above, the writer of this text uses several passive constructions. These are the mark of an impersonal register, which is often used to sound more formal, or to suggest a distance between reader and writer. This may be because of the controversial subject matter of the article in which the writer is criticising his country for not doing enough to support the Dutch language in Suriname. We also saw that the writer had chosen a more elaborate style by rearranging the word order of a sentence to start with a preposition phrase. He also uses complex sentences that sometimes have more than one subclause. This elaborate style of writing is generally considered to be more of an academic style than a journalistic one. As a translator you have a choice to make: you can reproduce it to give a flavour of the ST, or you can adapt it to a more conventional journalistic style, perhaps by breaking up some of the sentences to make them more easily accessible. While this kind of communicative translation is probably your safest option, if you translate according to the brief given above – that is, for academics and experts interested in languages in the Caribbean – this suggests a translation oriented towards the source language. Ultimately, the best translation policy is probably one of compromise, aiming to preserve some of the style and register of the ST while also making some changes to improve readability.

4. The first draft of the translation

We recommend the same approach for this text as for the first text in this chapter, which is that you use your first draft to ensure you have an accurate translation with all the information contained in the source text present in the target text. If you do this, you will also have a version that contains the elaborate structures of the ST.

5. Revising and improving your first draft

This part of the process is just as important as the transfer of information as it determines the readability and the character of the resulting piece of written English. With a difficult piece like Text 2, you may need to approach this in stages. In our sample translation, we aimed to implement the kind of strategy of compromise described at the end of section 3, that is to arrive at a balance between capturing some of the feel of the ST and ensuring that the meaning is conveyed in a single reading.

Sample translation of Text 2: *Meer aandacht voor de Nederlandse taal in Suriname*

Looking after the Dutch language in Suriname

Although Suriname is a member of the *Nederlandse Taalunie* (NTU) whose central mission is to promote co-operation in matters concerning the Dutch language, language policy is put into practice very differently here. The main areas of activity for co-operation are: language and language tools, technology, teaching in and of Dutch, literature and reading, the position of Dutch in Europe and in the world, and digitalisation of Dutch-language heritage. Aruba, Curaçao, the Netherlands, Sint-Maarten, Suriname and Flanders all work together on certain agreed areas.

    The Netherlands and Flanders are highly industrialised Western countries while Suriname can be counted among the so-called 'Third World' countries. For this reason, Suriname needs a great deal of assistance in the adequate formulation of a sound language policy. A very modest amount of such support is on offer from the other wealthier countries in the NTU. Suriname hardly makes any use of the subsidy arrangements, and it infrequently takes advantage of the possibilities for Surinamese Dutch Studies academics and linguists to make contributions in the media in order to provide public information. This is part of the reason why language skills in our country are so poor. This is clear from both the written and the spoken word. Digitalisation of our heritage is also in its infancy.

Dutch translation in practice

To round off this chapter, we have selected a second passage from the article by Bobby Roeplall from the *GFC Nieuws*. This passage continues the argument and points made in Text 2 with a particular emphasis on literature and promoting reading, so you will already have a good idea of what the piece is about. However, it goes into more detail about the position of the Dutch language in Suriname, and uses some linguistic terminology that may be new to you in Dutch more particularly, there are some technical terms that refer to different branches of language study. With the exception of *zinsbouw* (syntax), the Dutch and English terms are rather similar. Compare the following word pairs: *fonetiek* and 'phonetics', *fonologie* and 'phonology', *etymologie* and 'etymology', *grammatica* and 'grammar', *semantiek* and 'semantics'. For a sample translation of this passage, see p. 181.

Text 3: *Talige en culturele variatie*

Tussen de verschillende delen van het taalgebied bestaat er veel verschil in onder andere taal en cultuur. Dit kan als een verrijking, maar tegelijkertijd als een beperking worden ervaren. Immers als de Nederlandse taal in een bepaalde cultuur niet een dominerende factor is, kan dit mogelijk allerlei consequenties hebben voor de wetenschappelijke verdieping van deze taal. Op het gebied van de letteren en de leesbevordering dient veel meer aandacht gegeven te worden. Dit zou kunnen gebeuren door jaarlijks geoormerkte budgetten hiervoor beschikbaar te stellen in het taalgebied. Wellicht bestaan er al initiatieven maar het is niet zo bekend hoe deze aangeboord moeten worden. In de media merk ik dat er teveel de nadruk wordt gelegd op politiek-geëngageerde onderwerpen, en minder op de literaire stukken (kwaliteit) van de indieners. Vaak is aan de vormgeving ook weinig aandacht besteed. De Nederlandse taal is een effectief communicatiemiddel

(continued)

(continued)

in onze samenleving waardoor het ook belangrijk blijft aandacht te blijven schenken aan basale aspecten als fonetiek/fonologie, etymologie, grammatica, semantiek en zinsbouw. Het is raadzaam dat neerlandici en taalkundigen meer gaan samenwerken om het taalniveau in ons land te optimaliseren.

Source: Robby Roeplall, *GFC Nieuws*, Paramaribo. Linked from *Taalunie* website (accessed 13 July 2013) by GFC Nieuws. Online at: http://www.gfcnieuws.com/?p=176410.

3   Literature

Introduction: texts and contexts

In this chapter we take a look at translating literature. This is a complex and demanding branch of translation, but one that is growing in importance. Literary translation is a topic that we can give you only a taste of here, but there are workshops and courses for translators who want to learn more. A good place to start for students based in the UK is the British Centre for Literary Translation: http://www.bclt.org.uk/. In this chapter we will introduce you to some basic principles and techniques, and look at some of the ways in which literary translation differs from translation of informative texts.

The Netherlands and Flanders have a rich literary tradition stretching back into the Middle Ages. We have decided to focus on writing by contemporary authors, since this is the period for which there is most demand for translations. Translating older texts also requires additional skills and is more complex, requiring specialist training. The same applies to poetry, which is why we have chosen extracts from two novels to introduce you to literary translation.

Abdelkader Benali

The first text is by Abdelkader Benali and is taken from his novel *Laat het morgen mooi weer zijn*. Translating the title offers a glimpse of some of the challenges of literary translation. The literal rendering would be 'Let the weather be nice tomorrow'. The website of the *Nederlands Literatuurfonds* (Netherlands Literary Fund) uses 'Let Tomorrow Be Fine', which preserves some of the Dutch title's ambiguity. At the same time, however, the phrase refers to a saying of the main character's father, who is an incorrigible optimist, someone who perhaps rather unfeelingly propels his son onwards to the future. A better translation might be 'Tomorrow is another day', which is used in English to suggest that we can pick ourselves up and start again in the future. What this tells us is that when translating literature, you need to be an attentive reader and bring your understanding of character and thematic content to bear on your translation. This is of course difficult to do if you are translating a fragment – hence this introduction. If you are commissioned to translate a sample of a work it would be very unwise to attempt it without reading the whole book.

Abdelkader Benali was born in Morocco and moved to the Netherlands with his parents when he was four. He published his first novel, *Bruiloft aan zee* (Wedding by the Sea), at the age of 21 in 1996 and has maintained a regular output of fiction amounting to eight novels, volumes of poetry, plays, and also collections of journalistic writing. He has also become well known in the Netherlands and Flanders for his television work, particularly the series *Benali boekt* in which he interviews other writers. *Laat het morgen mooi weer zijn*, which focuses on a young man's relationship with his father, has a companion novel in *De stem van mijn moeder* (My Mother's Voice), which appeared four years later. This novel has a completely new main character, and pays much more attention to this young man's mother, as well as his relationship with his dead twin brother. However, in both novels, family relationships and the way they are affected by the different individuals' response to living in a new culture are an important preoccupation of Benali's.

Laat het morgen mooi weer zijn features Malik, a successful therapist to Amsterdam yuppies who simply allows them to talk about themselves. He is not qualified as a therapist, and sees his work as lending an ear to the kinds of problems that these people don't want to bore their friends and colleagues with. Malik is obese and his own life is rather empty. The story, told by a narrator who has intimate knowledge of Malik's life, can be described as his therapeutic life narrative. In it, his strange relationship with his equally strange parents is depicted in a deceptively easy, yet subtly barbed Dutch. The narrative allows us and Malik to see how his father had dominated his life. For example, for his 18th birthday, Malik's father gave him a single ticket for a cruise – hardly a suitable present for a lone young adult, who is seduced by an elderly Spanish woman during the trip. The novel ends with Malik deciding to change his life by losing weight and changing his career.

Margot Vanderstraeten

The second passage for translation is also taken from a novel on the theme of looking back at family. This time a 62-year-old man looks back at his younger self and his difficult relationship with his family. The novel is *Mise en Place* by the Flemish writer Margot Vanderstraeten; it is narrated by Victor, youngest of four brothers and sisters. His favourite sister Louise is deaf and dumb, and has become a nun. It is her death that provokes Victor's story. As well as portraying the life of the successful chef Victor has become, the novel gradually uncovers a terrible family secret connected with the tragic death of their father and a number of his employees in an underground accident in 1958. The father's sudden death and the family's subsequent poverty explains some of the mother's bitterness, but the secrets and silences surrounding responsibility for their father's death explain Victor's driven perfectionism as a chef and Louise's withdrawal from the world.

Margot Vanderstraeten is a Belgian writer who was born in 1967 in Hasselt in the Dutch-speaking part of Belgium. The first of her three novels, *Alle mensen bijten* (People Bite), appeared in 2002 and was awarded the *Debuutprijs*, a Flemish literature prize awarded to the best first novel in that year. *De vertraging* (The Delay) appeared in 2004, followed by *Mise en Place* in 2009. She also has a journalistic career writing a regular column for the Flemish daily newspaper *De morgen* and contributing to a range of other publications. Margot Vanderstraeten has also published two collections of interviews, one focusing on writers, the other on criminal lawyers.

Again, the title of the novel from which our extract is taken – *Mise en Place* – presents some interesting translation problems. For a start, it is in French rather than Dutch, so an important question is whether we can leave it in French, since this is the effect deliberately created by the author. However, French is one of Belgium's official languages, which gives the language a more recognisable status than it has in the English-speaking world. The next question is whether an English reader would know what 'mise en place' means, and a quick look at Wikipedia suggests that it is a concept from the domain of cooking that is also used in English. If we were translating the novel and decided against using the French phrase, we could go so far as to consider inventing a completely different title, perhaps in discussion with the author. This idea introduces us to one of the exciting aspects of literary translation: the possibility of working with a writer.

Text 1: Extract from *Laat het morgen mooi weer zijn*

The extract is the opening passage of Chapter 34. The narrator has been telling the story of Malik's life with his parents, interwoven with memories of Carmen Lopez de la Madrid, the Spanish woman he encountered on his cruise. By this stage in the novel, it has become clear to us that Malik's parents each responded very differently to their new cultural surroundings: his father became obsessed with making money, while his mother withdrew and refused to adapt. Malik, a 13-year-old boy at this point, has recently learned his parents' secret: that his father spied for the regime in order to get a visa – this may explain his mother's reference to mysterious men in Switzerland. But the turning point for the family has been the father's new interest in Christianity – this is what is upsetting Malik's mother in this passage. Just before this scene, Malik had been sent by both parents independently of each other to have a butcher's knife sharpened, and he is unsure of their intentions.

(continued)

> *(continued)*
>
> **Laat het morgen mooi weer zijn**
>
> Maliks vader had een richting gevonden in zijn leven. Hij kende nu, zoals hij het zelf formuleerde, een leidend principe en daarmee was een proces in gang gezet waar Maliks moeder ziek van werd. Ze werd elke dag een beetje zieker.
>
> 'Ik weet niet wie die twee mannen waren die we in Zwitserland zijn tegengekomen, maar ik weet wel dat het agenten van het regime zijn geweest. Ze moesten eens weten wat ze op hun kerfstok hebben,' klaagde zijn moeder.
>
> Zijn vader haalde de Rembrandt-bijbel in huis, de grootste editie. Zij beschouwde het als een oorlogsverklaring.
>
> 'We moeten hulp zoeken voor je vader,' zei zijn moeder. 'En daarbij heb ik jouw hulp nodig.'
>
> 'Ik ga geen messen meer laten slijpen,' sprak Malik vastbesloten.
>
> 'Je moet niet meer met hem praten. Niet meer naar hem luisteren. Je moet hem aankijken alsof hij zichzelf door het slijk gehaald heeft. Hem mijden alsof hij schurft heeft.'
>
> 'Ik begrijp het,' zei Malik.
>
> 'Ik wil niet dat je het begrijpt,' schreeuwde ze. 'Ik wil dat je het veroordeelt. In naam van het vaderland, veroordeel het! In naam van de gerechtigheid, veroordeel het! Hij houdt niet van je. Zie je dat niet. Hij houdt van andere zaken. Eerst hield hij van geld en nu is hij in Jezus. Hij heeft een leeg haart. Een kakkerlak heeft meer gevoel in zijn donder.'
>
> Malik, niet eens een adolescent in die dagen, besloot het hoofd koel te houden.
>
> 'Hoe wil je hem helpen?'
>
> 'Door te laten zien dat we echt van hem houden.'
>
> ---
>
> Source: Abdelkader Benali (2005) *Laat het morgen mooi weer zijn*. Amsterdam: Arbeiderspers, p. 153.

1. Translation strategies and techniques

Here are our two key questions to help you make a first analysis of the text. The first will help you develop your 'picture' or interpretation of the text, while the second involves reflection on your target audience.

i. *What are the first things you notice about the text?*

– *It consists largely of dialogue.*

   The first question to ask yourself is: What style is the conversation written in? Is it naturalistic – that is, is it written as people speak? Or is it stylised in some way? This leads on to the larger observation:

– *The text is written in short sentences, which sound slightly abrupt.*
Before you start translating, you need to decide how the style and tone of the novel come across and try to reproduce this. Both the dialogue and the linking narrative are written in a slightly alienated voice, which might sound a little abrupt. In the case of literature, your aim should be to recreate this voice even if it means using a style of English that feels a little uncomfortable. As a translator, you could opt for a different strategy in which you 'naturalise' the language of the text – that is, make it sound more like natural English. But be aware that, if you do this, you are changing the way the writer and his work come across in English.

– *The character of the mother is dominant.*
Malik's mother characterises herself through the way she speaks. Try to form a clear picture of what she is like. This will help you to create a consistent character in your translation. Although Malik doesn't say much, it is important that you also have a sense of the relationship between mother and son. For example, Malik is described as *niet eens adolescent in die dagen* – in other words, he is still quite young and impressionable.

ii. What do you know about your target audience and how will this affect your translation?

A likely brief for the translation might be that the writer's publisher or agent has asked for a sample translation to be used at book fairs. In actual fact, such a sample would normally be longer than this fragment, but you can use this brief to visualise your target audience. In other words, we are not thinking of a general English-speaking audience, but rather a specific one of individuals who work in the publishing industry. They are likely to be scouts, agents and readers working for publishers. The point is that they are experienced readers of literary texts, so the translation is not just for information: it must be good. This suggests that you will need to revise it very carefully.

2. Text and language

This step is crucial since it determines the accuracy of your translation.

i. Words and expressions

In gang gezet: in the dictionary you are more likely to find phrases with *aan de gang*, which means 'in motion'. This means that you will have to work out what this phrase – *in gang zetten* – means from the context.

Ziek van iets worden: a phrase expressing the cause of an illness, to be made ill by something.

Kerfstok: there are a number of expressions using *kerfstok* – e.g. *op zijn kerfstok hebben* – which originally referred to outstanding payments, but have gradually come to mean a more general kind of debt someone owes. In the case of *wat ze op hun kerfstok hebben* you would have to paraphrase to give an even more general meaning such as 'what they are responsible for'.

Rembrandt-bijbel: this is a culturally specific reference to Dutch versions of the Bible, which contain reproductions of Rembrandt's work as illustrations.

Mijden: the more usual verb would be *vermijden*; this gives *mijden* a particular 'feel' of an activity that is outdated, almost medieval.

Donder: this is very informal language and helps to convey the mother's anger. It is also quite funny, though not intentionally so on the mother's part and is in stark contrast to the old-fashioned language she has just used. In neutral English, *donder* means 'body', so you will have to be very inventive here if you want to convey the humorous effect.

ii. Sentences

There are not many complex sentences in the passage, but it is worth reminding you of the technique for analysing such sentences. Also, we touch on the important grammatical question of the Dutch word *er*, its various forms and related constructions. The Practical Tips section of this chapter also deals with how to translate *er*, so please refer to this as well.

Hij kende nu, zoals hij het zelf formuleerde, een leidend principe en daarmee was een proces in gang gezet waar Maliks moeder ziek van werd.

Start by asking yourself how many grammatical clauses this sentence contains. There are four, which can be analysed as follows: the two main clauses are *Hij kende nu een leidend principe* and *daarmee was een proces in gang gezet*. The subclause *zoals hij het zelf formuleerde* is embedded within the first main clause and tells us that *een leidend principe*, or 'guiding principle', is the phrase the father uses to refer to his new faith. The second subclause concludes the sentence: *waar Maliks moeder ziek van werd*. The second half of the sentence – *en daarmee was een proces in gang gezet waar Maliks moeder ziek van werd* – contains two examples of '*er*-constructions': *daarmee* and *waarvan*.

Ze moesten eens weten... Things to note here are that the past tense of *moeten* often translates as 'ought' and that the particle *eens* gives emphasis to the sentence meaning. 'Really' would be a fairly neutral rendering compared with 'jolly well', which is more informal.

En daarbij heb ik jouw hulp nodig. This clause uses a similar *er*-construction to the one introduced by *daarmee* discussed above. For a full discussion, refer to the Practical Tips section of this chapter.

3. Style, register and tone

i. Stylistic analysis of the source text

The text is written in a style that is emphatically plain. However, it is very carefully constructed, and although the grammatical structures are relatively simple and the sentences quite short, the text uses very subtle means to convey the mental states of the main characters. In fact, it is the very simplicity and business-like character of the style that alerts the reader to look more closely at the writing.

While the dialogue represents the characters' mood and ideas, it is important to remember that there is a narrator whose starting-point for his story is Malik in the present, an older man about to change his life. The narrator tells Malik's story as if he has privileged access to it, replaying Malik's memories of his strange childhood and difficult adolescence. In other words, the narrator tells the story in the knowledge of how Malik had been affected by his parents' contrasting behaviour: his mother's emotion and his father's lack of feeling. It is a similar lack of feeling that is conveyed by the narration.

The register of the text remains resolutely neutral and distanced. Even in the dialogue, the characters speak in sentences, they do not stutter with emotion. In fact, the mother's angry pronouncements come across as slightly laughable because of her mixing of linguistic registers.

The tone of the text is not only distanced; there is a hint of irony from time to time. Perhaps this is the only way to tell the story from the perspective of the older Malik, as it conveys the fact that he has been able to look critically at his youth in order to move on.

ii. Assessment of the style of writing appropriate to the target text

This aspect of translation is clear where literature is concerned: the main duty of a literary translator is to represent a writer and his or her work to new audiences outside the Dutch language area. Unless there are serious problems of cultural transfer, such as the use of local dialect, for example, the best strategy is one in which you aim to recreate the literary effects and thus the experience of reading the source text. This means forming a clear 'picture' of the text, its characters, its mode of narration, and its themes and preoccupations so that you can ensure that decisions you make about word choice and sentence structure all contribute to the bigger picture.

Sample translation of Text 1: *Laat het morgen mooi weer zijn*

Tomorrow is another day

Malik's father had found a direction for his life. He now possessed a guiding principle, as he himself put it, and it was this that set in motion a process which made Malik's mother ill. Every day the illness became a little worse.

(continued)

(continued)

'I don't know who those two men were that we encountered in Switzerland, but I do know that they were agents of the regime. They have a lot to answer for, if only they knew it,' his mother complained.

His father brought the Bible into the house, the largest edition with Rembrandt pictures. She regarded it as a declaration of war.

'We need to get help for your father,' said his mother. 'And I need your help for that.'

'I am not going to get any more knives sharpened,' Malik said decisively.

'You must stop talking to him. Stop listening to him. You must look at him as if he has dragged himself through the mud. Avoid him as if he has the mange.'

'I understand,' said Malik.

'I don't want you to understand it,' she yelled. 'I want you to condemn it. In the name of the fatherland, condemn it! In the name of justice, condemn it! He does not love you. Don't you see. He loves other things. First he loved money and now he has found Jesus. He has an empty heart. A bullet-proof cockroach has more feeling.'

Malik, not even an adolescent in those days, decided to keep a cool head.

'How are you planning to help him?'

'By showing that we truly love him.'

PRACTICAL TIPS: TRANSLATING *ER*

There is a grammatical construction that occurs widely in Dutch and is important for a full understanding of Dutch texts. It revolves around the small word *er* and does not have a counterpart in English. This is why it poses something of a challenge to translators, not least because it is vital for comprehending the source text in the first place. In what follows, we identify the four functions of *er* together with the different forms and usages of *er*, and suggest ways of translating it. You will also find more extensive explanations in most grammars of Dutch.

The small Dutch word *er* has four different grammatical functions. Understanding these is the first step towards ST comprehension. The most straightforward function of *er* is as an adverb meaning 'there' – for example, *Ze heeft er altijd gewoond* – 'She has always lived there.'

Er is also used to introduce sentences with an indefinite subject. This second function has a parallel in the English 'There is ...' or 'There are ...' and does not pose too many problems for translators. However, the range of possibilities in Dutch is greater. For example, in sentences with a passive verb and open subject the translation will depend on the register of the passage: *Er wordt gelachen* – 'There is laughter' or 'Someone is laughing'. Take this sentence from a story by Cees Nooteboom: *Er was heel veel met haar gebeurd, schreef ze.*[1] Literally, 'There had happened very much with her . . .' – however, English grammar does not invariably require use of 'There' to start a sentence with an indefinite subject. A better translation would be 'A great deal had happened to her, she wrote.'

In the third function of *er* it is used to refer to a part of a greater whole, and can be translated as 'of it' or 'of them'. For example: *Hoeveel broers heb jij? – Ik heb er drie.* How many brothers do you have? – I have three (of them). Whereas in Dutch, *er* must be present, in English you will most likely be able to leave out its translation. Here is another example from a story by Cees Nooteboom in which he uses *er* in the introductory and 'part' functions: *Er is er maar één, de man met de pet, die lacht.*[2] The sentence, which refers to a photo with seven people in it, opens with 'There is . . .'. It goes on to specify that 'only one of them' (*er maar één*) is laughing: 'the man with the cap'.

It is the fourth function of *er* which presents the biggest challenge to translators into English, mainly because the English language does not have a parallel construction, except in very high register legal documents where it is found in such words as 'theretofore' and 'thereinafter'. The fourth function of *er* is pronominal – in other words, it refers to a previously mentioned noun. The pronouns *het*, *hem* and *ze* cannot be used in Dutch after prepositions. Instead, the construction '*er* + preposition' is used: *De huisvrouw besteedt een dagtaak aan haar werk, maar toch krijgt ze er geen loon voor betaald.* Taken from a 1979 pamphlet on feminism, this sentence complains that 'The housewife spends a whole day on her work, yet she does not receive a wage for it.' Here, *ervoor* refers back to the noun *dagtaak* (day's work) in the first part of the sentence. Notice that *er* can be separated from the preposition it is used with – *er geen loon voor* – and that this does not affect the translation.

In this function, *er* can be replaced by *hier* and *daar*, which are translated by 'this' and 'that'. Compare: *Wat doe je ermee? Wat doe je daarmee? Wat doe je hiermee?* What are you doing with it? What are you doing with that? What are you doing with this? Now you can look back at the second sentence of Text 1 in this chapter:

Hij kende nu, zoals hij het zelf formuleerde, een leidend principe en daarmee was een proces in gang gezet waar Maliks moeder ziek van werd.

(continued)

(continued)

He now possessed a guiding principle, as he himself put it, and <u>with that</u> a process was set in motion by which Malik's mother became ill.

Note the special form of *met* in this construction. *Daar + met = daarmee.* Note also that, in the more sophisticated use of Dutch in the quote, the word *daar* (that) can refer back to the whole idea of Malik's father's new faith as well as the 'guiding principle'.

Here is another similar example from Text 1:

'We moeten hulp zoeken voor je vader,' zei zijn moeder. 'En <u>daarbij</u> heb ik jouw hulp nodig.'

In this example, *daarbij* refers back to the idea expressed by Malik's mother in the first half of the sentence: 'We must seek help for your father.' She tells Malik that she needs his help 'with that'.

Note that both *daarmee* and *daarbij* have been translated as 'with that'. The two different prepositions do indicate a difference in meaning that is masked in the translation. *Mee* refers back to the instrument of change – the 'guiding principle' – whereas *daarbij* suggests a process that could be expressed in English by saying 'to do that' instead of 'with that'. There is one more aspect to the fourth, pronominal function of *er*: it also functions as a relative pronoun. The English relative pronoun 'which' is normally rendered in Dutch with *die* or *dat*. For example, *Neem de pen die op tafel ligt* (Take the pen which is lying on the table) or *Het boek <u>dat</u> ik aan het lezen ben . . .* (The book which I am reading . . .). But as soon as a preposition enters the frame, a construction with *waar-* is triggered. For example, *De pen <u>waarmee</u> ik schrijf . . .* (The pen with which I am writing/The pen I am writing with) and *Wat vind je van het schilderij <u>waar</u> we nu <u>naar</u> kijken?* (What do you think of the painting at which we are now looking/What do you think of the painting we are looking at now?)

To conclude, let us return to the last clause in the sentence from Text 1 about Malik's father's guiding principle for an example of *waar* in the function of relative pronoun referring back to the noun *proces*:

. . . <u>waar</u> Maliks moeder ziek <u>van</u> werd.

The Dutch phrase *ziek worden van iets* contains the construction 'verb + preposition'. There are many of these constructions where a verb is followed by a set preposition. As we saw above, it is the presence of prepositions that triggers *er*-constructions, and the clause above provides an example. When analysing this example, note that '*waar* + preposition' do not have to occur side by side in the sentence.

You will remember that Malik's father 'now possessed a guiding principle, as he himself put it, and with that a process was set in motion <u>by which</u> Malik's mother became ill.

Literature 53

Text 2: Extract from *Mise en Place*

The extract is the opening passage of Chapter 6. In this chapter, Victor, who is narrating the story, looks back to when he was about 14 and was on his way to visit his sister Louise in the convent. When the book opens, we learn that he is a chef of 62 and that Louise has died, leaving a strange request in her will: that he provide a dinner for all the family on the evening before the funeral, at which they must read out a document that one of the nuns will bring. This is what happens at the end of the novel when the documents written by Louise are provided so that the reader can find out the true nature of the family secret.

Mise en Place

Toen ik, als enige van de vier, nog bij mijn moeder woonde, brachten we Louise maandelijks een bezoek in het klooster. We reden met de bus naar Heverlee. Dat vond mijn moeder niet prettig; als we opstapten, moest ik bij de chauffeur de tickets betalen, terwijl zij zich, met strakke blik, al een weg door de gang baande. Bussen waren voor arme mensen, en hoewel wij sinds de dood van mijn vader tot deze categorie waren afgezakt, weigerde zij deel uit te maken van dat deel van de bevolking dat hard moest werken om zich een ellendig bestaan te kunnen veroorloven. Liever bleef ze uren in bed liggen, tot het opnieuw donker werd. Dat was haar manier om onze status op te schroeven.

Andere moeders lieten hun kind aan de raamzijde zitten, maar niet de mijne. Zij eigende zich steevast de plek aan het raam toe. Tijdens de hele rit sprak ze geen woord. Met haar tas vastgeklemd op haar schoot tuurde ze naar buiten. Ze keek naar het voorbijglijdende landschap alsof ze een film volgde, of een tv-feuilleton waarvan ze geen enkel beeld wilde missen.

Op een van die maandelijkse bezoekdagen troonde Louise me mee naar de hostiebakkerij die achter in het klooster lag en waar zij, samen met haar medezusters en enkele verstandelijk gehandicapten, dagelijks duizenden ouwels bakte, die aan naburige parochiepriesters werden verkocht. De zusters, die goede contacten met missionarissen onderhielden, stuurden ook kilo's van dat flinterdunne brood de wereld rond. Congo en Rwanda rekenden ze tot hun grootste afnemers.

Source: Margot Vanderstraeten (2009) *Mise en Place*. Amsterdam/Antwerp: Atlas, p. 33.

1. Translation strategies and techniques

Below are our two key questions to help you make a first analysis. The first will lead you to reflect on the literary qualities of the text, while the second involves consideration of your target audience.

54 Literature

i. What are the first things you notice about the text?

– *It is told by a first-person narrator, an 'I' character.*
  This means that the main character is telling his own story, so in a way everything contributes to the picture of him. You will need to think about how to ensure you give him a consistent and convincing voice in your translation.

– *The text contains some specifically Roman Catholic references.*
  This is an important aspect of life in Flanders. If you are not familiar with Catholicism, you will need to do some research, in particular on the special bread that is made in the convent.

– *The narrative uses clear, measured language and even the long sentences are easy to follow.*
  With literary texts, such apparent clarity can be difficult to recreate. Ask yourself how the language functions. Which textual tasks is it performing here? Is it painting a picture? Is it dynamic or static? Does it seek to reveal or hide things from the reader? It certainly conveys a clear picture of Victor's mother as seen through his eyes.

ii. What do you know about the target audience for your translation and how will it affect your translation?

As with the first text, your target audience is most likely to be someone who knows about literature and works in the publishing industry. Given that they may well be looking to commission a translation of the whole novel, as the translator of a sample, you are responsible for the way the writer is perceived in English. This creates a particular kind of responsibility, which suggests you will take care over the literary quality of your translation.

2. Text and language

This step is crucial since it determines the accuracy of your translation.

i. Words and expressions

We begin with a group of expressions involving reflexive verbs. Below we cite them in their dictionary form – we suggest you go back to the text and underline them.

> *Zich een weg banen*: the basic expression here is *een weg banen*. With these everyday expressions it is sometimes difficult to know where to look them up: under *weg* or *banen*? A simple strategy is to start with the less frequent word – here *banen*. In the *Van Dale Groot Woordenboek*, you will find the combination immediately. In Text 2, the phrase is used with a reflexive verb since it denotes an action the mother performs for herself. How does English convey this element?
>
> *Zich iets kunnen veroorloven*: the basic meaning of *veroorloven* is 'allow', so taking into account the reflexive verb, a literal translation would be 'allow

oneself'. However, there may be English expressions more suited to the context of poverty. Especially with literary translation, give yourself the space to think creatively about vocabulary. The lexical items in the dictionary are less important than how the words come across in this very specific context.

Zich iets toeëigenen: again we are dealing with a reflexive verb phrase. The verb consists of the prefix *toe* and the base verb *eigenen*, and again your best strategy is first to give a literal translation and then to think about a more creative one.

Voorbijglijdende: this present participle of the separable verb *voorbijglijden* is used here as an adjective and can be analysed as follows: *voorbij* + *glijden* + *-d* + *-e*.

Hostiebakkerij and *ouwels*: there is clearly a relationship between *hostie* and *ouwels* since the text tells us they are both what the nuns bake. The fact that two different words are given should alert you to the need to do some research.

Enkele verstandelijk gehandicapten: this is a phrase that you would need to alter to something more currently acceptable if you were translating a factual text. Literature is different. Ask yourself when this part of the story is set and who is speaking. Remember that if you change a first-person narration you change the character too.

ii. Sentences

Bussen waren voor arme mensen, en hoewel wij sinds de dood van mijn vader tot deze categorie waren afgezakt, weigerde zij deel uit te maken van dat deel van de bevolking dat hard moest werken om zich een ellendig bestaan te kunnen veroorloven.

This sentence consists of a series of clauses. There are two main clauses: *Bussen waren voor arme mensen* (Buses were for poor people) and <u>*weigerde zij deel uit te maken van dat deel van de bevolking*</u> (she refused to be part of that part of the population). The second main clause begins with the verb, rather than the subject, because the first element of the clause is *hoewel wij sinds de dood van mijn vader tot deze categorie waren afgezakt* (though since my father's death we had descended to this category).

Ze keek naar het voorbijglijdende landschap alsof ze een film volgde, of een tv-feuilleton waarvan ze geen enkel beeld wilde missen.

This time we demonstrate the relatively straightforward sentence structure using brackets.

(*Ze keek naar het voorbijglijdende landschap*) (*alsof ze een film volgde, of een tv-feuilleton*) (*waarvan ze geen enkel beeld wilde missen*).

Note that the last clause is introduced by *waar* + preposition *van*, referring back to the noun *tv-feuilleton* in the previous clause. This can be translated literally as '... a TV series of which she did not want to miss a single image'. The question facing you is whether to render this in more everyday English, and the answer will depend on your assessment of the writer's style.

3. Style, register, tone

i. Stylistic analysis of the source text

The passage is composed in good, literary Dutch with a controlled style and balanced sentences. Although narrated by the character Victor, it maintains a neutral register, perhaps because the narrator is speaking of events that had a deep emotional impact and because he prefers to remain in control. The tone generally remains neutral even when he is describing his mother's seemingly selfish behaviour. There is only a subtle hint of anger or blame, for instance when he comments on his mother's tendency to stay in bed. He simply describes what he remembers. The memory of his mother is described in quite visual terms.

ii. Assessment of the style of writing appropriate to the target text

The challenge here is to recreate the literary text in the way it functions – as an account of a character's life that gives the reader a clear sense of what he is like, and as an account of his past experiences and his relationships with family members seen from his perspective.

Sample translation of Text 2: *Mise en Place*

The last supper

When, as the only remaining one of four, I lived at home with my mother, we paid Louise a monthly visit in the convent. We went by bus to Heverlee. This was not something my mother enjoyed; when we boarded, I had to pay the driver for the tickets, while she, staring straight ahead, made her way to her seat. Buses were for poor people, and although since the death of my father we had descended to this category, she refused to belong to that part of the population that had to work hard to eke out a miserable existence. She would rather lie in bed for hours, until it got dark again. That was her way of inflating our status.

Other mothers let their child sit by the window, but not mine. She insisted on taking the seat on the window side. During the entire ride she did not utter a word. Clasping her bag on her lap she peered out. She watched the passing landscape as though she were following a film, or a TV series, and did not want to miss a single image.

> On one of the monthly visitors' days Louise took me along to the host bakery behind the convent where she, together with her fellow nuns and some mentally handicapped individuals, baked thousands of wafers which were sold to neighbouring parish priests. The sisters, who had good contacts with missionaries, also sent kilos of this wafer-thin bread all round the world. Congo and Rwanda were counted among their main customers.

Dutch translation in practice

To round off this chapter, we have selected a passage taken from the companion novel to the book from which Text 1 was taken: Abdelkader Benali's *De stem van mijn moeder*. This book represents family life from a different perspective – that of a successful son, who is the narrator. The extract is taken from the beginning of the novel. It is the opening passage of the section entitled *De Schoonspringer*. For a sample translation of this passage, see p. 182.

Text 3: *De Schoonspringer*

Het is halftwaalf in de ochtend als de Schoonspringer mij belt.
  Ik bevries als ik zijn naam zie oplichten in mijn mobieltje. Het is precies vier maanden, zes dagen, acht uur en zestien minuten geleden dat hij mij gebeld heeft. Ik ben druk bezig op de fotoset, sta op het punt de modellen te vragen een andere positie in te nemen, heb net diep adem gehaald want het nu-of-nooit-moment is wel aangebroken voor deze glossy reportage.
  De Schoonspringer.
  Zo heb ik mijn vader genoemd sinds ik als jongen van een jaar of acht met mijn broer in een stapelbed lag en we de gesprekken afluisterden die hij met zijn vrienden voerde in de woonkamer, gelegen boven onze slaapkamer. Zijn vrienden kwamen steevast eens in de twee weken op bezoek. Wij zagen die vrienden nooit echt, want ze kwamen binnen als wij al in bed lagen en toch lukte het me om een glimp van ze op te vangen. Ik kroop, gehuld in de pyjama waar onze moeder ons voor het slapen gaan in hees, voorzichtig uit bed en sloop de kamer uit, en keek van onderaan de trap naar boven, waar ik ze, wanneer de kamerdeur geopend was, kon zien zitten. In de gang waar ik zat waren ze kort daarvoor binnengekomen en stonden hun vermoeide schoenen te wachten op hun terugkeer. Onze vierkamerwoning was ons het jaar daarvoor met een ruimhartig gebaar door de woningstichting toegewezen zodat we onze krappe tweekamerwoning achter ons konden

(continued)

> *(continued)*
>
> laten. We schrijven de eerste helft van de jaren tachtig. Tsjernobyl was nog niet ontploft. Maradona had nog niet met de Hand van God tegen de Engelsen gescoord. En mijn vader luisterde als het maar even kon elke dag naar klassieke Arabische muziek waarvan hij hele stukken meeneuriede.
>
> Source: Abdelkader Benali (2009) *De stem van mijn moeder*. Utrecht/Amsterdam/Antwerpen: Arbeiderspers, pp. 13–14.

Notes

1 Taken from Nooteboom, C. (2009) *'s Nachts komen de vossen* (The Foxes Come at Night). Amsterdam: De Bezige Bij, p. 18.
2 Ibid., p. 42.

4 Employment

Introduction: texts and contexts

In the course of the twentieth century, the society and culture of the Low Countries underwent considerable changes that altered irrevocably the role that work played in people's lives. This chapter explores how these changes have placed new pressures on the job markets in the Netherlands and Belgium over the past few decades, but also brought with them new opportunities for diversity, openness and innovation that will shape further developments in employment in the twenty-first century. Both countries are signatories on the Treaty on the Functioning of the European Union and the Treaty on European Union, which seek, among other things, to improve the working environment across Europe. They do so by establishing policies for workers' health and safety and their social protection both when in work and once their employment contract has been terminated. They combat discrimination based on sex, racial or ethnic origin, religion or belief, disability, age or sexual orientation, and are committed to ensuring that men and women are equal with regard to labour market opportunities, and are entitled to equal treatment at work.

In the Netherlands, the Criminal Code of 1971 contained the first legal instruments against discrimination, which took the form of provisions against racial discrimination. Subsequent EC directives on the equal treatment of men and women resulted in the *Wet Gelijke Beloning* (Equal Pay Act), which came into force in 1975. With the introduction in 1994 of the *Algemene Wet Gelijke Behandeling* (General Equal Treatment Act), the scope of anti-discrimination was extended further, given that 'unequal treatment' now constituted discrimination on the grounds of gender, marital status, race, nationality, religion, political opinion, and hetero- or homosexual preference. This law covers all aspects that pertain to employment, from the advertising of a position to recruitment processes and appointment criteria. It also covers the terms and conditions of employment, including initial salary level and increases, training and promotion opportunities. Dutch employers are also bound by law to submit annual reports documenting the proportion of ethnic minorities among their employees, to ensure the ongoing integration of non-Dutch citizens into the labour market in the Netherlands. With regard to gender discrimination, the

60 *Employment*

Dutch Parliament has been active in creating legislation that supports women in the workforce, including laws to combat discrimination against part-time employees (who tend to be female rather than male) and to increase the childcare responsibilities that employers must take on, thus ensuring that women are no longer tied to the home.

In Belgium similar legislation has been put in place to counter discrimination on the grounds of gender. On 12 January 2007, the Belgian government adopted a law that would promote the equality of men and women by integrating the gender dimension of employment into Belgian federal policy frameworks. 'Gender mainstreaming', the concept of examining the different implications for women and men of any given planned policy action, is therefore no longer something to which firms can voluntarily submit but is now a legal requirement. The *Instituut voor de Gelijkheid van Vrouwen en Mannen* (http://igvm-iefh.belgium.be/nl/), known in English as the *Institute for the Equality of Women and Men*, aims to 'guarantee and promote the equality of women and men and to fight against any form of discrimination and equality based on gender in all aspects of life'. The *Instituut* seeks to fulfil these aims in a number of different ways: by co-ordinating studies and research into gender inequality, formulating recommendations to make to public authorities with a view to improving relevant laws and regulations, supporting institutions in efforts towards achieving equality between men and women, and making individuals aware of their rights and their obligations. The *Instituut* is also a repository of documentation that might be of use in future legal cases and is located at the hub of networks actively related to prohibiting any form of gender discrimination.

Texts that deal with the subject of discrimination – whether on the grounds of race, gender or other category – are therefore likely to be encountered by translators working in a variety of different fields. Whether you consider yourself to have a specialism in business, law, marketing or finance, you may well be required to deal with texts that relate to equality in the workplace – and in areas such as education policy, or national and regional government, issues related to equal pay and equal working conditions are just as likely to crop up. From public-sector employers to private companies, multinationals to small businesses, all need to demonstrate that they have a policy of non-discrimination towards their employees. A code of ethics (*Code van Bedrijfsethiek*) is often made publicly available to read and download from the websites of a considerable number of high-profile employers, including European institutions such as the European Parliament, international banks and worldwide employers in the retail, fashion and car industries. By publishing such information in their online documentation and in their printed corporate literature, employers seek to demonstrate that they recognise the ethical obligations they have towards their employees, and that their departments of human resource management are aware of the need for non-discriminatory behaviour in the spheres of recruitment selection, performance appraisal, training and development.

Text 1: *Migratie*

The following text comes from a prize-winning work that appeared in 2008 with Van Gorcum, a publishing house that covers a range of titles that fall into the categories of care and welfare, culture, management and education. The authors of the book, Karen van Oudenhoven-van der Zee and Jan Pieter van Oudenhoven, are academics working at the Rijksuniversiteit Groningen, who specialise in organisational and cross-cultural psychology. They are particularly interested in questions of integration and social empowerment, as well as international relations and the factors that govern successful intercultural interaction. This book was commissioned by the *Nederlandse Stichting voor Psychotechniek* ('Dutch Foundation for Psychotechnology'), an organisation that aims to ensure that people use their capacities to the best of their ability in the world of work. The book addresses how globalisation and changes in the employment market have made diversity an economic necessity – something with which organisations must engage in order to keep pace with changes in society. The authors discuss what can be done to improve the position of foreign co-workers in the workplace, and to facilitate co-operation between Dutch and non-Dutch employees. They examine how organisations can benefit from the talent of foreign members of their workforce, and profit from the creativity and innovation that such people bring to their organisations. Taking diversity in the workplace as their central theme, the authors discuss how different forms of intervention – whether on an individual or a group level – can reconcile differences and allow employers and employees to make full use of the opportunities that a culturally diverse workplace can offer. The extract we have chosen for translation comes from a subsection of the Introduction in which the authors discuss cultural diversity and integration, and various stages of interculturalisation, as organisations move from being primarily monocultural to becoming multicultural.

Migratie

Van de huidige Nederlandse bevolking is 19% allochtoon, waarvan meer dan de helft niet-westers is (CBS, 2004). De belangrijkste niet-westerse groepen allochtonen zijn de Turken, Marokkanen en Surinamers die tezamen meer dan een miljoen inwoners bedragen. Op de arbeidsmarkt doen niet-westerse allochtonen het aanmerkelijk slechter dan autochtonen. De arbeidsparticipatie van 15- tot 64-jarigen bedraagt voor autochtonen 67% tegen 49% voor allochtonen, met de laagste participatie voor Marokkanen en de hoogste voor Surinamers. Hoe kunnen landen nu het beste omgaan met de verschillende groepen immigranten? Met uitzondering van Canada, dat misschien wel het enige land is met een duidelijk multicultureel beleid, neigen de meeste naties naar een assimilatie-ideologie, hetgeen wil zeggen dat men

(continued)

62 Employment

> *(continued)*
>
> van immigranten verwacht dat ze hun culturele en taalkundige identiteit inruilen voor die van de gastsamenleving. Meestal heeft de autochtone meerderheid ook een duidelijke voorkeur voor assimilatie. Nederland vormt hierop geen uitzondering. In een opiniepeiling uit 1996 vond 75% van de Nederlandse bevolking het 'belangrijk' of 'tamelijk belangrijk' dat immigranten 'Nederlandse normen en waarden aannemen'. In een peiling van 2002 was het percentage gestegen naar 85%. De voorkeur voor assimilatie is begrijpelijk. Zoals eerder aangegeven in dit hoofdstuk, kunnen verschillen in opvattingen, of die nu uit cultuurverschillen voortkomen of uit andere factoren, de communicatie bemoeilijken. Waarschijnlijk komt de groeiende druk tot assimilatie in Nederland, in vergelijking bijvoorbeeld met Canada en de Verenigde Staten, ook voort uit het relatieve gebrek aan ervaring met grote groepen cultureel verschillende immigranten. De hugenoten die in de 17e eeuw naar Nederland migreerden kwamen hier omdat zij hun godsdienst deelden met een groot deel van de Nederlanders. Bovendien waren zij relatief bemiddeld. De grote groep Indische Nederlanders die na de onafhankelijkheid van Nederlands-Indië hier kwamen, spraken Nederlands en waren Nederlands opgevoed. Zij waren immers de vertegenwoordigers en uitvoerders van de Nederlandse koloniale politiek.
>
> Source: Karen van der Zee and Jan Pieter van Oudenhoven (2006) *Culturele diversiteit op het werk: Achtergronden en interventies.* Assen: Van Gorcum, pp. 7–8.

1. Translation strategies and techniques

Below are our two key questions to help you make a first analysis. The first concerns background knowledge relevant for understanding the text, while the second involves reflection on your target audience.

i. What are the first things that you notice about the text?

– *It is written from a strongly Dutch perspective and references to foreignness equate to what is non-Dutch.*

   You will need to think about whether you can continue to adopt this perspective in your translation. Given the fact that you are translating it into English, you are automatically making the text accessible to a wider, international, public, which suggests that you are going to have to adopt a perspective that is less obviously Dutch-centric.

– *It frequently uses the terms* allochtoon *and* autochtoon, *which are not easily translatable into English.*

   You will have to think about which terms are most appropriate in the text that you are constructing, in terms of register as much as political correctness.

Dictionaries tend to offer translations such as 'immigrants' and 'foreigners' to describe those people who originate from another country and are therefore *allochtoon*, while 'indigenous' or 'native' are the translations that tend to be given for those whose origins lie within the country in question and are considered *autochtoon*. You may not necessarily think these English terms are the best words to choose, and you would need to be careful to select terms that are both accurate and do not cause offence. You may also find English-language websites helpful in deciding on the right vocabulary to use. In a British context, for example, the Centre on Migration, Policy and Society (COMPAS) at Oxford University could be helpful, particularly its pages on employment (see https://www.compas.ox.ac.uk/).

– *It refers to another source: 'CBS, 2004'.*
   This is a reference to the report 'Allochtonen in Nederland 2004' published by the *Centraal Bureau voor de Statistiek* and you would need to mention this in a footnote or a bibliography at the end of your translation, if you are commissioned to translate only this one extract from the work.

ii. What do you know about the target audience for your translation and how will this affect your translation?

Your target audience is most likely to be made up of readers from outside the Netherlands with a general interest in European employment policy, or those who have more specific questions about the labour market in the Netherlands and issues related to racial integration and (un)employment. We have mentioned above that the authors, writing within their given context, adopted a strongly Dutch perspective: you are probably coming to the text as a native speaker of English and will necessarily bring a different perspective to this text that should help you to contextualise it more broadly.

2. Text and language

This step is crucial since it determines the accuracy of your translation.

i. Words and expressions

De belangrijkste niet-westerse groepen allochtonen zijn de Turken, Marokkanen en Surinamers: you would need to consider whether you think it is politically correct to use the English term 'Turks' for *Turken*. While the English equivalent of *Marokkanen* is relatively easy to come by, what do we call the people of Suriname? How can you neatly refer to these three different groups in one phrase?

Assimilatie-ideologie: are you going to leave the hyphen in your translation of these two terms or do you think, after doing some research on the internet, that this word pair is more commonly used in English without one?

De gastsamenleving: this is a compound noun made up of *gast* and *samenleving* – but should the translation really be 'guest society'? Think about who is 'receiving' whom in the context of the sentence and therefore how the guest–host relationship is constructed. Think also about how words like *gastgezin* and *gastland* would be translated into English when used in sentences like *U bepaalt zelf of u bij een gastgezin wilt logeren, in een gemeubileerd appartement of in een hotel* and *Er werd van uitgegaan dat migranten zich tot op zekere hoogte moesten aanpassen aan de cultuur van het gastland*.

De hugenoten: the text already tells us that they emigrated to the Netherlands in the seventeenth century for religious reasons. Where did these émigrés come from and what is the English spelling of the group to which they belonged? Are you going to capitalise this term in English or leave it in lower case, as in the original Dutch?

Indische Nederlanders: can this really be translated as 'Indian Dutch', which would refer to people with a connection both to India and the Netherlands? Where is *Nederlands-Indië*, what are the historical ties between this part of the world and the Netherlands, such that it is called *Nederlands-Indië*, and what is the correct English translation for this region and the people who live there?

ii. Sentences

Van de huidige Nederlandse bevolking is 19% allochtoon, waarvan meer dan de helft niet-westers is.

Your initial translation of this sentence might be something like '19 per cent of the current population in the Netherlands were born abroad, of whom more than half are not of Western origin', but this would then mean that your sentence (and in this case the paragraph) would start with a figure, which is considered by some to be stylistically awkward. Can you think of how to reorder the elements in the sentence so that you can start with a word rather than a number?

Op de arbeidsmarkt doen niet-westerse allochtonen het aanmerkelijk slechter dan autochtonen.

The difficulty that you might have encountered in translating this sentence probably has to do with the expression *het slechter doen dan*. This construction can be used in a number of different ways to describe how one thing fares in relation to another. Sometimes it can be translated literally as 'to do worse than/not to do as well as', as in the sentence *Op het gebied van onderzoek en ontwikkeling doen we het slechter dan onze concurrenten*, which translates as 'In terms of research and development we are not doing as well as our competitors.' However, it can also mean 'to be worse off' or 'to be at a disadvantage', as in *Het drama in Joegoslavië resulteerde in povere leefomstandigheden voor het grootste deel van de bevolking, en veel mensen hebben het nu veel slechter dan in 1985*, 'The crisis in Yugoslavia resulted in poor living conditions for the great majority of the population and many people are now much worse off than in 1985.' A similar construction can be found in the sentence *Het is overduidelijk dat kinderen die in armoede opgroeien het op school veel slechter doen, een slechtere gezondheid hebben en veel minder mogelijkheden hebben op maatschappelijk gebied*, which means something like 'It is abundantly clear that children who grow up in poverty tend to perform much less well at school and have poorer health and far fewer opportunities in social terms.'

. . . hetgeen wil zeggen dat men van immigranten verwacht dat . . .

How are you going to translate the word *men*? Are you going to use the English equivalents 'one' or 'you', and how might that change the register of your translation? Or do you think that the sentence could better be restructured in English, using, for example, a passive verbal construction rather than the active one with a dummy subject that has been adopted in the Dutch?

Meestal heeft de autochtone meerderheid ook een duidelijke voorkeur voor assimilatie.

While the Dutch uses the singular verb form with *meerderheid*, in the English we tend to think of the 'majority' of people as a plural concept. So in the same way that in the first sentence we looked at in this section, *19% is allochtoon* is translated as '19% are foreign/were born abroad', you would need to think about the form of the verb that you take here. It is also worth noting how the Dutch sentence puts the stress on *assimilatie*, by placing it at the end. In English, you could think either about placing it at the start or at the very end of the sentence to produce a similar effect.

3. Style, register and tone

i. Stylistic analysis of the source text

The text has a reasonably high register, given that it is a piece of academic writing. It does use terms that belong within the specialist vocabulary of the field, such as *arbeidsparticipatie* and *assimilatie-ideologie*, but it does not presume much background knowledge of the subject, and compares Dutch employment policy with that in Canada to offer a more general introduction to the topic as a whole.

ii. Assessment of the style of writing appropriate to the target text

The formal features of the ST suggest that the translator should ensure that s/he creates a text in English that is stylistically similar, although as mentioned above, it is worth thinking about how to reorient the text towards an international, rather than a specifically Dutch-speaking, readership.

Sample translation of Text 1: *Migratie*

Migration

Currently 19% of the Dutch population are foreign born, of whom half are not from Western countries (CBS, 2004). The most important non-Western minority groups comprise people from Turkey, Morocco and Suriname, who together make up more than 1 million inhabitants. The situation on the job market for members of non-Western minority groups is significantly worse than for people of Dutch origin. The employment rate for 15- to 64-year-olds stands at 67% for those of Dutch origin and 49% for those from minority groups, with those from Suriname the most likely to find work, and those from Morocco the least. How can countries best deal with different groups of immigrants? With the exception of Canada, which is perhaps the only country with an unambiguously multicultural policy, most nations tend towards an ideology of assimilation, i.e. one in which it is expected of immigrants that they exchange their cultural and linguistic identity for that of the host society. The majority of those in that society also have a clear preference for assimilation. The Netherlands is no exception in this regard. In an opinion poll from 1996, it was found that 75% of the Dutch population considered it 'important' or 'quite important' that immigrants should 'adopt Dutch norms and values'. In a poll from 2002, that percentage had risen to 85%. The preference for assimilation is understandable. As we have mentioned earlier in the chapter, variations in interpretation as to whether this derives from cultural differences or other factors can complicate communication. The increasing pressure for assimilation in the Netherlands, in comparison with Canada and the United States, probably derives from the relative lack of experience with large groups of culturally different immigrants. The Huguenots who emigrated to the Netherlands in the seventeenth century came here because they shared their religion with a large proportion of the Dutch. Furthermore they were fairly affluent. The large group of immigrants who came here after the Dutch East Indies became independent, spoke Dutch and had been brought up as Dutch. They were, after all, the representatives and implementers of Dutch colonial policy.

PRACTICAL TIPS: TRANSLATING THE INDEFINITE PRONOUNS *MEN, JE* AND *ZE*

In Dutch there are a number of ways to refer to unspecified people, objects or places. In this section we will focus on the indefinite pronouns *men, je* and *ze*, which are used in Dutch to refer to an undefined person. We tend to think of these in English as the generic or impersonal 'you' or the indefinite pronoun 'one', which we often use in English to make general statements such as 'You should brush your teeth at least twice a day' or 'If one chooses to break the rules, then one must expect to suffer the consequences.' As you may have noticed from these sentences, the English word 'one' sounds extremely formal and perhaps even archaic, and definitely belongs more within the context of written rather than spoken language. By contrast the Dutch word *men*, which is the general equivalent of the English 'one', is used much more frequently and in a relatively wide range of situations. The Dutch term *men* always takes a verb in the third person singular, even if we might think of it in English as referring to a plural concept, so *Men is alleen verzekerd als men in Nederland woont* translates as 'People are only insured if they live in the Netherlands' or 'You are only insured if you live in the Netherlands.' The unstressed *je* or *ze* can be translated as 'you' or 'they' in English, and these are the terms found more commonly in conversation when referring to an unspecified subject, as in our first example, 'You should brush your teeth at least twice a day.' In the sections below we will think about the various options you have as a translator to put these terms *men*, *je* and *ze* into English, and about the verbal constructions you can use with them.

Men as 'one'

We noted that the translation of *men* as 'one' would depend very much on the context in which you were working: the register of the target text would need to be quite formal for this to work in English. In general if you are translating a piece for general public consumption – such as a website, a pamphlet or flyer – then 'one' is less likely to be appropriate. Have a look at the following examples of *men* translated as 'one' and see what kind of 'feel' the English translation has:

> *De geleverde diensten kunnen zowel betrekking hebben op de internetverbinding zelf als diensten die men op het internet kan gebruiken.*
> The services that are provided may either relate to the internet connection itself or to the services one can use on the internet.

> *Al kan men redetwisten over de grootte van de wereldreserves aan kolen, olie en aardgas, het staat onweerlegbaar vast dat de beschikbaarheid van deze brandstoffen beperkt is.*
> Although one can argue about the extent of the world's reserves of coal, oil and natural gas, it is indisputable that ultimately the supply of these fuels is limited.

Particularly the phrase 'one can use on the internet' sounds very formal and there would definitely be persuasive reasons for using 'you' here.

(continued)

(continued)

Using *men*, *je* and *ze* in subject-less sentences

There are two main ways of translating sentences that take *men*, *je* or *ze* as their subject. As we have seen in the discussion of *er* (another word that can be used as an undefined subject) in Chapter 3, subject-less sentences and those with a dummy subject tend to be translated into English either by giving the sentence a subject (this could simply be 'it' or another word that suits the context of the passage), or by using the passive.

Have a look at the different ways of translating the phrase *men verwacht dat* in the following sentences:

Men verwacht dat tegen 2020 het merendeel van de bevolking zal leven in zones met ernstige watertekorten.
It is expected that by 2020 the majority of the population will live in areas with a severe water shortage.

Men verwacht dat de eerste fase van het pilootproject tijdens het eerste kwartaal van 2015 voltooid zal worden.
The first phase of the pilot project is expected to be completed by the end of the first quarter of 2015.

Men verwacht dat die investering tot minstens 500 nieuwe banen zal leiden.
Projections are that at least 500 jobs will be created as a result of this investment.

In the first example, a passive construction, 'It is expected', has been used with the neutral subject 'it'. In the second example, 'first phase' is used as the subject and *men verwacht* is combined with the passive *voltooid zal worden* to avoid there being two separate passive constructions ('it is expected' ... 'shall be completed'). In the third sentence, the translator has essentially used a noun derived from the verb *verwachten* ('to expect', 'to anticipate') as the subject; while the translation 'expectations are that' is a good solution, the word 'projections' may better suit the economic context in which the sentence is being translated.

Some of the same strategies can be used to translate sentences using the construction *men kan*, as the examples below demonstrate:

Men kan ook zeggen dat filosofie door praktijk kan worden verduidelijkt en de praktijk door theorie kan worden verlicht.
It may also be said that philosophy can be clarified by practice and practice can be illuminated by theory.

Ook kan men op dat moment vragen stellen die in de bijeenkomst aan bod komen.

Questions can also be put at that point that will be dealt with at the meeting.

Van hieruit kan men een van de beschikbare spoelfuncties kiezen.
From here you can select one of the available rinse functions.

Here again we see the use of the neutral subject 'it' in the first example, 'it may also be said'. In the second sentence, the object of the Dutch sentence *vragen* has been made the subject of the passive construction in the English version, 'questions ... can be put'. In the final sentence, we see the use of 'you' to stand for *men*, as discussed above. In this sentence, the use of 'one' would have been stylistically inappropriate in any case, since the repetition of 'one' in 'one can select one of the available rinse functions' sounds rather clumsy.

Use of present participle form

So far we have essentially focused on using either a neutral subject or a passive construction in the English to translate sentences using *men* in Dutch. Depending on the other elements in the source text sentence, you might also want to consider using a present participle (stem + -ing) form in English. Have a look at the following sentences:

Dit kan leiden tot het gevoel dat men de controle over het eigen leven en lot verliest.
This can lead to the feeling of losing control over one's life and destiny.

Een andere route is dat men binnen een jeugdscene op een informelere manier in contact komt met personen die extremistische ideeën uitdragen.
Another route involves establishing more informal contact within a youth subculture with people who are propagating extremist ideas.

In the first we have dispensed altogether with using an English equivalent of *men*. A more literal translation of that sentence would have given us the phrase 'This can lead to the feeling that one loses', which we have compressed into 'the feeling of losing'. Similarly, at the start of the second sentence we have avoided translating the Dutch literally as 'Another route is that one comes into contact'. Instead we have used the verb 'involve' in combination with the present participle 'establishing' for *in contact komen met*, to offer a more fluent version in English.

(continued)

(continued)

Adverbial constructions

Another way to translate a *men* + verb construction may be to use a sentence adverb, i.e. an adverb modifying or commenting on the content of a sentence as a whole. Compare the following Dutch sentences and our suggestions for an English translation:

> *Men hoopt dat het verhaal een inspirerende film zou worden.*
> Hopefully the story will become an inspiring film.
>
> *Men kan begrijpen dat het op deze wijze moeilijk is om relaties aan te gaan en zeker om ze te bestendigen.*
> On this basis it is, understandably, difficult to enter into a relationship and certainly to maintain it.
>
> *Men zou kunnen zeggen dat er geen slechtere term bestaat dan 'geestelijke stoornis' om deze ziekte te beschrijven.*
> There could arguably not be a worse term than 'mental disorder' to describe this illness.

Given that it is now accepted that 'hopefully' can not only be taken to mean 'in a hopeful manner' but also 'it is hoped', we have used this in the first sentence to avoid the clumsier English construction 'it is hoped that'. In the second sentence we have condensed *men kan begrijpen dat* ('it is understandable that') into the adverb 'understandably' and in the third we have used 'arguably' to convey *men zou kunnen zeggen* ('it could be said that').

Idiomatic constructions with *men*

There are a few idiomatic constructions such as *naar men zegt* that you might want to think about translating rather differently from the literal 'according to what people say/one says':

> *Hij was naar men zegt een van de eerste zelfstandige componisten in de geschiedenis.*
> It is said that he was one of the first independent composers in history.
>
> *Or:*
> He is considered to have been one of the first independent composers in history.
>
> *Naar men zegt worden producten in vrij hoge mate herkend aan het merk.*
> It has been argued that products are to a fairly large degree recognised by their branding.

Naar men zegt zijn de meeste regionale en lokale overheden nu ook beter toegerust om gedecentraliseerde benaderingen te integreren in hun eigen planning van sociaal beleid.
Most regions and local authorities are also reported to have improved their capacity to integrate decentralised approaches into their own social policy planning.

Sayings with *men*

Since sayings tend to refer to general situations, it is not uncommon to find the word *men* in them, often at the beginning. In English we would either tend to use the pronoun 'you' or we would start with an imperative:

Men moet een boek niet beoordelen aan de kaft.
You should not judge a book by its cover.
Or:
Don't judge a book by its cover.

Men moet leven en laten leven.
You should live and let live.
Or:
People should live and let live.

Om een haar versteekt men geen boterpot.
[Literally: You don't hide a butter-dish for the sake of a hair.]
You shouldn't spoil the ship for a ha'p'orth [halfpennyworth] of tar.
Or:
Don't spoil the ship for a ha'p'orth of tar.

Text 2: *Discriminatie op de werkvloer*

This text is taken from an article that appeared in the journal *Over. Werk*, which is produced by the academic publisher *Acco*, based in Leuven in Belgium. This journal offers scholars the opportunity to publish research results and discussion articles that are aimed at a readership that includes professionals working on a range of topics related to the labour market. According to the website (http://www.acco.be/uitgeverij/nl/tijdschriften/over.werk), the audience for this journal is researchers at universities and research centres, social and sociocultural organisations, policy formulators, educators and students, and those working in human resources. The article

(continued)

(continued)
from which we have taken the extract here is written by Lieve Lembrechts, a researcher at the University of Hasselt, who is part of a group of scholars exploring issues around three aspects of diversity: in the workplace and organisations, in teaching, and in Belgian society. Diversity is studied from a number of different perspectives, including issues related to how self-employed people combine work and family, the careers that women pursue in the IT and financial sectors, and forms of discrimination that arise in relation to pregnancy. This working group also focuses on research related to diversity and equal opportunities in (higher) education, and at an organisational level in schools and universities. Another angle to its work involves the implementation of equal opportunities in Belgian society and the integration of ethnic minorities in Flanders. This extract comes from the opening paragraphs of Lembrechts' article, published in 2012, which is part of a larger study into the forms of discrimination to which pregnant women have been exposed in the workplace in Belgium.

Discriminatie op de werkvloer: een onderzoek naar de ervaringen van zwangere werkneemsters in België

Maar liefst drie vierde van de werkneemsters wordt in België gediscrimineerd naar aanleiding van haar zwangerschap. Dit blijkt uit de eerste omstandige studie die onderzoeksinstituut SEIN van de Universiteit Hasselt uitvoerde in opdracht van het Instituut voor de gelijkheid van vrouwen en mannen. In dit artikel stellen we de belangrijkste bevindingen voor.

Internationaal onderzoek toont aan dat zwangere werkneemsters en werkneemsters met jonge kinderen niet zelden te maken krijgen met discriminatie (Adams, McAndrew & Winterbotham, 2005; HALDE, 2009; James, 2004). Hoewel voor België tot nu toe geen onderzoek rond zwangerschapsgerelateerde discriminatie op de werkvloer beschikbaar was, deed het toenemend aantal klachten dat bij het Instituut voor de gelijkheid van vrouwen en mannen op dat vlak wordt neergelegd, vermoeden dat dit soort discriminatie ook in ons land voorkomt. Ruim een vijfde van alle klachtendossiers die het Instituut in 2008 verwerkte, had te maken met zwangerschap, bevalling of moederschap. Discriminatie is in het bijzonder problematisch omdat het aanstaande en jonge moeders ontmoedigt om hun professionele loopbaan verder uit te bouwen, ongeacht hun capaciteiten en ambities. Daarnaast gaat het in tegen de huidige maatschappelijke verwachting dat elk individu in de mate van het mogelijke dient deel te nemen aan de arbeidsmarkt. Onder meer naar aanleiding van het proportioneel grote aantal klachten gaf het Instituut voor de gelijkheid van vrouwen en mannen ons de opdracht om

Employment 73

> een verkennend onderzoek te voeren. Het doel van dit onderzoek bestond erin de verschillende facetten van zwangerschapsgerelateerde discriminatie waarmee werkneemsters in België te maken krijgen, in kaart te brengen. Hiertoe werd een empirisch onderzoek opgezet, bestaande uit twee delen. Het eerste deel van het empirische luik focuste op de ervaringen van werkneemsters, op basis van een schriftelijke enquêtebevraging en twee focusgroepgesprekken.
>
> Source: L. Lembrechts (2012) Discriminatie op de werkvloer: een onderzoek naar de ervaringen van zwangere werkneemsters in België. *Over.Werk. Tijdschrift van het Steunpunt WSE*, 22(1). Leuven: Steunpunt Werk en Sociale Economie/Uitgeverij Acco, pp. 30–35 (extract on p. 30).

1. Translation strategies and techniques

Below are our two key questions to help you make a first analysis. The first concerns background knowledge relevant for understanding the text, while the second involves reflection on your target audience.

i. What are the first things that you notice about the text?

– *It refers to national and local organisations like the* Instituut voor de gelijkheid van vrouwen en mannen *and the* onderzoeksinstituut SEIN, *which need further clarification.*

The *Instituut voor de gelijkheid van vrouwen en mannen*, which we mentioned in the introduction to this chapter, has an English-language website (http://igvm-iefh.belgium.be/en/), which gives the name of the organisation as the 'Institute for the Equality of Women and Men'. You will need to be careful in your translation to get the word order right, as in English we tend to talk more naturally of 'men and women', rather than ordering the sexes the other way round – so the very name of this institute makes us rethink the old orders and hierarchies.

While the website of SEIN exists in Dutch and English (see http://www.uhasselt.be/SEIN), it is difficult to establish what the acronym 'SEIN' stands for. Further research beyond the organisation's own web page suggests that the first three letters were originally 'Socio-Economisch Instituut', while the website for SEIN now gives 'Identity, Diversity and Inequality Research'. We have therefore kept the acronym but described the organisation as an 'institute for Identity, Diversity and Inequality Research'.

– *It is written from a strong Belgian perspective with turns of phrase like* ons land.

You will have to decide, on the basis of who commissions your translation and who you envisage your audience to be, whether you translate this as 'our country' or 'Belgium'.

ii. What do you know about the target audience for your translation and how will it affect your translation?

Your target audience could be an academic readership comprising other researchers who work on diversity and discrimination in the workplace. Alternatively, it would be of interest to those studying changes in employment from an economic or legal perspective, who want to learn more about the current situation in Belgium. You therefore need to ensure that all terminology is used accurately and that all elements in the text (including acronyms) are meaningful to an international audience.

2. Text and language

This step is crucial since it determines the accuracy of your translation.

i. Words and expressions

> *Zwangere werkneemsters en werkneemsters met jonge kinderen*: it is important to point out the fact that the text is about *werkneemsters met jonge kinderen* and not *werknemers met jonge kinderen*, and you will need to demonstrate that the word *werkneemster* is gendered and does not simply mean 'employee'. In this context, where gender is so crucial to the data presented and the conclusions being discussed, it is therefore essential that you translate *werkneemster* as a 'female employee'.

> *Dit blijkt uit*: there are a range of different possibilities here, including 'this can be seen from', 'this is apparent from', 'this is evident from' or 'this is evidenced by'.

> *Zwangerschapsgerelateerde discriminatie*: although this pairing looks tricky to translate, it can be easily broken down into its constituent parts *zwangerschap*, *gerelateerd* and *discriminatie*, which translates as 'pregnancy-related discrimination'.

> *Klachtendossier*: literally 'complaint file' or perhaps simply 'complaint'.

> *In de mate van het mogelijke*: literally 'in the degree of what is possible', which can be put into more fluent English as 'to the extent that this/it is possible' or 'as far as is possible'.

ii. Sentences

> *Internationaal onderzoek toont aan dat zwangere werkneemsters en werkneemsters met jonge kinderen niet zelden te maken krijgen met discriminatie.*

The construction *te maken krijgen met* means something like 'to deal with', 'to be exposed to' or 'to be confronted with'.

Hoewel voor België tot nu toe geen onderzoek [. . .] beschikbaar was, deed het toenemend aantal klachten [. . .] vermoeden dat dit soort discriminatie ook in ons land voorkomt.

Here we have the verb *doen* used as an auxiliary in the construction *het deed [...] vermoeden*. In this context, the form of *doen* is translated as 'to cause to', so 'caused people to presume/suspect that', or, if you want to avoid giving this phrase the subject 'people', simply use 'suggested' or 'implied'.

Daarnaast gaat het in tegen de huidige maatschappelijke verwachting dat . . .

This seems more complicated than it is. The adjectives *huidig* and *maatschappelijk* go with the noun *verwachting*, so 'the current social expectation'. The expression *het gaat in tegen de [. . .] verwachting* is harder to translate, but we are looking for a verb that is used in combination with the word 'expectation' to describe something that is in stark contrast to current expectation – something that 'counters' or 'goes against' expectation.

. . . de verschillende facetten [. . .] in kaart te brengen.

Here, too, you will need to find a verb that fits with the *verschillende facetten* ('different aspects' or 'different facets'). The expression *in kaart brengen* can literally mean 'to map', but also 'to chart' and, more abstractly, 'to identify'.

Het eerste deel van het empirische luik focuste op de ervaringen van werkneemsters.

Your dictionary might well give you 'hatch', 'shutter', 'skylight' or 'porthole' for the word *luik*, none of which is particularly helpful in this context. However, a *luik* can also be a 'section', 'element' or 'segment' of a study or undertaking, and these are the kinds of terms you need to be thinking about as you translate this sentence, choosing a word that will fit well with the adjective *empirisch*.

3. Style, register and tone

i. Stylistic analysis of the source text

The text has a high, formal register but is accessible by non-specialist readers.

ii. Assessment of the style of writing appropriate to the target text

Given that we have already decided that the target audience for this text is likely but not exclusively to be academic, the formal features of the ST suggest that the translator should ensure that s/he creates a text in English that is accessible by experts in the field as well as interested non-specialists.

76 *Employment*

> **Sample translation of Text 2:** *Discriminatie op de werkvloer*
>
> ***Discrimination in the workplace: a study of the experiences of pregnant employees in Belgium***
>
> As many as three-quarters of female employees in Belgium are discriminated against as a result of becoming pregnant. That is the conclusion drawn from the first detailed study carried out by the institute for Identity, Diversity & Inequality Research, SEIN, based at the University of Hasselt, and commissioned by the Institute for the Equality of Women and Men. In this article we present the most important findings.
>
> International research shows that it is not rare for female employees who are pregnant or who have small children to encounter discrimination (Adams, McAndrew & Winterbotham, 2005; HALDE, 2009; James, 2004). Although no research into pregnancy-related discrimination in the workplace was available up to now for Belgium, the growing number of complaints that were filed with the Institute for the Equality of Women and Men in that area suggested that this form of discrimination is also common in Belgium. Approximately one in five of all complaint files which the Institute processed in 2008 were related to pregnancy, birth or maternity. Discrimination is particularly problematic because it discourages expectant women and young mothers from further developing their professional career, regardless of their capacity and ambitions. Moreover it goes against the expectation held in today's society that every individual should, as far as is possible, be involved in the labour market. As a consequence of, amongst other things, the proportionately large number of complaints, the Institute for the Equality of Women and Men gave us the task of conducting exploratory research. The aim of this research was to map the different facets of pregnancy-related discrimination with which female employees in Belgium are confronted. To this end, an empirical study was launched that comprised two different parts. The first part of the empirical strand focused on gathering female employees' experiences, on the basis of a written questionnaire and two focus group interviews.

Dutch translation in practice

To round off this chapter, we have selected a passage that is taken from the book that we drew on at the start of this chapter, Karen van Oudenhoven-van der Zee and Jan Pieter van Oudenhoven's work on cultural diversity and employment. The extract represents a continuation of their discussion about which approaches Dutch employers can adopt to facilitate the further integration of ethnic minorities in the workplace. For a sample translation of this passage, see p. 183.

Text 3: *Immigranten*

Nederland kan niet om de vraag heen hoe het zich moet opstellen tegenover immigranten. Aan de ene kant omdat Nederland al veel immigranten kent en aan de andere kant omdat er altijd immigranten bij zullen blijven komen. Net als autochtone Nederlanders op hun culturele identiteit gesteld zijn, blijven immigranten in Nederland hun cultuur koesteren. Hierdoor wordt Nederland geconfronteerd met een aantal fundamenteel verschillende opvattingen die vooral op het gebied van man-vrouwrelaties, religieuze overtuigingen, en vrijheid van meningsuiting hevige emoties oproepen. Op zich hoeven verschillen in cultuur geen onoplosbare problemen op te leveren. Een samenleving kan hier wat aan doen. Een pluralistische politiek van een land – Canada is daar een voorbeeld van – kan het immigranten gemakkelijker maken zich met die samenleving te identificeren dan wanneer die samenleving assimilatie afdwingt. Een haalbare benadering is om immigranten een grote mate van vrijheid toe te staan om hun cultuur te uiten, maar een flinke mate van instrumentele aanpassing te verlangen op school en op de werkplek. Bij instrumentele aanpassing gaat het om cultuurgebonden vaardigheden die noodzakelijk zijn om het werk goed te kunnen doen. Vooral de beheersing van Nederlands is belangrijk. Het belang hiervan is alleen maar toegenomen, omdat de aard van de arbeid veranderd is. In de tijd dat de gastarbeiders naar Nederland kwamen, was er nog veel zware handarbeid vooral in de industriële en agrarische sector. Tegenwoordig is het aantal banen in de dienstsector relatief sterk toegenomen. Daarvoor zijn communicatieve vaardigheden extra belangrijk. De vraag is of die instrumentele aanpassing op het werk afgedwongen moet worden. De meeste immigranten doen dit spontaan omdat ze zelf de zin ervan inzien en graag aan het werk willen.

Het probleem van culturele diversiteit moet overigens niet overdreven worden. Te vaak wordt de schaduwzijde van immigratie benadrukt. Heel vaak echter zijn immigranten hardwerkende, ambitieuze en succesvolle burgers die een belangrijke bijdrage aan onze samenleving leveren.

Source: Karen van der Zee and Jan Pieter van Oudenhoven (2006) *Culturele diversiteit op het werk: Achtergronden en interventies*. Assen: Van Gorcum, p. 8.

5 Finance and economics

Introduction: texts and contexts

Although the Netherlands and Belgium are relatively small countries within Europe, they nevertheless both belong among the richest nations of the world. While the ongoing global financial crisis has hit their economies considerably in the course of the past decade, both continue to be prosperous, industrially innovative nations that depend heavily on foreign trade. The Dutch economy is noted for its stable industrial relations and relatively low unemployment and inflation. The Netherlands is home to a number of companies with an international reputation, not least the Anglo-Dutch multinational oil and gas company Royal Dutch Shell, which has its headquarters in The Hague, the multinational banking and financial services corporation ING Groep, and the technology company Koninklijke Philips NV, one of the largest electronics companies in the world, which was founded in Eindhoven in 1891. Maritime trade and shipbuilding has, of course, long been one of the pillars of the Dutch economy. The *Vereenigde Oost-Indische Compagnie*, or *VOC* (United East India Company), established in 1602, has often been considered one of the first truly multinational corporations in the world, which eclipsed all its European rivals in trade with Asia. It imported huge quantities of spices, silks, cottons and porcelain from the East Indies for trading in the company's warehouses in Amsterdam, as well as carrying supplies back out to the VOC settlements in Asia. This economic boom came to an abrupt end in the 1670s, although the VOC continued to operate until the end of the eighteenth century and was finally nationalised in 1796. The Netherlands was slow to industrialise and it was only at the beginning of the twentieth century that, for example, the port of Rotterdam was developed westwards to improve the connection towards the North Sea. A large canal, the *Nieuwe Waterweg* ('New Waterway'), was dredged to connect the Rhine and Meuse rivers to the sea. In the 1960s the completion of the first *Maasvlakte* extended the harbour and industrial area now known as 'Europoort' by reclaiming land from the North Sea. A 'Second Maasvlakte', or '*Maasvlakte 2*', heralded as one of the largest civil engineering projects in the Netherlands in the twenty-first century, is being created to construct a new port and surrounding infrastructure on more reclaimed land.

The Port of Antwerp, currently the second largest port in Europe in terms of freight volume, had already started to bring prosperity to Belgium in the first half of the nineteenth century. Emerging relatively undamaged from the two world wars,

Finance and economics   79

the port enjoyed a boom in the 1960s and has continued to expand along the bank of the River Scheldt. Its position makes it an important distribution centre in northern Europe: Flanders' main imports include food products, petroleum and petroleum products, clothing and textiles, while its exports include automobiles, iron and steel, finished diamonds, plastics and non-ferrous metals. Antwerp continues to be considered the main diamond market in the world and its diamond exports account for approximately one-tenth of all Belgian exports. Within the small area of two square miles, the Diamond Quarter houses more than 1,500 diamond companies and four diamond exchanges, and attracts an international public of specialised bankers, brokers and buyers. Brussels, home to many of the European institutions and to NATO, has a largely service-based economy. While these institutions draw business tourism, they also attract individuals in related professions such as lobbying, consultancies and the media. The presence of European and international institutions in Brussels also makes it one of the world's leading congress venues. Recent initiatives on the part of the Flemish government to boost the economy of the Dutch-speaking regions of Belgium have included the establishment of the *Departement Economie, Wetenschap en Innovatie* (Department of Economy, Science and Innovation) in 2006, which aims to support excellence in scientific research, foster an attractive and sustainable climate for businesses, and encourage entrepreneurship and innovation in society (http://www.ewi-vlaanderen.be/). Its goal is to promote the creation of partnerships between business, academia and government, which encourage researchers from diverse backgrounds to work together and maximise knowledge exchange and skill development. Flexibility, mobility and open communication therefore lie at the heart of the models now being adopted to ensure that Flanders can consolidate its place within the most innovative regions in Europe.

Text 1: *Zeehavens*

The following text comes from a report commissioned by the Dutch *Ministerie van Verkeer en Waterstaat* (Ministry of Transport, Public Works and Water Management), in collaboration with the *Stichting Nederland Maritiem Land* ('Dutch Maritime Network') or NML, an organisation that explores the developments that the Dutch shipping industry is undergoing, and the problems and challenges that it faces in the years ahead, and that also records staff movements across the sector. Published at regular intervals, this report offers a useful summary of the current state of affairs in the maritime sector in the Netherlands, and gives detailed accounts both in the form of textual information and of data presented visually in charts, tables and graphs, to illustrate short- and long-term changes in this sector. Given that a large percentage of the total value added by shipping is actually created onshore, this report also bears in mind how changes

(continued)

> *(continued)*
>
> in the shipping industry could have knock-on effects for employment on land. Like most of the promotional material that the NML produces (see http://www.maritiemland.nl/NL/1637/rapporten.html), this report is aimed at an audience of maritime specialists with an economic background, or those working in the financial sector who have a particular interest in shipping.
>
> ### Zeehavens
>
> De twee belangrijkste zeehavens in Nederland zijn Rotterdam en Amsterdam. De afgelopen jaren kenmerken zich door een sterke groei van de internationale handel. Als gevolg van die sterke groei is de overslag in de Rotterdamse haven tussen 2003 en 2005 met gemiddeld zo'n 6 procent gestegen, tot 370 miljoen ton in 2005. Internationaal gezien heeft Rotterdam haar marktaandeel daarmee weten te stabiliseren. Het grootste deel van de overslag wordt gerealiseerd in aardolie en aardolieproducten (39%), de belangrijkste groei komt echter van de containeroverslag. Door sterk te zijn in containeroverslag profiteert Rotterdam van de groeiende wereldhandel, vooral van de handel met China.
>
> Ramingen van eind 2004 geven aan dat voor de Rotterdamse haven de groei van de goederenstromen tot 2009 3,2 procent per jaar zal bedragen. Geraamd wordt dat tot 2009 60 procent van de groei van de overslag in de haven voor rekening van het containervervoer zal komen. De komende jaren zullen de zeehavens bij hun uitbreidingen steeds meer te maken krijgen met de beperkingen die hun omgeving en de maatschappij daar aan stelt. In dit kader spelen de aanleg van de Tweede Maasvlakte in Rotterdam en de sluis in Amsterdam een belangrijke rol. De aanleg van de Tweede Maasvlakte moet starten in januari 2008 en het eerste schip moet in 2013 aan de kade liggen. De Tweede Maasvlakte moet een verdrievoudiging van de containeroverslag mogelijk maken.
>
> Ook de Amsterdamse haven heeft de afgelopen jaren goede resultaten geboekt. De totale overslag bedroeg zo'n 75 miljoen ton in 2005, een groei van 2,3 procent, het jaar daarvoor. In 2004 werd zelfs een groei van 12,7 procent geboekt. De Zeeuwse havens Vlissingen en Terneuzen zijn samen goed voor ongeveer 30 miljoen ton, in Delfzijl en de Eemshaven werd bij elkaar ongeveer 7 miljoen ton overgeslagen.
>
> ---
>
> Source: Stichting Nederland Maritiem Land (2007) *Monitor Maritieme Arbeidsmarkt 2006*. Amsterdam: IOS Press BV, p. 16.

1. Translation strategies and techniques

Below are our two key questions to help you make a first analysis. The first concerns background knowledge relevant for understanding the source text, while the second involves reflection on your target audience.

Finance and economics 81

i. What are the first things that you notice about the text?

– *It uses a fair amount of specialist economic vocabulary such as 'containeroverslag', 'containervervoer' and 'goederenstromen'.*

You will need to ensure that you have the correct translations for these terms by looking them up in a specialist dictionary and then checking the usage of the English terms you have found in relevant sources on international cargo and freight transport.

– *It makes reference to places and phenomena that the non-specialist English reader might not have heard of, such as the 'Tweede Maasvlakte' and 'de Eemshaven'.*

You will have to decide just how explanatory you need to be in your translation, depending on how well informed you gauge your Anglophone readers to be. If you feel you are translating for a specialist readership with knowledge of European shipping then perhaps no further elaboration is required, whereas if your translation is to be presented to a non-specialist audience, you might want to add a footnote with more information or add brief details in brackets following the first use of these terms.

– *One sentence does not appear to make sense, namely the second sentence in the third paragraph*: *De totale overslag bedroeg zo'n 75 miljoen ton in 2005, een groei van 2,3 procent, het jaar daarvoor.*

We have copied the sentence in exactly the form that it was given in the original. While the first part of the sentence makes sense (*De totale overslag . . . een groei van 2,3 procent*), the final part (*het jaar daarvoor*) is linked only by a comma to the earlier part and it is not immediately clear how these two elements fit together. If we translate the first part of the sentence, then we come up with something like 'The total turnover amounted to around 75 million tons in 2005, a growth of 2.3 per cent'; the second part, *het jaar daarvoor*, means 'the previous year' and we can presume that the author was aiming to make a comparison between statistics for 2005 and 2004, i.e. 'a growth of 2.3 per cent on the previous year'. The sentence should probably have read thus: *De totale overslag bedroeg zo'n 75 miljoen ton in 2005, een groei van 2,3 procent tegenover het jaar daarvoor.*

It is not uncommon for there to be mistakes in source texts: authors writing annual reports such as the one we are focusing on here are often working under immense pressure of time and mistakes do creep in. If you think that there is an error in a text that you have been asked to translate, check for a list of errata (often at the back of a book, for example) or contact the author direct where possible. If it is not possible to liaise with the person who wrote the text, then you are simply going to have to use your common sense and translate the passage in such a way as to ensure that it makes sense. You would, however, be advised to point out to the person commissioning the translation that you have made these adjustments.

82 *Finance and economics*

ii. What do you know about the target audience for your translation and how will it affect your translation?

Given the strongly factual nature of the Dutch text, it was probably initially written for a fairly specialised readership with an interest in the ongoing development of the Netherlands as a maritime economy. The Anglophone audience for whom a translation is intended is almost certainly going to have some specialist knowledge either of the economic affairs of the Low Countries or of international shipping. You therefore need to assess how well they will know the geography of the Netherlands and how familiar they will be with recent developments in its ports.

2. Text and language

This step is crucial since it determines the accuracy of your translation.

i. Words and expressions

> *Zeehavens*: the title of this extract is not just *Havens* but *Zeehavens* and it is important to acknowledge that in your translation. The term *zeehaven* refers to a seaport – that is, a port on or very near the coast, such as Rotterdam and Amsterdam (NL), Harwich and Hull (England), Boston and Brunswick (United States), Durban and Port Elizabeth (South Africa). By contrast a *binnenhaven* is an inland port that is situated on an inland waterway such as a river, lake or canal. Examples of inland ports are the ports of Birmingham (England), Montreal (Canada), Virginia (United States) and Nairobi (Kenya).
>
> *Containervervoer* and *containeroverslag*: you need to make sure you find out exactly what these terms mean, since they come up a number of times in the passage. *Containervervoer* simply refers to the transportation of containers from one place to another, whereas *containeroverslag* refers to the 'transshipment' of goods, i.e. their shipment to an intermediate destination (such as a port), where they often change their means of transport and are sent on to another destination.
>
> *De groei van de goederenstromen [zal] 3,2 procent per jaar bedragen*: the term *goederenstromen* can be variously translated as 'flow of goods', 'freight flows' or 'cargo flows'. Although 'cargo' and 'freight' are closely related terms and their main purpose appears to be the same, it is important to bear in mind that 'freight' refers to the transportation of goods by train or truck, whereas 'cargo' refers to the transportation of goods by ship or by plane. In the context of this passage, we are looking at transportation by ship into the ports of Rotterdam and Amsterdam, so we are looking at 'cargo flows' or, more generally, the 'flow of goods'. You are undoubtedly aware that decimals such as '3.2%' are written with a decimal point in English rather than

the comma in Dutch – *3,2 procent* – although it is easy to forget to 'translate' this punctuation when working at speed.

De Tweede Maasvlakte: as mentioned in the introduction, this relates to the second stage of expansion that the port of Rotterdam is undergoing. The official English-language website for the Port of Rotterdam describes this project as 'Maasvlakte 2' (https://wwww.maasvlakte2.com), which suggests that this is the official English name and should be used in our translation. Depending on the context in which you are translating, you may want to add a brief description in your text – something like 'a large-scale extension to the Port of Rotterdam, using reclaimed land to construct a new port and terminal infrastructure', or put even more detailed information in a footnote, perhaps also with a link to the official web page.

De Zeeuwse havens Vlissingen en Terneuzen: Vlissingen belongs among the towns and cities in the Low Countries for which a different translation also exists in English. Its strategic location between the River Scheldt and the North Sea means that 'Flushing' (as it was called by seventeenth-century British visitors like Samuel Pepys and Sir William Temple) has been an important harbour for hundreds of years. Modern-day Anglophone guidebooks appear to have reverted to using the Dutch name 'Vlissingen', and indeed the English version of the website produced by the town itself repeatedly uses the name 'Vlissingen' rather than 'Flushing' (see http://www.vlissingen.nl/english/welcome.html). You could therefore either just put 'Vlissingen' and leave it like that or add 'Flushing' in brackets. The adjective *Zeeuws*, or 'Zeelandic', refers to the position of Vlissingen and Terneuzen in the south-western Dutch province of Zeeland.

Delfzijl en de Eemshaven: there is a reason why the article *de* precedes Eemshaven. *Delfzijl* is a city in its own right on the River Ems, but Eemshaven is a harbour that lies to the north-east of the city of Groningen. You might want to translate *de Eemshaven* simply as 'the Eemshaven', or you might want to elaborate on this by adding something like 'the largest seaport in the Northern Netherlands, situated on the Ems near Groningen'.

Goed zijn voor ongeveer 30 miljoen ton: the idiomatic construction *goed zijn voor* does not make much sense if we translate it literally here. It is commonly found in economic texts and means something like 'to account for', 'to represent' or 'to make up'. So, for example, the sentence *Enkele industriële sectoren zijn goed voor 40% van de totale uitstoot van broeikasgassen door de Europese Unie* could be translated as 'A few industrial sectors account for 40% of total greenhouse gas emissions in the European Union', and the sentence *De investering zou in een eerste fase goed zijn voor 30 tot 35 jobs* could be put into English as 'In a first phase, the investment should provide for 30 to 35 jobs'. The construction *goed zijn voor* can be used literally, in quite a different context, to mean 'to be good for something', as in sentences like *We willen goed zijn voor de mensen binnen het bedrijf én voor de wereld om ons heen*, meaning 'We aim to do good for/do our best for the people working in our company and the people in the world around us.'

Ongeveer 30 miljoen, zo'n 6 procent, zo'n miljoen ton: while it is important that you translate amounts and units correctly (see the Practical Tips section in this chapter), it is just as important that you translate the words before them that qualify the amounts in question – so 'roughly/approximately/about 30 million', 'around/about/some 6 per cent', 'roughly/approximately/about a million tons'. Check that you know what *om en bij*, *ruim*, and *rond* mean when preceding a figure.

ii. Sentences

Internationaal heeft Rotterdam haar marktaandeel daarmee weten te stabiliseren.
While the verb *weten* means 'to know', the construction *weten + te* is normally translated as 'to be able to', 'to manage to'. Further examples of this construction would be *In deze periode hebben de partijen hun marktpositie grotendeels weten te behouden*, which could be translated as 'The parties have largely maintained their market position throughout this period', and *Mijn vader vond het zeer belangrijk dat zijn medewerkers hem wisten te waarderen*, which could be put into English as 'It was very important to my father that his fellow workers respected him/could respect him.'

De komende jaren zullen de zeehavens bij hun uitbreidingen steeds meer te maken krijgen met de beperkingen die hun omgeving en de maatschappij daar aan stelt.

There are two constructions that make this sentence difficult to translate – *te maken krijgen met* and *de beperkingen... daar aan stelt*. The construction *te maken krijgen met* is normally translated as 'to be faced with', 'to cope with' or 'to deal with'. The sentence *De sportwereld zal vroeg of laat te maken krijgen met het verschijnsel van genetische doping voor de verbetering van de sportprestaties* could therefore be translated as 'The sporting world will sooner or later be faced with the phenomenon of gene doping to improve athletic performance', and the statement *De sector zal bovendien te maken krijgen met verdere hervormingen in de financiële regelgeving* could be put into English as 'The industry also faces the challenge of further reforms to financial regulations.' The second part of the sentence, *beperkingen... daar aan stelt*, needs further unravelling. The construction that underpins it is *beperkingen stellen aan iets*, namely to 'impose limitations/restrictions on', while the *daar* in *daar aan* refers to the process of expansion that the seaports are undergoing – *de uitbreidingen [van de zeehavens]*.

3. Style, register and tone

i. Stylistic analysis of the source text

The text has a high, formal register and includes a wealth of factual information. The translation needs to convey this same information accurately and unambiguously.

ii. Assessment of the style of writing appropriate to the target text

The translation needs likewise to be composed in a formal register and to make use of appropriate specialised vocabulary.

Sample translation of Text 1: *Zeehavens*

Seaports

The two most important seaports in the Netherlands are Rotterdam and Amsterdam. The last few years have been characterised by strong growth in international trade. As a result of this strong growth, the turnover in the port of Rotterdam rose between 2003 and 2005 by an average of around 6 per cent, to 370 million tons in 2005. From an international perspective Rotterdam has managed to stabilise its market share. Oil and oil products account for the largest proportion of the turnover (39%), but the main growth comes from container transshipment. Rotterdam profits from growing world trade, particularly trade with China, by proving strong in container transshipments.

Prognoses from the end of 2004 show that a 3.2% growth in the flow of goods is expected for the port of Rotterdam until 2009. By 2009 it is estimated that 60% of the growth in turnover for the port will be due to container transport. In the next few years, as the seaports expand, they will increasingly have to deal with restrictions imposed upon them by their environment and society. In this context the construction of Maasvlakte 2 in Rotterdam and the lock in Amsterdam will play an important role. The construction of Maasvlakte 2 must begin in January 2008 and the first ship has to dock in 2013. Maasvlakte 2 must enable container transshipments to triple.

The port of Amsterdam has also achieved good results in the past few years. The total turnover amounted to around 75 million tons in 2005, a growth of 2.3 per cent on the previous year. In 2004 growth even reached 12.7 per cent. The seaports of Vlissingen (Flushing) and Terneuzen in the province of Zeeland together deal with around 30 million tons, while in Delfzijl and the Eemshaven the turnover roughly amounts to 7 million tons in total.

PRACTICAL TIPS: DEALING WITH STATISTICS AND NUMBERS IN TRANSLATION

We might think that translating numbers is relatively easy – on the face of it, there is little that needs to be changed or 'translated' at all as numerical information is transferred from one language to another. But translating sentences that refer to numbers and numerical issues can be more complicated than you imagine, and any mistakes you make can have disastrous consequences – from an erroneous statement about a company's profits or losses, to the wrong dosage of a medicine to a patient. It is not only important to ensure that the right figures end up in your translation. It is also vital to read carefully the context in which a percentage or an amount or a volume is being presented in a given passage. When you have finished, double-check all percentages and proportions, volumes and distances, ages and years, to ensure that your translation conveys the same information as in the source text.

Punctuation: decimals, dots and commas

The most obvious occasions where you need to pay careful attention to the punctuation marks you use is in translating very large amounts (several millions, for example) or very small amounts (such as decimal places, signifying fractions of a whole). The general rule of thumb is that, where there is a comma in Dutch, you need a point/full stop in English, and vice versa. Take a look at the following examples:

> *Tussen 1972 en 2005 groeide de nietwesterse populatie met 1,5 miljoen, terwijl de totale bevolking groeide met 3,0 miljoen personen.*
> Between 1972 and 2005, the non-Western population grew by 1.5 million, while the total population grew by 3 million.

> *In 1997 daalde de winst tot 0,5 % om vervolgens te veranderen in een verlies van 1,5 % in 1998 gevolgd door een verlies van 9,8 % in het onderzoektijdvak.*
> In 1997 profits dropped to 0.5%, and subsequently turned into a loss of 1.5% in 1998, followed by a loss of 9.8% in the period under investigation.

We can therefore see that *1,5 miljoen* becomes '1.5 million' in translation and *0,5 %* in Dutch is '0.5%' in English. You may have noticed that *3,0 miljoen* has simply been given as '3 million', although '3.0 million' would mathematically be the same. Having ensured that you have used the right punctuation marks to transfer these amounts and percentages, it is important to go back to the original and look at the preposition being used in relation to these figures. In the first example we note that the population *groeide . . . met 1,5 miljoen* – so it grew '*by*' 1.5 million. Bear in mind that *groeien* +

met is not the same as *groeien + tot* and that your sentence (and the factual content it conveys) would be very different if you had mis-translated this as 'grew *to* 1.5 million'. Similarly, in the second sentence we read that profit *daalde ... tot 0,5 %* – so it dropped *to* 0.5% (and not *by* 0.5%).

Currencies

We have just looked at how to translate smaller and larger numerical quantities, but how do you deal with the units of currency, weight or measurement in which they are being given? The abbreviations for (milli)litres and (kilo) grams are essentially universal, although the singular form of these words is used in Dutch, where the plural is used in English, so *driehonderd gram vlees* is 'three hundred grams of meat' and *twee liter melk* is 'two litres of milk'. Dealing with currencies is more difficult. Have a look at the vocabulary and word order in the following Dutch sentence and its translation:

Vandaag wordt elk jaar 55 miljard dollar uitgegeven aan koffie, waarvan maar 7 miljard dollar (15 %) in de producerende landen blijft.
Today 55 billion US dollars is spent on coffee every year, of which only 7 billion stays in the producing countries (15%).

Or:
Today $55 billion is spent on coffee every year, of which only $7 billion stays in the producing countries (15%).

Note that if you decide to write the currency out in full, then those words come after the figures, whereas if you opt to use the dollar sign, then the symbol goes *before* the numerical amount in English. You will also have noticed that a *miljard* has been given as a 'billion' – that is, one-thousand million, or 1,000,000,000. British and American English used to vary in what it was considered that a 'billion' signified, although British English has now adopted the American figure. There also used to be discrepancies between British and American English over a 'trillion', which is now generally held to be equivalent to a million million (1,000,000,000,000). Disagreement continues to surround whether the Dutch *biljoen* is a thousand or a million millions.

Translating the names of currencies also requires some reflection. Take a look at the sentences below:

Voor 77% van de aandelen werd de werkelijk betaalde som van 9,0 miljoen Britse pond in rekening genomen.
The sum of 9 million pounds sterling which was actually paid was taken into account for 77% of the shares.

(continued)

(continued)

> *In totaal verkochten de instellingen in 1996 voor 100 miljoen gulden (ruim 45 miljoen euro) aan kunstwerken, waarvan de helft direct aan de kunstenaars werd uitbetaald.*
> In 1996, the institutions sold a total of NLG 100 million (over EUR 45 million) worth of artwork, with one-half paid direct to the artists concerned.
>
> *De belastingdruk in de periode 2001–2003 wordt jaarlijks met ongeveer 10 miljard BEF (0,25 miljard EURO) of 0,1% van het BBP verlaagd.*
> The tax burden in the period 2001–2003 will be reduced each year by about BEF 10 billion (EUR 0.25 billion), or 0.1% of GDP.

In the first example, we have not translated *Britse pond* literally as 'British pounds' but taken 'pounds sterling', which is the term usually used in financial texts. If we were translating for an audience of economic specialists, we could also have used 'GBP', since this is the abbreviation recognised by the International Organization for Standardisation (ISO). You will see these standard abbreviations used in the other two examples, where *100 miljoen gulden* becomes 'NLG 100 million' and *10 miljard BEF* is translated as 'BEF 10 billion', since NLG and BEF were the ISO codes for the Dutch guilder and the Belgian franc, respectively, before the euro (EUR) was introduced on to world financial markets as an accounting currency in 1999, and euro coins and banknotes entered circulation on 1 January 2002.

Compound adjectives

Numbers do not just appear in texts in numerical form, but are also written out as words, and often in combination with other parts of speech. In this section we look at compound adjectives, which are adjectives formed from a number and a noun. Read the next two sentences and find the compound adjectives:

> *De vijftigjarige monteur raakte zwaargewond met veel brandwonden, maar kon een aantal maanden later weer aan het werk.*
> The fifty-year-old technician sustained severe burns but was able to return to work a few months later.
>
> *Zijn bekendste werk is de geruchtmakende roman* Lolita *uit 1955, die de uitzinnige liefde van een veertigjarige intellectueel voor een jong Amerikaans meisje beschrijft.*
> His most famous work is the notorious novel *Lolita* from 1955, which describes the frenzied love of a forty-year-old intellectual for a young American girl.

The compound adjectives in the sentences above are *vijftigjarig* and *veertigjarig*. Note the use of the hyphen to connect the three elements ('x-year-old'), which make up the correct translation in English.

Compound adjectives can also be used in more complex constructions, as in the following example:

Meer informatie vindt u in de samenvatting van de 36-bladzijdes tellende conclusie met daarin de belangrijkste gegevens.
For more information read the résumé of the 36-page conclusion containing the most important data.

In English the adjective '36-page conclusion' neatly translates the *36-bladzijdes tellende conclusie* without having to stress what is obvious in English, that the conclusion 'numbers' (*tellend*) 36 pages. Other examples where we manage to compress the Dutch into a briefer English translation using a compound adjective are as follows:

Het object bestaat uit een huis met drie slaapkamers op twee woonlagen en met drie toegangsdeuren, aan de voor-, zij- en achterkant.
The property comprises a three-bedroom house on two levels and with three access doors, front, side and rear.

Voor alle producten geldt een geld-teruggarantie van 30 dagen.
All products are protected by a 30-day money-back guarantee.

Er is een verzoek ingediend voor de plaatsing van containers van drie verdiepingen om meer tijdelijke accommodatie te creëren.
Additional space in the form of three-storey containers has been requested in order to provide more temporary accommodation.

In each of the above cases, the genitive construction in Dutch using *van* or *met* (*met drie slaapkamers, van 30 dagen, van drie verdiepingen*) has been compressed in English into a hyphenated adjective ('three-bedroom', '30-day', 'three-storey').

Text 2: *Nieuwe regionale economische vooruitzichten 2008–2014*

This extract comes from an online press release by the Brussels-based Federaal Planbureau (FPB) or Federal Planning Bureau. This is a Belgian public agency under the authority of the prime minister and the Ministry

(continued)

(continued)

of Economic Affairs, which enjoys a certain autonomy and intellectual independence within the Belgian public sector. The activities of the FPB are primarily focused on macro-economic forecasting, and the analysis and assessment of policies in economic, social and environmental areas. The macro-economic forecasts it makes are used by the Belgian federal government to draw up the budget. Together with the National Bank of Belgium, it also compiles the general government account within the national accounts. The FPB also publishes a medium-term economic outlook every spring for the Belgian economy. While the extract we shall be concentrating on below focuses on economic growth and the labour market, the FPB's website also contains a wealth of information on demographic change and ageing in Belgium, energy and transport, productivity and long-term growth, as well as analyses of individual economic sectors. Given its central function in providing economic analyses and forecasts, its publications tend not to be oriented towards the general public but rather towards those with a more specialised knowledge of the European economy. The extract below is taken from a press release dating back to July 2009, which presented results derived from a regional and sectoral macro-economic model developed by a number of organisations specialising in statistical analysis to forecast economic developments for the period from 2008 to 2014.

Nieuwe regionale economische vooruitzichten 2008–2014

Economische groei

In 2009 zou de economische recessie de drie Belgische gewesten op een vrijwel identieke wijze treffen: de inkrimping van de economische activiteit zou bijna 4% bedragen, zowel in Brussel als in Vlaanderen en Wallonië. De belangrijkste kanalen waarlangs de economische crisis zich verspreidt, zouden echter verschillen van gewest tot gewest. In het Brussels Gewest zou vooral de financiële sector sterk terugvallen, terwijl in Vlaanderen en Wallonië de industriële bedrijfstakken het hardst getroffen zouden worden; toch zouden ook de diensten niet gespaard blijven. In 2010 zou het geleidelijk verdwijnen van de crisis zich vertalen in een nulgroei in Vlaanderen, een zeer zwakke (positieve) groei in Wallonië en een nog licht negatieve groei in Brussel. Op middellange termijn (periode 2011-2014), zouden de gewesten opnieuw een groei laten optekenen die vergelijkbaar is met die voor het uitbreken van de crisis. Het gemiddeld jaarlijks groeitempo van het bbp zou zo 2,4% bereiken in het Vlaams Gewest, waarmee deze regio zou genieten van een iets krachtiger herstel dan in de twee overige gewesten, die een gemiddelde groei van 2,2% noteren over de periode 2011-2014. In de projectieperiode zou dus een

> groeiverschil tussen de drie gewesten in het voordeel van Vlaanderen blijven bestaan, maar het zou verminderen in vergelijking met vroeger.
>
> **Arbeidsmarkt**
> De daling van de regionale bbp's in 2009 en de stagnering in 2010 zouden gepaard gaan met grote verliezen voor de binnenlandse werkgelegenheid. Vlaanderen zou over die twee jaar ongeveer 44 500 jobs verliezen, terwijl Wallonië en Brussel respectievelijk 29 000 en 16 000 arbeidsplaatsen zouden verliezen. De werkgelegenheid zou pas vanaf 2011 aangroeien in de verschillende gewesten (voor Brussel pas vanaf 2012, er zouden nog ongeveer 1 800 banen verloren gaan in 2011). De jobcreatie zou hoger liggen in Vlaanderen dan in de twee overige gewesten.
>
> Source: Federaal Planbureau, Brussels, http://www.plan.be/press/communique-837-nl-64-67-regionale+economische+vooruitzichten+2008+2014 (accessed 29 November 2013).

1. Translation strategies and techniques

Below are our two key questions to help you make a first analysis. The first concerns background knowledge relevant for understanding the text, while the second involves reflection on your target audience.

i. What are the first things that you notice about the text?

- *The tense seems rather odd and there is constant use of different forms of the verb* zullen *in the conditional* zou *form.*

    In contextualising where the extract comes from, we stressed the fact that it presents economic forecasts and prognoses for the five years after its publication. It therefore does not offer a summary of what has already happened and lies in the past, but instead aims to give some indication of how the Belgian economy could develop in the future. The statements that are made using *zou* are therefore all hypothetical, suggesting what is expected to happen and what is likely to take place. You have probably already encountered *zou(den)* in 'if'-clauses – such as *Dat zou ik niet doen als ik jou was* ('I would not do that if I were you'). This text likewise indicates a series of possibilities, rather than certainties, which is why this tense is used throughout. Your text needs to reflect this by constantly using formulations that indicate the provisional nature of the statements made – constructions like 'is expected to' or 'is likely to'.

- *It contains a number of specialised terms such as 'nulgroei', 'groeitempo' or 'projectieperiode'.*

    As with the previous text, you will need to ensure that you have found the right terms, not only by looking them up in a specialised dictionary but also by checking their use in similar contexts.

92 Finance and economics

ii. What do you know about the target audience for your translation and how will it affect your translation?

Given the quite specialised nature of this text, it is most likely that it would be commissioned by a financial institution with an interest in the economic affairs of Belgium. Your translation therefore needs to demonstrate familiarity with the appropriate vocabulary.

2. Text and language

This step is crucial since it determines the accuracy of your translation.

i. Words and expressions

> *De inkrimping*: this can be translated in a variety of different ways in an economic context, although in all cases it refers in some way to a reduction in size or a drop. In an employment context it could mean 'cutbacks', so *de inkrimping van het personeelsbestand* could be translated as 'cutbacks/a reduction in staffing/the workforce', whereas in financial terms *de inkrimping van de exportmarkten* could be translated as 'the contraction of export markets'. Here we are looking at *de inkrimping van de economische activiteit*, which we could translate as 'a reduction in economic activity' or 'shrinking economic activity'.
>
> *Sterk terugvallen*: there are a number of different adverbs you could use to complement the verb *terugvallen*, which signifies a 'drop' or 'fall'. Depending on what best fits the sentence you are constructing, you could use 'substantial fall', 'steep decline', 'major slump' or 'significant drop'.
>
> *Het bbp*: this stands for *het bruto binnenlands product*, which equates with gross domestic product (GDP). Other financial abbreviations you are likely to come across are *BTW*, which stands for *Belasting over de Toegevoegde Waarde*, which is the equivalent of VAT, or 'Value Added Tax', in English. At the end of company names you encounter the abbreviation *NV*, which stands for *Naamloze vennootschap*, the corresponding concept being 'plc', or 'public limited company', in the UK and Ireland. You may need to think about whether to translate this abbreviation if it is actually part of a company's designated name, so the firm 'Oranjewoud NV' would still be called this in translation into English. A number of other abbreviations do not actually change in English, since the words they represent happen to start with the same letter in Dutch and in English – for example, the 'ECB' is both the *Europese Centrale Bank* and the 'European Central Bank', and the 'IMF' stands for the *Internationaal Monetair Fonds* as well as the 'International Monetary Fund'. Abbreviations of international organisations you might not immediately recognise are the 'OESO', which is the *Organisatie voor Economische Samenwerking en Ontwikkeling* or in English the OECD (Organisation for

Economic Cooperation and Development), the *EG*, which is the *Europeese Gemeenschap* or EU (European Union), and the *NAVO* or *Noord-Atlantische Verdragsorganisatie*, which is NATO (North Atlantic Treaty Organization).

ii. Sentences

De belangrijkste kanalen waarlangs de economische crisis zich verspreidt.

This sentence uses language metaphorically to compare the developing economic crisis with a liquid flowing through channels. You need to come up with an expression that draws on similar imagery: 'the channels/routes along/down which the crisis will spread'.

3. Style, register and tone

i. Stylistic analysis of the source text

The text has a high, formal register and a strongly factual, informative character, and is intended to be read by those with a reasonably specialised understanding of economics.

ii. Assessment of the style of writing appropriate to the target text

The formal features of the ST suggest that the translator should ensure that s/he creates a text in English that appeals to an audience that has a similarly specialist interest in Belgian or European finance and economics.

Sample translation of Text 2: *Nieuwe regionale economische vooruitzichten 2008–2014*

New regional economic outlook 2008–2014

Economic growth

In 2009, the economic recession is likely to hit the three Belgian regions in almost identical ways: the reduction in economic activity is expected to reach almost 4%, both in Brussels and in Flanders and Wallonia. The most important routes along which the economic crisis will spread are, however, likely to be different from region to region. In the Brussels-Capital Region, it is primarily the financial sector that is expected to experience a steep decline, while in Flanders and Wallonia the industrial sector is likely to be hit the hardest. Public services are not expected to go unscathed either. In 2010, the crisis should gradually fade and translate into zero growth in Flanders, very weak (positive) growth in Wallonia and still slightly negative growth in Brussels. In the middle term (the period from 2011 to 2014) the regions are

(continued)

(continued)

once again likely to experience growth comparable with that before the outbreak of the crisis. It is anticipated that the average annual GDP growth rate will reach around 2.4% in the Flemish Region, with this region enjoying a slightly more powerful recovery than in the two other regions, which should record an average growth of 2.2% between 2011 and 2014. In the period covered by the projection, the growth differential between the three regions should therefore continue to be to the advantage of Flanders, but is expected to be less than in comparison with previous years.

Labour market

The drop in regional GDPs in 2009 and the stagnation in 2010 are expected to be accompanied by large losses in domestic employment. Flanders is likely to lose around 44,500 jobs in those two years, and Wallonia and Brussels 29,000 and 16,000 jobs respectively. Employment is only expected to grow from 2011 onwards in the various regions (not until 2012 for Brussels, where further job losses of around 1,800 are likely in 2011). It is anticipated that job creation will be higher in Flanders than in the two other regions.

Dutch translation in practice

To round off this chapter, we have selected a passage that is taken from the same publication as the previous extract on the Dutch ports, and likewise falls within the same section that focuses on the various types of employment that make up the maritime sector. This passage is taken from an early part of the section in which recent developments are assessed in areas such as shipbuilding and civil engineering, the navy, offshore employment and inland navigation, as well as the water sports industry. Towards the end of the section, the authors reflect on the prognoses for employment in these areas as well as the expected expansion demands. For a sample translation of this passage, see p. 183.

Text 3: *Visserij*

De visserij richt zich op de productie, in het bijzonder de vangst van vis en het oogsten van schelpdieren. De sector bestaat voornamelijk uit kottervissers en een klein aantal trawlerrederijen. Met uitzondering van de rederijen zijn er in de visserijsector met name maatschappen, dat wil zeggen dat de meeste werkzame personen in de kottervisserij een positie als zzp'er hebben (zelfstandige zonder personeel).

De visserijsector heeft het tij tegen, dit ondanks de toename van de visconsumptie en stijging van de verkoopprijzen. De sector wordt geconfronteerd met een aantal ontwikkelingen die de bedrijvigheid negatief beïnvloeden. Ten eerste zijn er ontwikkelingen op het gebied van wet- en regelgeving, zoals vangstbeperkingen, beperken van de effecten op niet-doelsoorten, voedselveiligheid, et cetera. Een belangrijk thema in het overheidsbeleid van de laatste jaren voor de visserij is de eis dat de sector duurzaam moet zijn. In dat licht zijn er per 2005 geen vergunningen voor de kokkelvisserij in de Waddenzee meer uitgegeven. Deze vorm van visserij is daarom inmiddels uit de Waddenzee verdwenen. De mosselvisserij daarentegen heeft wel voldoende toekomst.

Ten tweede worden de visserijen geconfronteerd met de hoge branstofprijzen, die gezien de beperkte marges in de visserij relatief zwaar drukken op de winst. Ten slotte wordt bij ruimtegebrek op het land steeds meer naar de zee gekeken (windmolenparken, Maasvlakte 2, mariene natuurreservaten). Hierdoor verliest de visserij een deel van zijn visgronden.

Als gevolg van deze ontwikkelingen is de afgelopen jaren het aantal bedrijven afgenomen, van bijna 800 in 2001 naar 730 in 2005 (zie tabel 2.10). [. . .]

De deelsectoren binnen de visserij waar de vooruitzichten minder slecht zijn, zijn de trawlervisserij (grotere schepen die in verre, buiten-Europese wateren vissen) en de mosselvisserij. Ook in deze sectoren is de werkgelegenheid afgenomen, zij het minder sterk (respectievelijk 4 en 5 %).

Source: Stichting Nederland Maritiem Land (2007) *Monitor Maritieme Arbeidsmarkt 2006*. Amsterdam: IOS Press BV, p. 18.

6 Media and communications

Introduction: texts and contexts

After the Second World War, society in the Netherlands began to change gradually at first and then in far-reaching ways. The overall process is referred to by sociologists and historians as depillarisation (*ontzuiling*). Until this point, Dutch society had been structured in vertical groupings according to people's religion (Dutch Reformed Church or Catholic) or ideology (liberalism, socialism). Each of the 'pillars' had its own social and political organisations. It also possessed its own media: newspapers and magazines, followed by radio and, later, television. As the social and cultural boundaries between the pillars began to break down, so the market opened up, particularly for the various printed media, which were faced with serious competition. This competition came from newspapers and magazines that had been associated with the other pillars, but since the late 1950s it had also come from television.

To illustrate the shift that took place we can look at the two main daily newspapers in the Netherlands: *De Volkskrant* and *NRC Handelsblad*. *De Volkskrant* was originally the newspaper of the Roman Catholic pillar of Dutch society, based in the Catholic south of the country. When it relaunched after the Second World War, it moved to Amsterdam, and in the 1960s and 1970s became known for its left-wing leanings. It now occupies a position in the centre ground. *NRC Handelsblad*, frequently known by its first three letters, was the result of a merger in 1970 of two papers: the *Algemeen Handelsblad* and the *Nieuwe Rotterdamsche Courant*. The merger made sense as they were both newspapers of the liberal pillar, based in Amsterdam and Rotterdam, respectively. *NRC* has maintained this political position and is well known for the rigour of its journalism. It was the first newspaper in the Netherlands to launch a digital edition.

Similar processes were at work in the Dutch-speaking part of Belgium, though it is important to remember that it was a unitary country until the period 1970–2001 when a number of state reforms resulted in federalisation, which gave rise to the Dutch-speaking federal state of Flanders. This development provided a new social and political framework for the Dutch-language media. Taking, for example, the major daily newspaper *De Standaard*, we can see that the publication also underwent a political and cultural shift, moving from a position as the daily paper associated with the Christian Democratic, i.e. Catholic and conservative sector of society, to that of a more independent commentator, especially on foreign affairs, in the 1960s and 1970s. Today it occupies a centre-right position in the media landscape of Flanders. *De Morgen* currently presents itself as a progressive newspaper experimenting with new formats and advanced greener printing technology. It was formed from the merger of two socialist newspapers.

No sooner had the market for news media in both the Netherlands and Flanders adjusted to the post-war social and political changes than a fresh wave of change was instigated by the arrival of the internet, which offered new ways of delivering the full range of journalistic coverage of current affairs, culture and sport. The internet also posed a threat to the publishing industry and to traditional broadcast media, but at the same time it created countless new possibilities for the delivery of reading matter and audio and visual material. In the twenty-first century, all of these media companies have their own web presence, and multiple means of delivery seem to both promote and cater for the new internet-based democracy in which there is something for all groups, whether defined by age, politics, sexuality, religion, hobbies, interests and so on. In other words, not only did the arrival of the internet change the media landscape, it also brought a new kind of democratic culture by opening up new possibilities for individual citizens to gain access to vast amounts of information. For example, in Chapter 1 of this book, we looked at how a museum can give people information ahead of their visit and those who are unable to visit in person a taste of what is on offer in the museum. As translators, you need no longer experience the frustration of getting stuck with a translation for want of information, and you are saved the time of having to visit libraries in person. In addition, the internet has brought new ways for people to communicate with one another, starting with email and developing into a range of methods: Facebook, Skype, chatrooms, blogs and Twitter.

Such dramatic changes have had a tremendous impact everywhere, but for speakers of what are sometimes called 'smaller' languages, there has been a particular sense of threat to their language. Dutch is a case in point. In recent decades there have been different aspects to this threat, including a concern that the survival of the language itself could be at stake. We can relate this concern to (i) European enlargement, which has meant that Dutch became only one of many smaller languages, and (ii) the growth of English as a global *lingua franca* in combination with a positive attitude on the part of many Dutch speakers to this neighbouring language.

Against this background is a different kind of concern for the future of the Dutch language: that speakers are losing their awareness of correct Dutch and that this might damage the actual language in some way. The difficulty here is to assess whether this is just another case of the older generation disapproving of the way a younger generation uses language, and, given that language is always subject to change, to understand precisely what changes are occurring and as a result of what processes. Text 2 addresses this question, particularly in relation to the way texting and Twitter may be affecting the Dutch language.

Text 1: *De virtuele krant. Samenleving in beweging*

This text is taken from a collection of essays on journalistic culture in the Netherlands in the twentieth century. These essays began life as academic papers at a conference on journalism held in Amsterdam. The final section of the book deals with new developments in the field, asking whether the availability of the internet means the end of journalism as it was then known in the Netherlands, and it attempts to explore the changing relationship between journalists and the public. We have chosen the essay by Lou Lichtenberg from this section, in which he looks at developments leading up to the presence of newspapers in digital form. As director of the *Stimuleringsfonds voor de pers*, his role was to advise ministers of media and culture in the Netherlands about new developments in the field and how to encourage press innovation through government policy. He was concerned about how to preserve freedom of expression and diversity of opinion against a background of disappearing local newspapers. The passage below is the opening part of the article in which the author summarises important developments in Dutch journalism immediately after the Second World War.

De virtuele krant
Samenleving in beweging

De diepgaande veranderingen in het communicatiebestel in de tweede helft van de vorige eeuw vonden hun wortels in de eerste plaats in maatschappelijke ontwikkelingen, waaronder de ontzuiling. In dit proces werden de verschillen tussen de zuilen als het ware ingeruild voor een ander soort verscheidenheid, bestaande uit toenemende verschillen tussen individuele burgers in de samenleving. De samenleving werd aldus steeds pluriformer, maar, anders dan tijdens de verzuiling, was het vaak niet eenvoudig in deze nieuwe pluriformiteit een bepaalde structuur of een zeker patroon te onderkennen. Er ontwikkelde zich, wat we kunnen noemen, een 'mosaic democracy', een democratie gebaseerd op een sterk heterogene samenleving. Het dagblad ontwikkelde zich van een betrekkelijk kleinschalig massamedium met een dominante rol in het debat van de verzuilde samenleving, naar een grootschalig, op commerciële basis geëxploiteerd communicatieproduct dat zijn positie te midden van concurrerende media elke dag opnieuw moet bevechten. Met minder zelfstandige reacties en titels – de echte 'zuilenbladen' verdwenen en kleine kranten trachtten door samenwerking te overleven – maar met een kwalitatief sterker journalistiek product ging de dagbladpers in de afgelopen decennia de concurrentie met andere media aan. Journalistiek gezien was de ontzuiling een interessante periode. Kranten durfden en konden de autoriteiten vrijmoediger tegemoet treden, al waren ze nog niet geheel losgekomen van de neiging politieke idealen na te jagen. In de jaren tachtig nam tevens de politieke polarisatie

> af. Het accent bij de dagbladen verschoof van een politieke opstelling naar meer journalistieke afwegingen.
> Daarbij speelde in het communicatiebestel nog een andere belangrijke maatschappelijke ontwikkeling een rol, namelijk de opkomst van de televisie. De 'kijkkast' verwierf een dominante positie bij mediagebruikers, waardoor er steeds minder tijd aan kranten, boeken en tijdschriften werd besteed. Informatievoorziening en opinievorming waren en zijn niet langer voorbehouden aan de gedrukte media.
>
> Source: Lou Lichtenberg (2002) De virtuele krant, in Jo Bardoel, Chris Vos, Frank van Vree and Huub Wijfjes (eds) *Journalistieke cultuur in Nederland*. Amsterdam: Amsterdam University Press, pp. 427–428.

1. Translation strategies and techniques

Below are our two key questions to help you make a first analysis. The first question concerns background information relevant for understanding the text, while the second involves reflection on your target audience.

i. What are the first things you notice about the text?

– *It consists of long sentences and requires an effort to read.*
   It is written in an academic style of Dutch and in order to comprehend it you will have to think more deeply than you might with a journalistic text.

– *It uses terms and concepts from media studies and sociology.*
   If you are not familiar with these disciplines it is a good idea to find similar texts in English to orient yourself in the terminology and the particular style of writing.

– *It assumes a significant background knowledge of Dutch society in the twentieth century.*
   If this historical background is something you are not familiar with, you are well advised to do some research on the topic, as this is very important knowledge for dealing with a wide range of texts, since many do assume a general historical understanding of Dutch society in this period. History books frequently give good explanations of pillarisation since this is a distinguishing feature of Dutch society at the end of the nineteenth and beginning of the twentieth century.

ii. What do you know about the target audience for your translation and how will it affect your translation?

This is the kind of text where it helps to give yourself a brief. Here is an example of a situation that would give rise to the need to translate this piece: a group of European academics in comparative media studies have decided to publish a volume of selected essays on the history of the media in different EU countries, and Text 1 is taken from the article that has been chosen for inclusion.

Now you know that your audience is an academic one, so you will definitely have to orient yourself in this area of study. This is normal procedure for translators of academic texts. The next consideration is the fact that your audience will consist of academics and students from all over Europe for whom English is not their first language, but a language of academic communication. This means that you could consider simplifying some of the longer sentences.

2. Text and language

This step is crucial since it determines the accuracy of your translation.

i. Words and expressions

Het communicatiebestel: this is a word that you will find via Google, but not if you look it up in dictionaries or in the IATE database. We suggest that you proceed by looking at texts on a similar topic in English and defining the usage of the Dutch term to see if you can find a match. One possible equivalent is 'media landscape'.

De ontzuiling, de zuilen, de verzuiling, de verzuilde samenleving, de echte zuilenbladen: the common element in all these words and expressions is the noun *zuil*, or 'pillar'. The fact that there are so many expressions involving *zuil* should make it clear to you that you are dealing with a discourse on the topic, i.e. a well-developed set of concepts and positions shared among a group of academics. This is why we recommended above that you research this topic, rather than simply looking up words, because this will give you the deeper understanding required for such a discourse. The last of the terms – *zuilenbladen* – is probably made up for this specific text since it appears in inverted commas, so you will have to come up with something that fits the context.

Een betrekkelijk kleinschalig massamedium: starting with the noun *massamedium* in the first instance you may think of the term 'mass media'; however, note that the correct English translation, which denotes the singular form, is 'mass medium'. In addition, it is difficult to identify the word class of *betrekkelijk* and *kleinschalig* since *massamedium* is a *het*-word and any adjectives preceding it are therefore uninflected, i.e. without -*e*. Remember that, in Dutch, adverbs are identical to uninflected adjectives, creating potential for confusion. Be alert to the possibility that *betrekkelijk* is an adverb qualifying *kleinschalig*, and not an adjective, and so is translated as 'relatively small-scale'.

Kijkkast: this noun appears in inverted commas because it denotes a vocabulary item associated with a different, more informal register. It is probably clear to you from the context that it is referring to television, so the translation task here is to think of an English equivalent from a lower register.

ii. Sentences

Since most of the sentences in this text are long and relatively complex, it will only be possible to illustrate typical problems. We have chosen a couple of samples that illustrate key aspects of the style of writing in this passage, and that highlight separable verbs, which will be discussed in more detail in this chapter's Practical Tips section.

> *Het dagblad ontwikkelde zich van een betrekkelijk kleinschalig massamedium met een dominante rol in het debat van de verzuilde samenleving, naar een grootschalig, op commerciële basis geëxploiteerd communicatieproduct dat zijn positie te midden van concurrerende media elke dag opnieuw moet bevechten.*

This is an example of a sentence that is difficult to follow because of its length. Since it is difficult to see how it might be broken up, you will need to translate its component parts and then see if you can reformulate it to make it a little more accessible. Use bracketing to find the sentence components – in this case clauses:

> (*Het dagblad ontwikkelde zich van een betrekkelijk kleinschalig massamedium met een dominante rol in het debat van de verzuilde samenleving, naar een grootschalig, op commerciële basis geëxploiteerd communicatieproduct*) (*dat zijn positie te midden van concurrerende media elke dag opnieuw moet bevechten*).

Surprisingly there are only two! We can also use bracketing to isolate the components of the first clause:

> (*Het dagblad ontwikkelde zich*) (*van een betrekkelijk kleinschalig massamedium* (*met een dominante rol in het debat van de verzuilde samenleving*)), (*naar een grootschalig,* (*op commerciële basis geëxploiteerd communicatieproduct*)).

This shows that the complexity comes from preposition phrases embedded in the first clause, so it will not be possible to break it up, unless you do a radical rewrite.

> *Kranten durfden en konden de autoriteiten vrijmoediger tegemoet treden, al waren ze nog niet geheel <u>losgekomen</u> van de neiging politieke idealen <u>na te jagen</u>.*

In this sentence are two examples of separable verbs. Like the constructions with *er* discussed in the Practical Tips section of Chapter 3, the challenge posed by separable verbs lies not in their actual translation into English, but in detecting and comprehending them. This is because we do not have a parallel construction in English, so you have to sensitise yourself to their usage, the problem being that these verbs consist of two elements, a prefix and a verb, which are not always found together in a sentence. The final verb in the example above is *jagen*. If you look up this item in a dictionary you will find that it describes the act of hunting or chasing. However, if you identify the element *na* as a separable prefix belonging with *jagen*, and look up the infinitive *najagen* this will place you in a different semantic field related to actual hunting, but only figuratively – 'to strive after', 'to aim for'. Similarly, the infinitive of the past participle *losgekomen*, which is not so difficult to identify, is *loskomen*.

3. Style, register and tone

i. Stylistic analysis of the source text

The text is written in an academic style with terminology taken from specific disciplines. It focuses on conveying complex ideas rather than on readability. The register is consistently high, except where the author is citing a word in everyday use.

ii. Assessment of the style of writing appropriate to the target text

The brief given above suggests that you should maintain the academic style, register and tone of the ST since the target audience is an academic one. At the same time, bearing in mind that English may only be a second or third language for some of the target audience, you may consider improving the readability of the text by breaking up some of the longer sentences.

Sample translation of Text 1: *De virtuele krant*

The virtual newspaper

Society on the move

The far-reaching changes in the media landscape in the second half of the last century had their roots primarily in social change, which includes depillarisation. In this process the differences between the pillars were as it were exchanged for a different kind of variety consisting of growing differences among individual citizens in society. In this way, society became increasingly pluriform but, other than in the case of pillarisation it was frequently not easy to discern a particular structure or distinct pattern in this new pluriformity. What we might call a 'mosaic democracy' developed – a democracy based on a highly heterogeneous society. The daily newspaper developed from a mass medium on a relatively small scale with a dominant role in the debates of a pillarised society to a large-scale media product exploited on a commercial basis which has to defend its position afresh each day among competing media. In recent decades, the

> daily press confronted the competition with other media armed with fewer independent reactions and titles (the real 'pillar dailies' disappeared and small newspapers attempted to survive by working together) but with a qualitatively stronger journalistic product. From the point of view of journalism the period of depillarisation was an interesting one. Newspapers dared to take on the authorities more openly and had the ability to do so although they had not completely let go of the tendency to pursue political ideals. In the 1980s political polarisation was simultaneously decreasing. The daily papers shifted their emphasis from a political stance to more journalistic considerations.
>
> In this process another important social development played a role in the media landscape – the arrival of television. The 'box' acquired a dominant position among media users with the result that less and less time was spent on newspapers, books and magazines. The provision of information and opinion was no longer the preserve of the printed media.

PRACTICAL TIPS: TRANSLATING SEPARABLE VERBS

Separable verbs, a distinct category of Dutch verbs consisting of a separable prefix and a base verb, present translators with a particular problem. They can be difficult to identify in a source text, and failure to do so often leads to problems in ascertaining the correct meaning of the verb. The main reasons for this are practical ones: the prefix may be some distance away from its verb in a sentence, and if you have not located it and placed it in front of the verb in order to form the infinitive, you will probably be looking in the wrong place in the dictionary. This may sound rather basic, but it is of great importance for accurate comprehension. Once you are able to identify separable verbs, translating them should not pose too many problems.

The infinitive

Here are some examples based on the verb *nemen*:

afnemen	decrease
innemen	take in
meenemen	take along
toenemen	increase
wegnemen	take away

(continued)

(continued)

Note that separable prefixes are always stressed. Some of the prefixes used in separable verbs can also be used without stress: unstressed prefixes <u>are always</u> <u>inseparable</u>. There are two examples of this unstressed use of a prefix in Text 1: *overléven* (to survive) and *onderkénnen* (to discern) (the accent is the conventional way of indicating stress in Dutch spelling, used solely in order to avoid ambiguity). Verbs with unstressed and therefore inseparable prefixes form the past participle in a different way from separable verbs.

The past participle

The prefix *ge-*, which denotes the past participle, is placed between separable prefix and verb. The participle is written all as one word:

> *afgenomen, ingenomen, meegenomen, toegenomen, weggenomen*

Verbs with unstressed, inseparable prefixes form their past participles without the insertion of *ge-*: *overleefd* and *onderkend*.

Monolingual Dutch dictionaries have many uses and all practising translators should make use of them. If you feel uncertain about a particular past participle you can normally find it between brackets after the infinitive of the verb in one of these dictionaries.

Separable verbs in sentences

Below you will find some examples of separable verbs in use in the translation texts. The main difficulty with separable verbs in sentences is in main clauses where the prefix is placed at the end of the sentence, while the verb is in second place. Translators must adopt a wait-and-see reading strategy that resists ascribing meaning to the verb until the end of the sentence has been reached.

> *In de NT <u>werken</u> Aruba, Curaçao, Nederland, Sint-Maarten, Suriname en Vlaanderen op enkele afgesproken gebieden <u>samen</u>.* (Chapter 2, Text 2)

This example using the verb *samenwerken* demonstrates just how far apart a verb and its prefix can be.

> *Zij <u>eigende zich</u> steevast de plek aan het raam <u>toe</u>.* (Chapter 3, Text 2)

The reflexive and separable verb *zich iets toeëigenen* does not occur frequently so you are more likely to need to look it up. The example demonstrates the importance of the reading strategy described above, because the small element *toe* at the end of the sentence can only be a separable prefix. This means you will look up the verb under 't' rather than 'e'.

> *Hoewel voor België tot nu toe geen onderzoek rond zwangerschapsgerelateerde discriminatie op de werkvloer beschikbaar was, deed het toenemend aantal klachten dat bij het Instituut voor de Gelijkheid van Vrouwen en Mannen op dat vlak <u>wordt neergelegd</u>, vermoeden dat dit soort discriminatie ook in ons land <u>voorkomt</u>.* (Chapter 4, Text 2)

The two underlined examples illustrate different usages of separable verbs:

wordt neergelegd is a passive verb consisting of the passive auxiliary verb in the present tense, *wordt* (is being), and the past participle of *neerleggen*, *neergelegd* (filed/lodged). It subject is het *toenemend aantal klachten* (the growing number of complaints).

dat dit soort discriminatie ook in ons land voorkomt – here we have an example of what happens when a separable verb is used in a subclause. This is a relative subclause introduced by *dat*. When the separable verb is placed at the end of its clause, prefix and verb are written as one word.

Text 2: *Veranderen nieuwe media de taal? Over sms'jes, chats en tweets*

This text is taken from an article that appeared in the internet magazine *Taalcanon*. It is written by Vivien Waszink, who is a lexicographer and has written a book about the language of hip-hop in Dutch, and Marc van Oostendorp who is a professor of language studies at the University of Leiden. The article itself questions whether computers and social media are really having a negative impact on the Dutch language. *Taalcanon* publishes a wide range of articles and questions-and-answers dealing with *alles wat je altijd had willen weten over taal* – everything you ever wanted to know about language. It has five themes: learning a language; using language; describing language; making language; and language and meaning.

Veranderen nieuwe media de taal? Over sms'jes, chats en tweets

De mobiele telefoon en het internet hebben ons allerlei nieuwe manieren van communiceren gebracht. Betekent dit ook dat we de taal op een andere manier gaan gebruiken of zelfs dat de taal daardoor verandert? Veel mensen lijken dat te denken, maar uit onderzoek blijkt dat het nog maar helemaal de vraag is.

(continued)

(continued)

Niemand zou het twintig jaar geleden hebben durven voorspellen, maar er wordt tegenwoordig meer geschreven dan ooit tevoren. Iedereen lijkt eraan mee te doen. In bus en trein zit al snel de helft van de mensen op een schermpje te kijken en berichten in te tikken. Veel mensen denken dat dit grootschalig gebruik van moderne media de taal wel moet veranderen – al is niet iedereen het erover eens of dat nu een gunstige ontwikkeling is of juist niet. Betekent het een uitbarsting van taalcreativiteit, of het begin van een totale taalregelloosheid die alleen maar kan eindigen in een totale taalchaos?

Twitter: kort en krachtig?

Om zulke vragen te kunnen beantwoorden moeten we eerst weten of – en zo ja op welke manier – taal nu precies verandert onder invloed van de moderne media. En dat is nog niet zo gemakkelijk. Zo hoor je vaak zeggen dat de nieuwe media het gebruik van afkortingen in de hand werken. Voor Twitter blijkt dat maar helemaal de vraag. Het is waar, de limiet van 140 lettertekens voor een tweet eist een zekere beknoptheid. Maar dat resulteert lang niet altijd in het gebruik van korte(re) woorden. De Amerikaanse taalkundige Mark Liberman vergeleek eind 2011 de woordlengte van honderd tweets van zijn studenten met de woordlengte in *Hamlet* van Shakespeare en in de verhalen van P. G. Wodehouse. Uit die vergelijking bleek dat de gemiddelde woordlengte op Twitter langer is dan die bij de literaire schrijvers.

En ook in een verzameling van twitterteksten van de Nederlandse taalkundige Folgert Karsdorp valt op dat twitteraars niet per se korte woorden gebruiken. Het komt eigenlijk juist vaker voor dat zij woorden extra nadruk meegeven door er letters aan toe te voegen, zoals in *Weeeeeeeeekeeeeeeeeeend, Laterssssssssssssssssssss, Goooooooooedemorgen* en *Dankuuuuuuuuuuuuuuuuuuuuuuu.*

Source: Vivien Waszink and Marc van Oostendorp (2012) Veranderen nieuwe media de taal? *Taalcanon*, http://www.taalcanon.nl/themas/maken (accessed 15 April 2014).

1. Translation strategies and techniques

Below are our two key questions to help you make a preliminary analysis of Text 2. The first concerns background knowledge relevant for understanding the text, while the second involves reflection on your target audience.

i. What are the first things that you notice about the text?

– It contains very up-to-the-minute vocabulary related to social media.
    This may not be a problem for those translators who regularly use social media in both languages. For those who do not, it is a good idea to follow some Dutch-speaking users of Twitter, or find a Dutch Facebook friend. Similarly, you could ask a Dutch student to exchange text messages with you,

to give you a feel for the medium. Background research is never a waste of time, even if it sometimes helps only indirectly with a particular translation.

- *It looks very varied, with questions, the use of dashes, recognisable names such as Shakespeare and P.G. Wodehouse, and some unrecognisable words in italics.*

    This liveliness is a feature of the article and is in keeping with the contemporary topic. The words in italics may well require some research among people who send text messages, mainly in the English language. Can you assume that a Dutch person using an English word will use it in the same way as an English person? And how recognisable is the name P.G. Wodehouse to a worldwide English-speaking audience? Do you yourself have a sense of why he is mentioned here? If your answers to such questions are 'no' or 'don't know', this is a sure sign that you need to undertake some research. While on the subject of name recognition, how will you tackle the name of the Dutch linguist referred to in the article – Folkert Karsdorp – since it will not mean anything to your audience? You may conclude that the article itself includes sufficient information, but it may still be worth doing a little research on him, as this may give you a better sense of the kind of research he undertakes.

- *The second subheading uses a fixed expression.*

    You will need to check the meaning of this expression in Dutch to make sure that it really matches any phrases you may think of in English. Ask yourself – is it as simple as finding the nearest expression in English? Are there other things to take into account?

ii. What do you know about the target audience for your translation and how will it affect your translation?

Judging by the liveliness of the ST, its intended audience is quite wide, and includes younger people. There are plenty of websites devoted to language and language learning, which list articles of general interest. You could translate a sample of this article to send to one of the sites to see if they are interested in publishing the whole piece. In this case, your audience will be very similar indeed to the ST audience, though you will have to decide whether to present the text as specifically relating to the Dutch scene or as being of more general relevance.

2. Text and language

This step is crucial since it determines the accuracy of your translation.

i. Words and expressions

> *sms'jes, chats en tweets*: although *sms* derives from the English phrase 'short message service', the term is not usually used in British English, which

prefers 'text (message)'. For more discussion of the use of loan words from English in Dutch texts, turn to the 'Introduction: texts and contexts' section of Chapter 8. Although this chapter focuses on loan words in texts about fashion, the discussion will nevertheless help you reflect on the problems that loan words cause for translators, together with possible solutions. In this text, *sms* is used in its diminutive form, hence the addition of *'je*. For an explanation of the use of the apostrophe, see http://taaladvies.net/taal/advies/vraag/1206/smsen_smsen/.

Chat is clearly the English word in use in Dutch, but is it used in exactly the same way? In the Dutch text it appears as a plural: *chats*. Can it be used in English as a plural noun, or does 'chat' itself denote an exchange of multiple messages?

Tweet: the same questions can be asked here.

Taalregelloosheid: this compound noun consists of the following elements: *taal + regel + -loos + -heid*. Working backwards, *-heid* is used to create a noun denoting a particular state of affairs; the suffix *-loos* denotes an absence of something – in this case *regel* (rule). This state of being without rules applies to *taal* (language). Since English does not have an equivalent compound noun, you will have to think of ways of paraphrasing the meaning.

Weten of – en zo ja: the phrase after the dash is a kind of extension to *weten of* 'know whether' (something is the case) indicating a further question – 'if so, …'.

In de hand werken: this is a set expression meaning to assist someone or promote something.

Blijkt, bleek: the verb *blijken* is used to denote that something is demonstrated to be the case. It occurs three times in this chapter because the authors are trying to take stock of recent research and comment on what it shows about language use.

ii. Sentences

Niemand zou het twintig jaar geleden hebben durven voorspellen, maar er wordt tegenwoordig meer geschreven dan ooit tevoren.

The question here is how to translate the four verbs that occur in the first clause. Leaving aside the phrase *twintig jaar geleden* (20 years ago), we have *Niemand zou het hebben durven voorspellen*. The finite verb is the auxiliary *zou* used with the perfect tense auxiliary *hebben* = 'would have'. There appears to be no past participle. This is because a certain group of verbs – modal verbs and certain others that are used together with an infinitive – form their perfect tense with the infinitive rather than a past participle (see, for example, *Dutch. An Essential Grammar*, section 14.6.2, p. 115). In other words, the combination *zou hebben durven* gives us 'would have dared' in English, and the final infinitive *voorspellen* tells us that 'no one would have dared to predict ...'.

> *Het komt eigenlijk juist vaker voor dat zij woorden extra nadruk meegeven door er letters aan toe te voegen ...*

These multiple clauses can be analysed using brackets: (*Het komt eigenlijk juist vaker voor*) (*dat zij woorden extra nadruk meegeven*) (*door er letters aan toe te voegen*). Starting with the main clause we have an example of a separable verb – *voorkomen* – 'occur' or 'happen' – where the verb is in second place and its prefix is placed at the end of the clause. In between is the adverb *vaker*, the comparative form of *vaak*. It is preceded by *eigenlijk* and *juist*, which both add emphasis to *vaker*, 'in actual fact more frequently' to give the translation: 'In actual fact it happens more frequently'. The second phrase also contains a separable verb, but since this is a subclause we find it at the end written as one word: *meegeven*, 'to give, provide with'. Following on from the first clause this gives: 'that they provide words with extra emphasis'. The third clause is introduced by *door*, 'by' used with an infinitive construction, where English uses a verb with the suffix '-ing'. Note that the infinitive in Dutch is another separable verb: *toevoegen*, 'to add', but with the prefix and verb separated by *te*. *Door ... toe te voegen* = 'by adding ...'. In addition, this clause contains a construction with *er*: *eraan*. In this case, the word *er* refers back to the noun in the previous clause – *woorden*. Putting all three clauses back together results in the following English translation: 'In actual fact it happens more frequently that they provide words with extra emphasis by adding letters to them ...'.

3. *Style, register and tone*

i. *Stylistic analysis of the source text*

Although it is a discussion of academic research, the register of the text is not particularly high or formal. The choice of vocabulary suggests that a neutral register has been chosen, though some of the contemporary words do suggest an accessible and lively style. The tone is fairly neutral, and perhaps a little didactic.

ii. *Assessment of the style of writing appropriate to the target text*

Given the context for the translation discussed above, it would be appropriate to aim to match the style, register and tone of the source text in English, perhaps bearing in mind that the audience is not only wide in terms of age and educational background, but also linguistic background.

Sample translation of Text 2: *Veranderen nieuwe media de taal? Over sms'jes, chats en tweets*

Are new media changing the language? On texts, chat and tweets

The mobile phone and the internet have brought us all kinds of new ways of communicating. Does this also mean that we are starting to use the language in a different way, or even that the language itself will be changed by this? Many people appear to think so, but research seems to show that this is still highly questionable. Twenty years ago, no one would have dared to predict that nowadays more is being written than ever before. Everyone seems to be doing it. Half the people on the bus or the train waste no time before consulting their screens and typing in a message. Many people think that this wide use of modern media is bound to change the language – though not everyone agrees whether this is a good development or the opposite. Does it bring a burst of linguistic creativity or the start of a total linguistic anarchy which can only end in language chaos?

Twitter: short and to the point?

To answer this kind of question we first need to know exactly whether language does change under the influence of modern media, and if so, how. And that is not such an easy task. For example, you often hear it said that the new media encourages the use of abbreviations. This is highly doubtful in the case of Twitter. It is true that the limit of 140 characters per tweet requires a certain conciseness. But this certainly does not always result in the use of short(er) words. In 2011 the American linguist Mark Liberman compared the length of words in a hundred of his students' tweets with Shakespeare's *Hamlet* and the stories of P.G. Wodehouse. The comparison showed that the average word length on Twitter is greater than in the work of the two literary writers. It is also striking that in a collection of twitter texts assembled by Dutch linguist Folkert Karsdorp Twitter-users do not make especial use of short words. Actually, it more frequently happens that they give words extra emphasis by adding letters as in *Byeeeeeee, soooooooo, whaaaaaaaaaaat* and *grrrrrrrrrrreat*.

Dutch translation in practice

To round off this chapter, we have selected a passage that is taken from the article we drew on for the first text: Lou Lichtenberg's 'De virtuele krant'. The extract comes from the closing pages and brings the account of the Dutch media up to the time of writing. For a sample translation of this passage, see p. 184.

Text 3: *De virtuele krant*

Uitgevers putten vaak uit eigen ervaring voor succesvolle strategieën. Zo verkondigt een aantal uitgevers de opvatting dat hun internetproducten, om werkelijk kansrijk te zijn, niet zozeer een elektronische editie of samenvatting van het gedrukte product moeten zijn, maar een 'value added feature'. Internetactiviteiten hebben volgens hen meer succes wanneer ze functioneren als een op zichzelf staand en met hun eigen, gedrukte, product concurrerend medium. Dit kan door de specifieke eigenschappen van internet optimaal te benutten: interactief, multimediaal en met gebruik van hyperlinks.

Andere ervaringen wijzen eveneens op mogelijk succes. Online projecten moeten dan niet louter beschouwd en gepresenteerd worden als experiment binnen krantenbedrijven, maar elektronische producten dienen als zelfstandige exploitaties te functioneren. Pas na uitwerking van businessplannen en met een weloverwogen planning worden de producten op de markt en op internet geïntroduceerd. Het doel is dan niet de krant slechts online uit te brengen, maar in samenwerking met partners binnen en buiten de perswereld, uitgebreide informatiesites aan te bieden. Zo verwacht de *Wall Street Journal* vooral veel succes van de samenwerking met andere spelers in het veld. Via diverse websites werkt de krant op verschillende manieren samen met andere ondernemingen die het een en ander te bieden hebben. Deze *allianties* kunnen gezamenlijk een product of dienst promoten, de inhoud van de site aanleveren of vervaardigen, door derden vervaardigde specifieke redactionele inhoud verspreiden en e-commerce service aanbieden. Volgens de *Wall Street Journal* kan zelfs samenwerking met een grote concurrent voor beide partijen lucratief zijn, wanneer ze kunnen profiteren van elkaars naamsbekendheid. Maar om dergelijke allianties succesvol te laten zijn, is het zaak telkens de weloverwogen doelen voor ogen te houden, en te accepteren dat *beide* partijen met de samenwerking hun voordeel (moeten) kunnen doen.

Source: Lou Lichtenberg (2002) De virtuele krant, in Jo Bardoel, Chris Vos, Frank van Vree and Huub Wijfjes (eds) *Journalistieke cultuur in Nederland*. Amsterdam: Amsterdam University Press, pp. 433–434.

7 Art history and exhibitions

Introduction: texts and contexts

In this chapter we will be looking at texts on art and art institutions in Belgium and the Netherlands. This is a subject area that translators encounter most often when they are asked to translate exhibition catalogues for museums and art galleries, material for auction houses, or manuscripts of academic monographs in the field of art history and architecture. When we think about Dutch art and artists, we might most immediately call to mind the work of the prolific late-nineteenth-century painter Vincent van Gogh (1853–1890), whose paintings were characterised by bold colour, rough texture and dramatic brushstrokes. While Van Gogh's depictions of sunflowers, peasant farm labourers and Mediterranean landscapes did not gain him great recognition during his lifetime, his works have subsequently earned him immense international acclaim and now hang in museums across the world, including the National Gallery in London, the Museum of Fine Arts in Boston, the Johannesburg Art Gallery and the National Gallery of Canada. Belgian contemporaries of Van Gogh include James Ensor (1860–1949) and Fernand Khnopff (1858–1921), whose works are frequently circulated internationally for display in exhibitions on the symbolist and expressionist movements. The close of the nineteenth century saw the Belgian painter, architect and interior designer Henry van de Velde (1863–1957) become one of the most important representatives of the art nouveau movement in Europe: his buildings and design objects are the subject of regular exhibitions across the Low Countries and Germany.

By the start of the twentieth century, artists in the Netherlands and Flanders had turned away from neo-impressionist forms of representation to those that advocated pure abstraction and a reduction to the essentials of form and colour. You might well know the work of artists such as Piet Mondrian (1872–1944), whose most famous paintings consist only of vertical and horizontal lines and the use of bold primary colours. 'De Stijl' ('The Style'), an artistic movement that Mondrian established with Theo van Doesburg (1883–1931) in 1917, also included the work of the architect and interior designer Gerrit Rietveld (1888–1964), whose functional furniture reflects his interests in new materials, production methods and standardisation. Painting, design and sculpture continued to flourish in the Netherlands and Flanders throughout the twentieth century, with the CoBrA group of avant-garde artists (an acronym for 'Copenhagen', 'Brussels' and 'Amsterdam') setting a new course towards abstract impressionism. The best-known twentieth-century graphic artist in the Low Countries was M.C. Escher (1898–1972). Contemporary Dutch and Flemish art is reflected in work by Jan Snoeck, Christoph Fink and Wim Delvoye. Modern art continues to thrive in the Netherlands and Flanders, with art fairs such as 'Art Rotterdam' and 'Art Brussels' attracting an international audience. Modern art museums – notably the Municipal Museum of Contemporary Art, 'S.M.A.K.' (*Stedelijk Museum voor Actuele Kunst*), in Ghent, and the Stedelijk Museum Amsterdam – similarly offer exhibitions dedicated to cutting-edge art and design.

But the rich history of art in the Netherlands and Flanders starts well before the nineteenth century. Flemish painting of the fifteenth, sixteenth and early seventeenth centuries was characterised by immense technical skill: artists were masters of oil painting, and used it to portray a realistic, astonishingly detailed vision of the world around them. The fifteenth-century Van Eyck brothers produced portraits of contemporary figures, images of saints and biblical figures, and church interiors. The Renaissance painter and printmaker Pieter Bruegel (*c.*1525–1569) produced powerful portrayals of peasant life, including festivals, dances and games, which offer us an authentic window on folk culture and social interaction in the period, making his work relevant to art critics and social historians alike. Bruegel's two sons inherited his artistic talent but developed in different directions: his elder son Pieter was nicknamed 'Hell Bruegel' for his fiery paintings of damnation, while Jan was known as 'Velvet Bruegel' for the accuracy and almost tangible qualities of his still-life painting. However, it was really in the so-called Golden Age – the *Gouden Eeuw* – of Dutch painting, spanning the period from roughly 1575 to 1725, that many of the painters we now consider to be 'Old Masters' were working. These included Frans Hals (*c.*1583–1666), Anton Van Dyck (1599–1641), Pieter de Hooch (1629–1684) and Pieter Paul Rubens (1577–1640), whose works continue to be seen as an important part of the artistic cultural heritage of the Low Countries. Johannes Vermeer (1632–1675), whose painting 'Meisje met de parel' formed the basis for the 2003 film of Tracy Chevalier's novel *Girl with a Pearl Earring*, was even voted by readers of the daily newspaper *Trouw* in 2006 to be the most beautiful painting in the Netherlands. These artists fostered a diversity of painting styles and subjects, including historical figures, portraits, representations of everyday life, landscapes and still life. The sheer mass of work produced – several million paintings are estimated to have been made in this period – graced walls across the Low Countries as well as the farther reaches of Europe. This reflects the aesthetic creativity and vibrancy of a period in which Dutch art was truly being reinvented to meet the needs and challenges of a new Dutch Republic (1588–1795), which swiftly became the most prosperous nation in Europe.

Text 1: *Een voorzichtig begin*

The first text in this chapter needs to be understood within the context of artistic developments in the Dutch Golden Age. It is a short extract from a scholarly monograph on Dutch art in the seventeenth century, written by the art historian Lyckle de Vries, which seeks to understand the narratives behind the paintings in this period. Although it was long assumed that such paintings were essentially the seventeenth-century equivalent of photographs of everyday life, de Vries argues that painters actually represented fictitious scenes of stereotypical communities. While, as we shall see in the passage below, various dissolute figures such as drunkards, womanisers and predatory females all had their part to play in such paintings, these were exaggerated characters who captured an image of the offending 'other' from which morally correct observers could distance themselves. The following passage is taken from the opening of a larger section on de Hooch and Vermeer.

Een voorzichtig begin

In 1655 werd Pieter de Hooch als schilder bij het Delftse gilde ingeschreven, maar vóór 1658 heeft hij geen van zijn werken gedateerd. In dat jaar lijkt hij zijn eigen stijl te hebben gevonden. Zijn eerdere schilderijen doen enigszins aan Sorgh en Saftleven denken, maar De Hoochs figuren waren vooral 'officieren'; hij combineerde de kortegaard dus met het stalinterieur. De afgebeelde ruimten zijn, op z'n boers, uit ondiepe en diepere gedeelten samengesteld en achterin staat soms een raam of deur open. Deze doorkijkjes zijn altijd gelijkvloers en hebben geen treden à la Maes.

In een interieur uit 1658 is met passer en liniaal een kamer getekend waarvan twee muren en een stukje zoldering te zien zijn. Als basis voor de simpele constructie dient een vloer met vierkante tegels van ongeveer een voet breed. Een kaartend stel en twee toeschouwers zitten in de hoek bij het raam, zodat grote delen van het vertrek leeg blijven. De opwinding die dit spel soms veroorzaakt, blijft hier achterwege. Wat dit schilderij toch spannend maakt, is het licht dat schuin van achter door deur en ramen binnenvalt. Hierdoor is de drinker links een silhouet geworden met glimlichtjes langs de contouren; zo behandelden italianiserende landschapschilders hun koeien als ze met tegenlicht werkten. De toepassing van de nieuw verworven vaardigheid is nog bepaald niet virtuoos en de schaduw van de stoel lijkt te zijn geschilderd met het wiskundeboek in de hand. Het doorkijkje naar een zonnige binnenplaats is gebruikt om de vertelling te ondersteunen. De waardin komt een nieuwe kan wijn brengen, want ondanks de schijnbare rust is hier een losbandig gezelschap weergegeven.

Source: Lyckle de Vries (2005) *Verhalen uit kamer, keuken en kroeg: het Hollandse genre van de zeventiende eeuw als vertellende schilderkunst*. Amsterdam: Salomé/University of Amsterdam Press, p. 124.

Art history and exhibitions 115

1. Translation strategies and techniques

Let us go back to our standard two key questions about the text to help us make a first analysis. The first concerns background knowledge relevant for understanding the text, while the second asks you to reflect on the audience for whom the text was originally written, who you imagine your own target audience to be, and the differences between the two.

i. What are the first things that you notice about the text?

- *It looks as if this is an academic text, written in a high register, using some terminology from art history, but also maintaining a style that is readable and idiomatic.*

  This suggests that you will need to go to reference works on art history – and preferably do some background reading on Pieter de Hooch.

- *In the second paragraph, one particular painting – 'een interieur uit 1658' – is described and analysed in some detail.*

  It would be important either to get hold of a copy of this painting or at least to acquaint yourself with similar pieces of indoor scenes by de Hooch to get a feel for style, content and the 'narratives' behind the kinds of scenes commonly found in his work. While you are doing your research, you might well come across the painting which de Vries describes, namely 'De Kaartspelers', known in English as 'Cardplayers in a Sunlit Room' and now kept in the Royal Collection in Windsor Castle. It is in the public domain on Wikimedia Commons and can be viewed and downloaded as 'Pieter de Hooch 014.jpg'.

- *It mentions several names.*

  These include Pieter de Hooch, who is one of the best-known painters of the Dutch Golden Age, but also Sorgh, Saftleven and Maes. Had you been commissioned to translate the whole of de Vries' book, then you would already have encountered the painters Hendrick Sorgh (c.1610–1670), Cornelis Saftleven (1607–1681) and Nicolaes Maes (1634–1693) in earlier chapters. For the purposes of this exercise, you should have a quick look at their work to gain a sense of the comparisons that de Vries is making. Wikimedia Commons is particularly useful for this. While you are surfing through a virtual gallery of the Old Masters, take a moment to look at Nicolaes Maes' 'An Eavesdropper with a Woman Scolding' of 1655 to understand what de Vries means when he talks about steps being important in Maes' work.

ii. What do you know about the target audience for your translation and how will it affect your translation?

Your audience might comprise art historians who are interested in ideas about space and place in (Dutch) art; alternatively, you might have been asked to

116   *Art history and exhibitions*

translate the text for a more general audience, interested in the kinds of scenes on which Dutch painters focused in the Golden Age.

2. Text and language

This step is crucial since it determines the accuracy of your translation.

i. Words and expressions

Having read the text, you will have found a number of pieces of vocabulary that are in some way difficult. Some could be terms you have simply never encountered before and cannot easily guess – *kortegaard* might well fall into that category. Others might be words that you feel are terms specific to art history – *tegenlicht, stalinterieur, italianiserende* – or are words you understand but cannot neatly translate, such as *doorkijkjes* or *glimlichtjes*. And then there are words that you might think you know, since they look very much like English terms – *virtuoos* would be a good example – but that could well wrong-foot you in other contexts: *virtuoos* does not mean 'virtuous'. Here are some examples of tricky words together with suggestions for approaching them:

> *Kortegaard*: a standard Dutch-English translation dictionary, such as *Van Dale*, is not of much help here, and a simple Google search generates many links to Danish uses of this word, but very few that enlighten us about what this word means as a term used in Dutch texts on art history. One online resource is, however, particularly useful. A digital copy of Petrus Weiland's art history dictionary, the *Kunstwoordenboek, of verklaring van allerhande vreemde woorden, benamingen, gezegden en spreekwijzen*, published in Rotterdam in the nineteenth century (available in its third edition from 1858 through the Digitale Bibliotheek voor de Nederlandse Letteren website, http://www.dbnl.org) informs us that a *kortegaard*, also spelt 'kortegard' or 'corps-de-garde' (from the French), is 'een wachthuis; stadsgevangenis enz., te Amsterdam'.
>
> *Stalinterieur*: this is actually relatively easy to deal with. It is a compound noun composed of *stal* and *interieur*, and can therefore be translated as a 'stable interior'. On the internet you will find a number of paintings from the eighteenth and nineteenth century of equine scenes that use precisely these terms in the title.
>
> *Doorkijkje*: this is clearly derived from the verb *doorkijken*, meaning 'to look through'. We might immediately think of the term 'peephole' or 'eyehole' as a way of translating the noun, and this would certainly be appropriate if we were thinking of a small aperture, such as a keyhole, through which to view a scene on the other side of a door or wall. But de Vries' text is clearly referring

Art history and exhibitions 117

to spaces larger than keyholes. He is thinking about doors or windows, which separate the immediate foreground from the background and give us visual access to other rooms in the painting. No single term in English seems to fit neatly: the best solution seems a phrase like 'spaces through which we look'. Fortunately this term comes up only twice in the given extract so this wordier solution is not too awkward.

Glimlichtjes: this compound noun, with its diminutive ending *-tjes*, can easily be broken up into two parts, *glim* and *licht*, the first part relating to the verb *glimmen* meaning 'to glow, gleam, shine' and the second meaning 'light'. Here again no one word in English conveys all these notions together, so we will need a series of words like 'small gleams of light'.

Italianiserende: this is a present participle with the adjectival ending *-e*. It comes from the verb *italianiseren*, meaning to 'italianise', so, to paint in an Italian style. You will notice that there are other present participles used adjectivally in this text, such as *een kaartend stel*. You will also have read *de afgebeelde ruimten*, which similarly makes use of a participle (this time a past participle) to describe the interiors. The participle *afgebeeld* derives from the separable verb *afbeelden*, to 'depict' or 'portray'.

Tegenlicht: a quick search in a translation dictionary will give you 'backlight' or 'contre-jour', which online reference works (including the *OED*) confirm as light coming from behind the subject, which distinguish it from the background and give it a silhouetted effect.

ii. Sentences

Zijn eerdere schilderijen doen . . . denken.

The verb *doen* is used here as a kind of auxiliary in combination with another infinitive and in this combination conveys a new concept in English, namely 'to remind' someone of something (see Donaldson, 1997: 183).

De toepassing van de nieuw verworven vaardigheid.

As we saw in Chapter 2, this is a complex adjectival construction that is particularly common in Dutch. This sentence therefore starts with the construction *de toepassing van de . . . vaardigheid* (literally: the application of the . . . skill'), with *de . . . vaardigheid* qualified by *nieuw verworven* (recently/newly acquired).

De waardin komt . . . brengen.

The verb *komen* is an auxiliary that, in combination with the verb *brengen*, is difficult to convey in English without appearing to use more words than are strictly necessary (what is known as a 'pleonasm'). If someone is bringing you something, then the fact that they are actually 'coming' to bring it to you is implicit in English. So, in this context, it makes more sense either to use the verb 'coming', so the innkeeper's wife 'is coming with a new flagon of wine' or 'bringing', so 'is bringing a new flagon of wine'.

> ... waarvan twee muren en een stukje zoldering te zien zijn.

This is an infinitive construction in Dutch – *zijn* ... *te zien*. This is best translated as an impersonal English passive, so something like 'can be seen' (see Donaldson, 1997: 193).

> *Wat dit schilderij toch spannend maakt* ...

The modal particle *toch* is an important word in this context because it creates a sense of contrast with the previous sentence in which we have just learned that it is not the card game that appears exciting. This sentence confirms that the painting is exciting, but in other ways – namely in the painter's handling of light. In English you might want to use the words 'however', 'yet' or 'but'. You could, alternatively, use the auxiliary 'do' for emphasis – 'what does make this painting exciting'.

3. Style, register and tone

i. Stylistic analysis of the source text

The use of language tells us that this is a form of scholarly writing that nevertheless seeks to be accessible. The text uses sophisticated vocabulary and complex sentences. Its register is quite formal and colloquialisms or contractions would not be appropriate.

ii. Assessment of the style of writing appropriate to the target text

The formal features of the ST do suggest that the translator should ensure that s/he creates a text in English with a high register, which accurately conveys the artistic effects described in the text (*het licht dat schuin van achter door deur en ramen binnenvalt*, for example) and understands the author's argumentation about 'narrative' and scene-setting in de Hooch's paintings.

At the same time, there are some target audience considerations, especially the need to make the content of the text accessible to someone unfamiliar with art from the Dutch Golden Age. This may mean including small amounts of additional information, such as the first names of the artists Sorgh, Saftleven and Maes, if the commission does indeed only involve translating this extract and no previous passages from de Vries' book. You could also consider bringing in information – textual and visual – about the dates during which these artists were working and the kinds of scenes they reproduced. Either way, it is important to make the translated passage instructive but not so fact laden that it loses the highly readable qualities of the ST.

Sample translation of Text 1: *Een voorzichtig begin*

A cautious beginning

In 1655 Pieter de Hooch was registered as a painter with the Delft guild, but before 1658 he did not date any of his works. That was the year in which he appears to have found his own style. His earlier paintings to some degree remind us of Sorgh and Saftleven, but de Hooch's figures were above all 'officers'; he therefore combined the guardhouse with the stable interior. The rooms depicted are, in their provincial manner, constructed of parts that have lesser and greater depth and at the back a door or window is sometimes open. These spaces through which we look are always on the ground floor and do not have steps as is the case with Maes.

In an interior from 1658 a room has been drawn with compasses and a ruler, of which two walls and part of the ceiling can be seen. A floor with square tiles approximately one foot wide provides the basis for the simple construction. A card-playing pair and two onlookers sit in the corner by the window, leaving large parts of the chamber empty. The excitement which this game sometimes causes is not evoked here. But what does make this painting exciting is the light that falls through the door and window diagonally from behind. As a result, the drinker to the left has become a silhouette with small gleams of light along his contours; that was how Italianising landscape artists treated their cows when they worked with backlight. The application of this newly acquired skill is certainly not done with a masterly touch and the shadow on the chair appears to have been painted with a book on mathematics in the other hand. The view through to a sunny inner courtyard is used to sustain the narrative. The innkeeper's wife is bringing a new flagon of wine since, despite the apparent tranquillity, the company portrayed here are carousers.

PRACTICAL TIPS: PASSIVE CONSTRUCTIONS

In the passage we have just read and translated, we encountered a number of different instances of the passive: we found passives in the Dutch that we translated using the passive in English (*Pieter de Hooch [werd] ingeschreven, de ruimten zijn [. . .] samengesteld*), as well as other

(continued)

(continued)

constructions in Dutch that we would not consider to be passive constructions, but that we put into English using passive forms (*twee muren [zijn] te zien*). In this section we therefore explore how passive forms are used in Dutch and consider when they can be translated using the passive in English and when an active form might be more advisable, as well as looking at which other constructions in Dutch favour a passive form in English.

Passive forms with a subject

Where in a passive sentence in Dutch there is a clear subject, the sentence can generally be translated using a passive in English too:

> *Een groot deel van het schilderij wordt ingenomen door de achterkant van het doek waarop hij werkt.*
> A large part of the painting is taken up by the back of the canvas on which he is working.

> *De bonte kleuren van het interieur werden na de restauratie nauwgezet opnieuw aangebracht.*
> The bright colours of the interior were carefully reapplied after the restoration.

> *Het beeld zal driemaal vergroot worden en 90 graden gedraaid worden.*
> The image will be enlarged three times and rotated through 90 degrees.

Here we can see that each of these sentences has an identifiable subject – *een groot deel*, *de bonte kleuren*, *het beeld* – which makes transferring them into English relatively straightforward. In each case the Dutch passives – *wordt ingenomen*, *werden [. . .] aangebracht*, *zal [. . .] vergroot worden* – are translated using similar passive constructions in English – 'is taken up by', 'were [. . .] reapplied' and 'will be enlarged' – and in each case the same tense is retained in translation.

Passive forms without a definable subject

Sentences in Dutch where the subject is not so easily defined tend to be harder to translate. Take a look at the following examples and think about how you would tackle putting them into English:

> *In juli 1931 werd begonnen met de sloop van de kathedraal.*

> *Opnieuw werd opgemerkt dat het schilderij niet per se in Rotterdam blijft na verkoop.*

In de BBC-uitzending werd vastgesteld dat het werk van Chagall in ieder geval nooit rond 1910 kon zijn gemaakt, wat de verzamelaar vermoedde.

There is a similar difficulty in each of these examples. We do not know in the first sentence who exactly undertook the demolition of the cathedral or who commented in the second sentence that the painting would not stay in Rotterdam. In the third sentence we know the context (*de BBC-uitzending*) within which the painting by Chagall was discussed, but we do not know precisely who was contesting previous claims about its age.

In English we tend to avoid formulating subject-less sentences. Instead we prefer to come up with a subject that fits the context in which the sentence is being used. Depending on the context, the translation of the first example could be something like 'In July 1931 demolition of the cathedral began', making 'demolition' the subject of the sentence, or 'In July 1931, they began to demolish the cathedral', if the 'agents' in the demolition process are clear from previous sentences in the passage. The second sentence could also be translated in a number of different ways – for example, 'It was once again commented that the painting would not necessarily stay in Rotterdam after its sale' or 'Mention was once again made of the fact that the painting would not necessarily stay in Rotterdam after its sale', each of which restructures the sentence to give it a subject, in this case 'it' and 'mention'. The same goes for the third sentence, which could be translated as 'In the BBC programme it was established that the work by Chagall could not, in any case, have been made around 1910, as the collector had presumed.' If you know more about the context, you might actually be able to take a subject much less neutral than 'it' and translate this sentence as 'researchers/art historians/specialists established that . . .', thus making it into an active, rather than a passive sentence. We are generally advised to avoid making passive statements, since they conceal from the reader who the subjects of 'agents' of the given action are. You can, within reason, make active statements of passive ones, although you should be careful to whom you attribute which actions. The author of the text you are translating may indeed have deliberately used the passive to construct a text that diplomatically avoids making open accusations or assertions.

Impersonal English passives

We now have a better idea about how to tackle sentences in Dutch that themselves make use of passive forms. There are, however, other constructions in Dutch that we would not classify as using the passive voice, but that often require us to use it in English. The constructions on which we will focus here all use the infinitive, i.e. 'te + verb' form, in Dutch. They are often accompanied by an impersonal subject. Take a look at the following sentence:

(continued)

(continued)

> *Het hoeft niet te verbazen dat dit monumentale meesterwerk latere componisten heeft geïnspireerd.*

Here, too, we have no properly defined subject, since it is simply the neutral pronoun *het* that is paired with the verb *hoeven*. In English we would tend to come up with a more definite subject to make this sentence read fluently. A possible translation would therefore be 'No one is/needs to be surprised that this monumental magnum opus inspired later composers' or we could use the English subject 'it' to produce the sentence 'It is hardly surprising that this monumental magnum opus inspired later composers.'

The sentences below offer similar examples of a 'te + infinitive' construction that can be translated using the passive in English:

> *Het is te hopen dat dit ontwikkelingsland uiteindelijk langzamerhand de weg zal inslaan naar de zo broodnodige vrede en voorspoed, ten behoeve van al zijn burgers.*
> It is to be hoped that eventually this developing country will gradually set itself on the path to much-needed peace and prosperity, for the benefit of all its citizens.
>
> *Or:*
> One hopes that eventually this developing country will gradually set itself on the path to much-needed peace and prosperity, for the benefit of all its citizens.
>
> *Deze illustraties zijn afzonderlijk te verkrijgen in kleur onder de vorm van diapositieven en transparanten.*
> These illustrations can be obtained separately in colour in the form of slides and overhead transparencies.
>
> *Sinds half 2000 hebben de prijzen zich een beetje hersteld, maar een duurzaam herstel van de wereldmarktprijzen valt niet te verwachten.*
> Prices have recovered slightly since the middle of 2000, but a sustainable recovery of the world market prices is not something to be expected.

Note that, with regard to the first sentence, the context in which it appears might enable you to be more specific in your choice of subject, so you could possibly have 'I hope that . . .' or 'We hope that . . .', if it is stylistically appropriate to attribute this sentence to an individual speaker or group of speakers. The same goes for the third sentence, where it might also be possible to state that 'a sustainable recovery of the world market prices is not something we expect'.

Text 2: *Het onstaan van de musea voor schone kunsten in België*

This extract is taken from the first part of a two-volume work on the history of the Royal Museums of Fine Arts of Belgium, and charts their history throughout the past 200 years. This is a richly illustrated book, published by one of the major Belgian publishers, Lannoo, in collaboration with the financial institution Dexia Bank. It clearly seeks to attract an educated audience of non-specialists who are interested in the history of Belgium, its cultural heritage and its contribution to art history in the West. The preface to this collection tells us that it was put together following celebrations to commemorate 200 years since the opening to the public of these museums at the very start of the nineteenth century. The extract itself comes from the beginning of one of the chapters in the first section, where particular emphasis is placed on the French influence on Belgian museums in the eighteenth century, so in the Enlightenment period up to the French Revolution.

Het onstaan van de musea voor schone kunsten in België

De eerste musea voor schone kunsten ontstonden in België tijdens de politieke, religieuze en artistieke omwentelingen in de Franse tijd. De onstaansgeschiedenis van het museum in Brussel is enigszins – doch niet helemaal – vergelijkbaar met die van de musea in de andere departementshoofdplaatsen: Antwerpen, Brugge, Gent, Luik, Bergen en Namen. Deze instellingen verschenen niet *ex nihilo*, want in Brussel waren er zowat twintig jaar eerder, onder het Oostenrijkse bewind, al verschillende plannen geweest voor de oprichting van een openbaar museum. Zulke projecten pasten in het tijdskader: in de Eeuw van de Verlichting had zich namelijk een nieuwe artistieke gevoeligheid en een bekommernis om de conservatie van kunstwerken ontwikkeld.

In de tweede helft van de 18de eeuw kwamen talrijke liefhebbers uit binnen- en buitenland naar de Oostenrijkse Nederlanden om er de schitterende meesterwerken van de prestigieuze Vlaamse school te bewonderen. Toeristische gidsen zoals die van Guillaume Mensaert en Jean-Baptiste Descamps, respectievelijk verschenen in 1763 en 1769, richtten zich tot die bezoekers. De auteurs beschreven hoofdzakelijk het kunstbezit van de kerken, die dikwijls als echte "schilderijenkabinetten" beschouwd werden. Dankzij de kunstwerken die ze vergaard hadden, fungeerden ze sinds vele eeuwen als bewaarplaatsen van het artistieke erfgoed. In die tijd was er in de Oostenrijkse Nederlanden nog geen enkel echt museum. Die gidsen vermeldden enkele privé-collecties, maar zonder veel details over de inhoud ervan. Bovendien was hun toegankelijkheid beperkt en

(continued)

124 *Art history and exhibitions*

> *(continued)*
> hun bestaan dikwijls kortstondig, omdat ze meestal bij de dood van de eigenaar verspreid raakten.
> Tijdens het bewind van keizerin Maria Theresia begonnen kunstenaars en connoisseurs de religieuze werken vanuit esthetisch oogpunt te bekijken en de rol die de kerkelijke instellingen op artistiek vlak vervulden, te bekritiseren.
>
> Source: Christoph Loir (2003) Het onstaan van de musea voor schone kunsten in België, in Michèle van Kalck (ed.) *De Koninklijke Musea voor Schone Kunsten van België: twee eeuwen geschiedenis*. Brussels: Dexia Bank/Lannoo, 2 vols, vol. 1, pp. 33–40 (extract on p. 33).

1. Translation strategies and techniques

Our standard two key questions about the text, which are helpful in making an initial analysis and reflecting on how to tackle the translation, focus on the background knowledge relevant for understanding the text and the kind of audience for whom the ST was composed, which could well be different from the assumed readership of the TT.

i. What are the first things that you notice about the text?

– *It appears to be an academic text, written in a high register but also maintaining a style that is readable and idiomatic, which assumes some knowledge of historical periodisation in Europe.*

   This suggests that it is worthwhile reading up on the history of the Low Countries in the eighteenth century to have some sense of the political changes in the period that might have influenced how artists and collectors operated. It would also be helpful to have a look at what kind of artistic heritage the Low Countries could lay claim to. What was the *prestigieuze Vlaamse school*?

– *There are frequent references to historical moments and periods.*

   You probably did your reading on the history of the Low Countries in English. Now it is time to work out what the correct English terms are for the *Franse tijd*, the *Oostenrijkse Nederlanden*, and the *Eeuw van de Verlichting*. Does the *keizerin Maria Theresia* change her name in translation and what exactly is her title in English?

– *In the first paragraph a series of place names are mentioned.*

   On the face of it, this might not seem like a major problem. In Chapter 2 we looked at how some Flemish cities such as *Antwerpen*, *Brugge* and *Gent* are translated into English. But what should you do with *Luik*, *Bergen* and *Namen*? Pick up a couple of English-language tourist guides to Belgium and see what they do with the names of these places.

Art history and exhibitions 125

– In the second paragraph the art historical term *'schilderijenkabinetten'* crops up.

A Dutch-to-English dictionary may provide you with terms like 'collections of pictures' or 'collections of paintings'. Do these adequately reflect what the word means? Where else do you find the word *schilderijenkabinet* (or sometimes *schilderijen-kabinett*) and what does it mean in that context?

ii. What do you know about the target audience for your translation and how will it affect your translation?

Your audience might comprise (art) historians who are interested in the development of museums in Belgium or readers who are more generally interested in the cultural history of Belgium.

2. Text and language

Analysing the text and language of this extract is crucial since it determines the accuracy of your translation.

i. Words and expressions

Having read the text, you will have found a number of pieces of vocabulary that are in some way difficult. The first of these might actually be the title itself – the *musea voor schone kunsten in België*. Other nouns that do not immediately lend themselves to translation are *tijdskader, ontstaansgeschiedenis* and *kunstbezit*.

Here are some examples of tricky words together with suggestions for approaching them:

> *Omwentelingen*: the plural of the noun *omwenteling*, meaning 'upheaval' or 'revolution'. Since the passage not only refers to the French Revolution of 1789, but also to the more general unrest in this period, 'upheaval' would be a better choice than 'revolution'. While the Dutch noun is in the plural, the singular noun 'upheaval' in English reflects just as well the state of chaos and change in the southern Low Countries in this period.

> *Musea voor schone kunsten in België*: an official title for these institutions does exist in English and it is this that you should be using in your translation. The 'Royal Museums of the Fine Arts of Belgium' – note that the capitalisation differs from the original Dutch – have an extensive English-language homepage (www.fine-arts-museum.be), which is helpful in understanding how this institution has already established an international profile for itself.

> *De Franse tijd*: literally 'the French period'. We know that the museum was founded at the turn of the nineteenth century. From this context we can deduce that the *Franse tijd* referred to here is the period from 1794 to 1815, when the

French occupied the southern provinces of the Low Countries. Their government was brought to an end by the defeat of Napoleon at Waterloo in 1815.

Ontstaansgeschiedenis: this is a compound noun composed of *ontstaan* and *geschiedenis*, and can therefore be broken up into elements meaning 'creation' or 'genesis' or 'origins' and 'history'. Given that we are looking at this word in relation to a museum, which is 'founded' or 'established' – a Google search suggests the former is more common than the latter – then we are looking at the 'history of the founding' of the museum in Brussels.

Onder het Oostenrijkse bewind, the *Oostenrijkse Nederlanden* and *keizerin Maria Theresia*: these refer to the period in which the Austrian branch of the House of Habsburg was in control of the southern Netherlands, from 1714 until 1780. The 'Austrian Netherlands' was ruled by Empress Maria Theresa (note that her name is spelled in English without an 'i') from 1741 until her death in 1780.

Tijdskader: literally 'time frame', but here 'historical context', 'context of the time' or something similar would be more appropriate.

De Eeuw van de Verlichting: literally the 'Century of the Enlightenment', but in English we tend to speak more frequently of the 'Age of Enlightenment' since this intellectual movement is considered to have begun in the late seventeenth century and lasted until around the close of the eighteenth century.

De prestigieuze Vlaamse school: this refers to the Flemish school of painters whom we mentioned in the introduction to this chapter, including Van Eyck and Rubens.

Kunstbezit: a compound noun formed of *kunst* and *bezit*, the former perhaps best rendered either by the noun 'art' or the adjective 'artistic', and the latter meaning 'belongings', 'property' or 'holdings'.

Schilderijenkabinetten: the literal translation 'cabinets of paintings' probably reads oddly at first sight. Yet a Google search shows that wealthy art collectors and connoisseurs in the eighteenth and nineteenth centuries did possess 'cabinets of paintings' – not unlike the 'cabinets of curiosities' of the sixteenth and seventeenth centuries, which contained all sorts of weird and wonderful objects. Such 'cabinets' essentially housed a small gallery of paintings that reflected the taste (and purse) of the individual collector. Travellers voyaging through the Low Countries in the late Enlightenment and early Romantic periods would write home enthusiastically of the 'cabinets of paintings' they had seen either on public view or in private collections. In 1820, the royal cabinets of paintings and rarities moved into the Mauritshuis in The Hague. A search of the web shows that both 'Royal Cabinet of Paintings' and 'Royal Picture Gallery' are used to describe this collection, the latter sounding decidedly more modern, which is perhaps why the Mauritshuis uses it on its own English-language website (www.mauritshuis.nl).

ii. Sentences

> *Deze instellingen verschenen niet* ex nihilo *want in Brussel waren er zowat twintig jaren eerder . . . al verschillende plannen geweest . . .*

These phrases have been lifted out of what is a much longer and much more complicated series of constructions to demonstrate that what is at the heart of this sentence is a construction using the indefinite subject *er* in combination with the verb forms *waren . . . geweest*. This 'repletive' use of the word *er* can be conveyed in a number of different ways (see Donaldson, 1997: 284–285): here we made *verschillende plannen* the subject of the English sentence and used a passive verbal construction, retaining the pluperfect of the original *waren . . . geweest*. If you are really lost in a sentence, start by underlining all the verbs to identify how they hang together, look next for the subjects that go with them, then the direct and indirect objects, until the meaning becomes clearer and the elements of the sentence fall into place.

> *Toeristische gidsen zoals die van Guillaume Mensaert en Jean-Baptiste Descamps, respectievelijk verschenen in 1763 en 1769, richtten zich tot die bezoekers.*

The word order in English tends to be different around the word 'respectively'. It more often comes at the end of what has been numerated, rather than at the beginning, so 'which appeared in 1763 and 1769 respectively'. It is also worth pausing for a moment to look at the small word *die* in this sentence. It is used to emphasise the fact that the guidebooks were composed especially for those visitors to the Austrian Netherlands who came to look at the works by the artists of the Flemish School.

> *In de tweede helft van de 18de eeuw kwamen talrijke liefhebbers uit binnen- en buitenland naar de Oostenrijkse Nederlanden om er de schitterende meesterwerken . . . te bewonderen.*

You may well be wondering what the small word *er* is doing in this sentence. We have just looked at how it can be used repletively (i.e. as an indefinite subject, often at the start of a sentence), but it can also be used with numerals and adverbs of quantity, and pronominally in connection with prepositions, as discussed in some detail in Chapter 3. Here it is used locatively, so it refers to a sense of place, and simply stands as an unstressed form of *daar*, 'there' (Donaldson, 1997: 287–288).

3. Style, register and tone

i. Stylistic analysis of the source text

The use of language tells us that this is a form of scholarly writing that is fairly factual. The text uses sophisticated vocabulary and complex sentence structures.

128 *Art history and exhibitions*

Its register is quite formal, and colloquialisms or contracted forms ('these institutions didn't appear *ex nihilo*') would not be appropriate.

ii. Assessment of the style of writing appropriate to the target text

The formal features of the ST do suggest that the translator should ensure that s/he creates a text in English with a high register that is suitable for the academic art market. At the same time, there are some target audience considerations that need to be taken into account, especially the need to make the historical context of the passage clear to someone unfamiliar with the complexities of political allegiances and shifts in political power in the Southern Low Countries. This may mean that you feel justified in including small amounts of additional information, such as explanations of when the *Franse tijd* was, who belonged to the *Vlaamse school* and why *keizerin Maria Theresia* has an important part to play in this period.

Sample translation of Text 2: *Het onstaan van de musea voor schone kunsten in België*

The founding of the Museums of Fine Arts of Belgium

The first museums of fine arts were established in Belgium during the political, religious and artistic upheaval in the French period. The history of the founding of the museum in Brussels is to some degree – but not entirely – comparable with that of museums in other regional capitals: Antwerp, Bruges, Ghent, Liège, Mons and Namur. These institutions did not appear *ex nihilo* since various plans had already been made in Brussels some twenty years earlier, under Austrian rule, to establish a public museum. Such projects corresponded with the preoccupations of the time, given that in the Age of Enlightenment a new form of artistic sensibility had emerged and concern had arisen about the conservation of works of art.

In the second half of the eighteenth century, numerous devotees from home and abroad came to the Austrian Netherlands to marvel at the stunning masterpieces of the prestigious Flemish School of painting exhibited there. Tourist guidebooks such as those by Guillaume Mensaert and Jean-Baptiste Descamps, which appeared in 1763 and 1769 respectively, were aimed at precisely those visitors. The authors primarily described the artistic property of the churches, which were often considered true 'cabinets of paintings'. Through the masterpieces which they had amassed, they had functioned for many centuries as repositories of artistic heritage. At that time no single proper museum existed in the Austrian Netherlands. The guidebooks recorded a few private collections, but gave very few details about their contents. Furthermore access to them was limited and their existence often short-lived, since they were often dispersed on the death of their owner.

During the reign of Empress Maria Theresa, artists and connoisseurs began to view religious works from an aesthetic standpoint and to criticise the role which the religious institutions played on an artistic level.

Dutch translation in practice

To round off this chapter, we have selected a second passage that is taken from the same work on art history as we examined right at the beginning of the chapter, namely de Vries' book on seventeenth-century painters and the 'narratives' behind their work. For a sample translation of this passage, see p. 185.

Text 3: *Een schilderswerkplaats*

Een schilderswerkplaats had meestal hoge vensters op het noorden waarvan de onderhelft met luiken werd afgesloten. Schilders zetten hun modellen hier zo neer dat ze schuin van links voor werden belicht met korte, naar rechts achter wijkende schaduwen. Een compositie met figuren die op deze manier zijn geobserveerd, maakt De indruk alsof het licht schuin van voren door de lijst het schilderij binnenvalt. Dit 'atelierlicht' werd soms gecombineerd met een lichtbron in het schilderij, zoals ook Dou had gedaan, maar aan die gewoonte heeft De Hooch een einde gemaakt. Hieruit blijkt hoeveel belangrijker lichteffecten voor hem waren, dan voor zijn voorgangers.

Johannes Vermeer handelde wat in kunst maar zijn hoofdberoep was herbergier. Daarnaast schilderde hij, maar hij leverde gemiddeld slechts eens per jaar een schilderij af. Er zijn een paar vroege historiestukken van hem bekend en in 1656 maakte hij een genrestuk dat zowel aan Van Honthorst als aan een Rembrandt-leerling doet denken. Waarschijnlijk heeft Vermeer beide voorbeelden uit de tweede hand leren kennen, zonder intensief contact met een leermeester. Dat viel ook niet te verwachten, want zijn opleiding tot historieschilder was al jaren eerder afgerond. Een tweede proeve van bekwaamheid bij de omscholing tot genreschilder doet door licht en kleur nog sterker aan een Rembrandt-leerling als Nicolaes Maes denken. In beide composities dient een oosters tapijt om het mislukte perspectief van een tafel te verhullen. Pas met hulp van De Hooch zou het Vermeer lukken om zijn beginnersproblemen te overwinnen.

(continued)

(continued)

Twee van Vermeers genrestukken hebben zoveel aan De Hoochs werk uit 1658 te danken dat de een de leerling van de ander lijkt te zijn geweest maar in feite ging het om de ontmoeting tussen twee beginnelingen van nog geen dertig; na dit kortstondige experiment is elk van beiden zijn eigen weg gegaan.

Source: Lyckle de Vries (2005) *Verhalen uit kamer, keuken en kroeg: het Hollandse genre van de zeventiende eeuw als vertellende schilderkunst*. Amsterdam: Salomé/University of Amsterdam Press, pp. 125–126.

8 Fashion and design

Introduction: texts and contexts

In this chapter we will be looking at the contribution that fashion and design have made culturally, socially and economically to the Netherlands and Belgium over the past half-century or so. When we think of the fashion capitals of Europe, it is probably Paris and Milan that most spring to mind. Yet, as the texts in this chapter show, designers in the Netherlands and Flanders have established an impressive reputation in the international fashion and design industry, not only as creative, imaginative inventors of new ways to clothe the body and to rethink the spaces in which we live and work, but also as instructors of the next generation of designers in the Low Countries. The fashion industry in the Netherlands is now a true force to be reckoned with: the fashion house Viktor & Rolf, established by the designer duo Viktor Horsting and Rolf Snoeren who met at the Arnhem art academy, is known worldwide for its highly theatrical fashion shows and its striking, extravagant collections. The Dutch designer Addy van den Krommenacker, knighted for his services to fashion, is also an internationally acclaimed figure in the world of haute couture. His creations, which have been worn by royalty and stars of stage and screen, are designed to be elegant and to capture the essence of femininity rather than to shock. But innovation in the Dutch fashion industry not only depends on the shows and collections put on by its most famous names – non-profit organisations such as the Dutch Fashion Foundation (DFF), supported by the Dutch Ministry of Economic Affairs, Agriculture and Innovation, aim not only to promote Dutch fashion per se, but also to organise cultural projects, fashion shows and presentations. Other initiatives, such as the *Cultuurfonds Mode Stipendium*, the highest grant awarded annually to an individual fashion designer in the Netherlands, has helped to bring Dutch fashion to media attention and demonstrate how innovative Dutch design can be. The Netherlands Institute for Design and Fashion is also a key national organisation that brings together those working in art and architecture, craft and cinema, performance art and textile design, to provide both real and virtual platforms for the exchange of ideas.

Flanders shares with the Netherlands a long history in cloth trading, and the architectural legacy left by 'cloth halls', such as the *Lakenhal* in Ypres, demonstrates how much the textile industry contributed to the prosperity of Flemish cities as early as the thirteenth century. From the sixteenth century onwards, Flanders became an important centre for lacemaking, an industry that required skill, innovation and the ability to adapt quickly to the demands of an ever-changing market. In the eighteenth century, Flemish lacemakers used linen thread to produce the exceptionally fine lacework required for the cravats, frills and cuffs fashionable at the time. Brussels, Bruges, Aalst and Mechelen enjoyed an international reputation as centres of needle and bobbin lacemaking until the start of the twentieth century, when fashions changed and mechanised forms of lace production came into being. New impulses in fashion in the 1960s placed the international spotlight on Flanders once again, as the Royal Academy of Fine Arts introduced a number of more 'applied' subjects to the syllabus, in line with the institution's expansion to include a department of fashion design. In the 1980s the 'Antwerp Six', a fashion collective of six Flemish designers about whom we shall read more in one of the sample texts in this chapter, presented new radical visions for fashion that made them important cultural ambassadors for Belgium on an international scale. Today, the Flanders Fashion Institute (also its name in Dutch!) aims to advise up-and-coming fashion designers, promote the work of Belgian designers abroad and advertise label launches, maintain links to flagship stores and co-ordinate 'meet and greet' sessions for Belgian designers and potential business partners. The *Design Platform Vlaanderen* (Design Platform Flanders) is similarly concerned to ensure that the success that Flemish designers enjoy on an artistic level feeds in to the success of Flanders in regional terms as a creative, competitive and versatile knowledge economy.

It may seem as if English already dominates the fashion industry in the Low Countries: the Dutch-language edition of *Vogue* magazine proudly promises to offer 'Het laatste fashion nieuws, trends, catwalk shows en cultuur'. Dutch fashion websites abound with terms like 'het label' and 'de styling', their 'designers' offer browsing customers 'sneakers' and 'hoodies' in their 'webshops' and 'flagshipwinkels', while in their 'homewearlijn' you may find 'sweaters' and 'damesshirts' in colours that range from the more traditional 'rood' and 'zwart' to 'off-white' and 'pastel'. The sheer number of loan words from the English that can be found in Dutch-language texts on fashion and design confirms the fact that the fashion industry in the Netherlands and Belgium demands a high level of internationality from its consumers. Readers of its Dutch-language web pages and magazines are therefore expected to take terms like 'casual' and 'urban dandy' in their stride. Yet traditional terms are very much still in evidence in haute couture, where the latest styles of 'avondjapon' coming off the Paris and Milan catwalks are enthusiastically discussed. Articles on more casual fashion also continue to require readers to know basic terms that are not (yet!) in circulation in a more anglicised form, such as 'stropdas', 'pantalon', 'windjack' and 'veters'. Names of more modern textiles such as 'fleece' and 'polyester' are essentially universal and crop up regularly in Dutch-language texts, but older fibres such as 'zijde', 'wol' and 'linnen' have not ceded to the English 'silk', 'wool' and 'linen'. As textiles companies increasingly acknowledge the need to produce material in ways that are both ethically correct and environmentally sound, terms such as 'biologische katoen' are becoming more widely used in the language of fashion in the twenty-first century.

This 'blending' of English with Dutch is, of course, not only a feature of articles written for consumption by those working or interested in the fashion industry. Texts generated for use within IT, banking or the automotive sector also display a high level of language blending, which can facilitate translation, but there are also plenty of false friends out there of which you should beware. The Dutch word 'heel' does not refer to a part of a shoe (that would be 'hak' as in 'schoenen met hoge hakken') and 'stof' does not mean 'stuff' but 'fabric' or 'material' (as in 'katoenen stof' or 'wollen stof'). A 'rug' has nothing to do with floor coverings (that would be a 'vloerkleed'), but instead indicates the back or reverse of something. If a piece of material is described as 'uni', this has nothing to do with universities: 'uni' indicates that material has no patterning, so 'uniblauw' would mean 'plain blue'. And a 'gulp', which in English relates to how you swallow your food, refers in Dutch to the front fly opening on a pair of trousers.

Text 1: *Mode, of de kunst van het alledaagse*

The following text comes from a richly illustrated, vibrant collection of almost 30 short contributions that form part of a monograph on the interconnection between fashion and interior design. These articles, together with their illustrations, give us an insight into the private lives and spaces of a range of Flemish designers from different regions and backgrounds, some younger, some more well established. The author of this article, Véronique Heene Thielemans, is the co-ordinator of the *Modo Bruxellae* association (Latin for 'In Brussels fashion'), an association founded in 1994 by the Minister for the Economy of the Region of the Capital City of Brussels (website of the Brussels Hoofdstedelijk Gewest: http://www.brussels.irisnet.be/) to promote those working in the Brussels fashion sector, whether they number among its more avant-garde designers or those employed by traditional fashion houses.

Mode, of de kunst van het alledaagse

De modeontwerper werkt met communicatiemiddelen. Hij vertaalt emoties, hij gebruikt kleren als taal met de buitenwereld. Zijn werk houdt niet op met het eenvoudige samenbrengen van stoffen en modellen: het is een enscenering die het de drager mogelijk maakt om zich te tonen zoals hij is, zoals hij zich op een bepaald moment voelt en zoals hij zich aan de omstandigheden aanpast. Doorheen zijn loopbaan vertelt

(continued)

134 *Fashion and design*

> *(continued)*
>
> de ontwerper het verhaal van zijn verleden en heden, zijn verlangens, invloeden en wereldbeeld. Hij vernieuwt zich zonder zijn stijl – zijn hoogst unieke handelsmerk – te verloochenen.
>
> De inspiratiebronnen van de modeontwerper zijn legio: ze melden zich aan in het straatbeeld of in andere kunstdisciplines. Behalve de stijl van de kledingstukken zelf bedenkt de ontwerper ook een imago voor zijn collectie – een bezigheid die van hem een artistiek directeur maakt. Hij moet de juiste beelden selecteren voor zijn catalogus, zijn kledinglijn presenteren in de showroom en op de catwalk, de inrichting van zijn boetieks op de voet volgen, als hij de decoratie al niet persoonlijk in handen neemt.
>
> Het zou dus bepaald verwonderlijk zijn dat deze professionele estheet met zijn geoefend oog geen aandacht zou hebben voor zijn eigen leefruimte. Als zoeker en trendsetter observeert hij zijn medemens zonder ophouden, doet zo inspiratie op en brengt al die indrukken samen in zijn interieur, ver van de argusogen van het publiek, en beter dan hij het elders zou kunnen.
>
> De binnenhuisinrichting ontdekken van de mensen die zich uit de naad werken om ons uiterlijk aan te kleden is een ware belevenis. Herken je de intieme omgeving waarin je favoriete ontwerper op adem komt uit de duizend? Begrijp je zijn collecties beter door een gestolen blik op zijn interieur, waar anders alleen zijn naasten komen?
>
> ---
>
> Source: Véronique Heene (2006) Mode, of de kunst van het alledaagse, in Barbara Witkowska (ed.) *Thuis bij modeontwerpers*. Tielt: Lannoo, pp. 7–9 (extract on p. 7).

1. Translation strategies and techniques

Below are our two key questions to help you make a first analysis. The first concerns background knowledge relevant for understanding the text, while the second involves reflection on your target audience.

i. What are the first things that you notice about the text?

– *It does not appear to be gender-neutral, since it constantly refers to the fashion designer using the masculine pronoun 'hij', reflecting the fact that this noun is masculine in Dutch.*

It is unlikely that the author of the text has any particular gender-focused axe to grind. Rather she is using the pronoun *hij* to refer back to the masculine noun *ontwerper*. Until relatively recently it would not have been considered wholly unacceptable to use similarly gendered terms in English. So in formulations like 'the designer . . . he', the masculine pronoun would have been tacitly understood to stand for male and female designers, much in the same way that 'mankind' is still taken to represent the whole of humanity. But how we think about language and gender has changed radically over the past few decades, and organisations are now very careful to avoid such potentially discriminatory forms of language. You therefore need to spend a couple of minutes thinking about what your approach is going to be, given that your translation will be taken to reflect the gender politics of the institution that has commissioned it. So how loyal can you be to the ST in this case? Where do you stand as a translator on the ethics of translation? What is your target audience and how do you think they would respond to a gender-marked translation? If you do opt for a gender-neutral, 'inclusive' form of translation, how are you going to deal with the technical problems that this presents? In their section on 'The ethics and responsibilities of the translator', in *Translation: An Advanced Resource Book*, Basil Hatim and Jeremy Munday consider how an apparently male-oriented view can best be circumvented (Hatim and Munday, 2004: 104–106, 314–316). They give examples that show how a use of the plural can help to eradicate most of the gender-related problems that arise in translation. This is generally the approach we have taken in our sample translation of this text.

– *It is quite abstract in places.*

Comments like *hij vertaalt emoties* might seem rather strange and you have to decide to what extent you leave them as they are by translating them literally and therefore place the responsibility for interpreting them with your reader, or whether you try to make them more immediately comprehensible by injecting your own interpretation into the sentence. We have attempted to find a middle ground in this translation as a whole.

ii. What do you know about the target audience for your translation and how will it affect your translation?

You might be commissioned to translate this passage within the context of the whole book being put into English. Alternatively, you might be asked to translate it as part of a text for an exhibition on the relationship between fashion and interior design. The audience is likely to comprise people who are generally interested in art and design, but who are not necessarily specialists.

2. Text and language

This step is crucial since it determines the accuracy of your translation.

i. Words and expressions

Het eenvoudige samenbrengen van stoffen: this is an example of a verb (*samenbrengen*) not actually being used as a verb at all, but as the noun *het samenbrengen*. Verbal nouns are common in Dutch and can be translated in a number of different ways. The sentence *Het hebben van een huisdier is goed voor je gezondheid* could be translated as 'Owning a pet is good for your health' or 'It is good for your health to own a pet', both of which use a verb (either the present participle 'owning', or the infinitive 'to own') in English in place of the noun in Dutch. In the sentence in our extract, you might therefore like to consider whether *het eenvoudige samenbrengen* can be translated using a verb rather than a noun construction to make your translation flow better.

Zijn hoogst unieke handelsmerk: this translates literally as 'his most highly unique trademark'. Either something is 'unique', and therefore beyond compare, or it is not. The superlative *hoogst* is therefore unnecessary and, purists would argue, bad style. You would have to exercise a certain amount of diplomacy here – perhaps you would simply mention to the person commissioning the translation that you have felt it necessary to 'improve' the translation stylistically at this point or perhaps you would just tacitly correct it in your translation.

In het straatbeeld: literally 'in the streetscape', although you might find that the term 'streetscape' sounds awkward in the sentence that you produce and that a turn of phrase simply involving the word 'street' might read better.

Kledinglijn: be careful not to translate this as 'clothes line', which has a decidedly practical function when you are doing your laundry. A search of the internet confirms that 'clothing line' and 'fashion line' are equally common terms in the fashion business.

Op de voet volgen: an idiomatic expression meaning 'to follow something closely', 'to stick to something', 'not to lose track of something'.

Argusogen: a translation dictionary may give you 'to look at something with Argus eyes', which would certainly test your readers' knowledge of Greek mythology. The giant Argus, fabled to have had more than 100 eyes, is now taken to represent a very vigilant person, someone who watches over others or who is their guardian. In English we have verbs like 'to scrutinise', 'to watch like a hawk' and then, more negatively connoted, 'to eye someone with suspicion'.

Zich uit de naad werken: this is an intriguing play on words, given that the word *naad* actually refers to the seam of a piece of clothing. The expression means something like 'to work yourself to death' or 'to work your socks off'.

Op adem komen: we have a similar expression in English that involves the notion of 'breath' – 'to catch your breath' or 'to take a breather'.

Zijn naasten komen: you almost certainly already know *naast* as 'next' or 'closest'. *Zijn naasten* is an adjectival noun formed in the same way as *de rijken* ('the rich') and *de blinden* ('the blind') and means something along the lines of 'those people who are close to him' (Donaldson, 1997: 98–99).

ii. Sentences

Hij vertaalt emoties, hij gebruikt kleren als taal met de buitenwereld.

The comma here is used to join two independent clauses: *Hij vertaalt emoties* and *Hij gebruikt kleren als taal met de buitenwereld*. This is called a 'comma splice' in English. While it is acceptable in some languages, it is considered to be a stylistic error in formal English prose (poetic uses of language being an obvious exception). In this case, you have several options, one of which is to make two sentences out of this. Another would be to link the sentences with a conjunction such as 'and'. Finally, another option would be to use a dash to set off the second sentence from the first but show that it is connected to it.

Hij gebruikt kleren als taal met de buitenwereld.

You may feel comfortable with translating this literally as 'He uses clothes as a language with the outside world', but you might find the 'language with' juxtaposition rather odd. In that case it would be worth considering whether you should add a verb in the English to create a construction that makes the sentence read more naturally.

3. Style, register and tone

i. Stylistic analysis of the source text

The text has a high, formal register but also frequently uses idiomatic expressions. The author clearly varies the style of her writing to produce a text that engages the attention of her readers: the rhetorical questions at the end of this extract are an important feature that you would want to consider reproducing in the TT.

ii. Assessment of the style of writing appropriate to the target text

As we have mentioned above, it would be important to produce a translation that is inclusive and gender-neutral, perhaps with a stronger focus on producing a text that is easily readable by the target audience than on a more literal translation of the original Dutch.

Sample translation of Text 1: *Mode, of de kunst van het alledaagse*

Fashion, or the art of the everyday

Fashion designers work with forms of communication. They translate emotions – they use clothing as a language to speak to the outside world. Their work does not stop at simply bringing together materials and

(continued)

(continued)

models: it is a form of enactment that enables wearers to show themselves as they are, as they feel at a particular moment and as they adapt themselves to circumstances. Throughout their career, designers tell the story of their past and present, desires, influences and world-view. They update themselves without renouncing their style – their highly unique trademark.

There are many sources of inspiration on which the fashion designer draws: they can be found on the street or in other artistic disciplines. Designers not only have to think about the style of the clothes themselves but also about an image for their collection – an activity that makes them artistic directors. They have to select the right pictures for their catalogues, present their clothing line in the showroom and on the catwalk, and keep a close eye on how their boutiques are being furnished, if they do not actually take a direct personal interest in how they are decorated. It would therefore be particularly strange if these professional aesthetes did not – with their trained eye – pay any attention to their own living space. As seekers and trendsetters they continually observe the people around them, thereby gaining inspiration, and bring all these impressions together in their interior spaces, away from public scrutiny, and better than they could have done elsewhere.

Exploring the interior design of the people working hard to clothe our exterior is in itself an experience. Can you recognise from amongst a thousand others the intimate environment in which your favourite designer takes a breather? Do you understand his or her collections better by snatching a glance at the interior which otherwise only those nearest and dearest enter?

PRACTICAL TIPS: PUNCTUATION

Generally the use of punctuation marks in Dutch and English does not vary enormously. However, there are some key differences that need to be considered when you are translating into English and, while it is your job as a translator to convey the meaning and register of the source text accurately, you must remember to follow punctuation conventions in English rather than automatically staying faithful to those you find in the Dutch text. It is also worth bearing in mind that the punctuation in your source text might not, in fact, be particularly accurate and could well be improved upon in your own translation as you set out to create a piece of English that reads fluently and unambiguously.

Commas: the comma splice

Commas are used in all sorts of ways. We use them most often to separate elements in lists, to distinguish subclauses from main clauses and before certain conjunctions. Earlier in this chapter we mentioned the 'comma splice' – the misuse of a comma in English to join two sentences together. While Dutch style guides do not wholeheartedly endorse this use of the comma in Dutch either, and advise that a full stop or a semi-colon should be placed to separate these units of meaning, it is not uncommon to find sentences in which this use of the comma occurs:

Ze hebben geweldig goed gespeeld, de overwinning was dik verdiend!
They played extremely well and their victory was well deserved!

Digitale vaardigheid komt niet zomaar aanwaaien, het moet geleerd worden.
Digital competence is not acquired automatically – it has to be learned.

Het onderzoek was gebaseerd op zelfevaluaties, de studenten werden niet getest in een uitvoeringssituatie.
The research was based on self-evaluations: the students were not tested in a performance situation.

Ik mag hem niet, hij praat te veel en is eigenwijs.
I dislike him: he talks too much and is conceited.

In these examples above, you will see that we have gone about dealing with the potential problem of the 'comma splice' in various ways. In the first, we have opted to link the two sentences with the conjunction 'and', but we could equally well have used 'so' in this case. In the second sentence we have used a dash to separate the elements more emphatically and stress the contrast between skills that are acquired naturally and those that have to be consciously learned. In the third and fourth sentences, we have used a colon. This is a less abrupt way of setting two sentences apart and tends to be used to indicate that what follows the colon elaborates on the statement made before it. We can therefore see that there are a number of ways of dealing with the problem of two juxtaposed sentences. The option we choose depends as much on how we interpret the source text and which points we feel the author is emphasising, as on what fits within the context of the translation we are creating.

Commas: commas for emphasis

Making clear connections between ideas in texts tends to depend on the use of relevant conjunctions. Extremely common words such as 'and' and 'but',

(continued)

(continued)

as well as longer transitional expressions such as 'however', 'nevertheless' and 'on the other hand', enable transitions to be made between sentences which enable a text to be read more fluently. Transitional devices (also known as conjunctive adverbs or adverbial conjunctions) are an important feature of writing, and can convey addition ('furthermore', 'in addition'), concession ('of course', 'naturally'), emphasis ('indeed'), illustration ('in other words'), summary ('all in all') or time sequences ('at that time', 'in the first place'). These are often set between commas, or, if placed at the start of a sentence, are followed by a comma in English, where that would not necessarily be the case in Dutch. Look at the following examples:

Natuurlijk kunnen niet alle ideeën worden verwezenlijkt en voor sommige valt nog te bezien in hoeverre ze realistisch en uitvoerbaar zijn.
Not all of the ideas can, of course, be put into practice and for some it remains to be seen if they are realistic and feasible.

Ze waren uiteraard van onze vergadering op de hoogte, maar waren de afgelopen twee jaar niet aanwezig.
They were, of course, informed about our meeting, but have not been present for the last two years.

Bedenk echter wel dat wij in dienst van onze klanten staan en dat het ons doel is de best mogelijke oplossing en service te leveren aan onze klanten, waardoor het soms nodig is om overuren te maken.
Bear in mind, however, that we work for clients and our aim is to deliver the best possible solution and service for our clients, so sometimes an assignment necessitates you working overtime.

Kleine boeren kunnen dit geld bijvoorbeeld gebruiken om de opbrengst van hun land te verhogen en de kwaliteit van hun thee te verbeteren.
Small growers can use this money, for example, to improve the productivity of their land and therefore the quality of their tea.

You therefore need to think about the punctuation you use in English when translating words like *bijvoorbeeld* and *natuurlijk*, *echter* and *uiteraard*, as well as related terms like *in feite* ('in fact/in reality') or *al met al* ('all in all').

Apostrophes

It is essential that you are clear in your own mind about the use of the English apostrophe ('it's' and 'its', for example) before you set about translating any passage. Wrongly using apostrophes not only creates ambiguity and confusion in texts. It also gives a poor impression of you as the translator. Bear in mind that it is not always the case that where an apostrophe is used in Dutch, one is also used in English. As you are almost certainly aware, it is used in English to signal possession (Henk's cat) and to signal omission ('we're running late today'). In Dutch it can also be used to signal a plural:

> *Beschrijf CD's niet met een potlood of een balpen.*
> Do not write on CDs with a pencil or ballpoint pen.
>
> *In ons dorp zelf is een klein restaurant met een kleine kaart, maar vele vers gemaakte pizza's.*
> In our village is a small restaurant with a small menu, but many freshly made pizzas.
>
> *De menselijke kwaliteiten van de dagelijkse samenwerking tussen collega's, klanten en partners verschaffen een klimaat van waardering en vertrouwen.*
> On a human level, the quality of daily dealings with colleagues, customers and partners creates an atmosphere of appreciation and trust.

You will notice from these sentences that the English plurals are all written without an apostrophe – CDs, pizzas, colleagues – where these nouns in Dutch (*CD's, pizza's, collega's*) need the apostrophe + s ending to signal a plural. This is extremely uncommon in English, where an apostrophe is only used to show the plurals of single letters – 'there are two m's in *Amsterdam*' – or to show the plurals of single numbers – 'there are two 3's in the postcode for Dordrecht'. Note that there are no apostrophes in English for the plural of abbreviations ('two MPs have just been appointed') or to indicate decades ('the 1990s').

Accents

Unlike some other European languages, Dutch uses relatively few accents. The trema (¨) is used to indicate that sounds need to be separated, as in *tweeën* ('twee-en') or *beëindigen* (be-eindigen). A few accents from French loan words and loan expressions are also used in Dutch, as in *café, rosé* and *à la carte*. If you are using these French terms in your English translation then you probably need to retain these accents in the same places. Where you do need to be particularly alert is in translating Dutch texts where accents are used to provide extra emphasis. So in a sentence like *We gaan vandaag naar het zwembad én naar het theater*, the writer is emphasising that this is going to be a busy day, involving a trip to the swimming pool

(continued)

(continued)

and to the theatre as well. You will need to signal this in some way in your translation: 'We're going to the swimming pool today and the theatre too' or 'Today we're going both to the swimming pool and the theatre' would be possibilities. You could also think about using italics: 'Today we're going to the swimming pool *and* the theatre.'

Have a look at the following examples, pick out the word that is signalling emphasis and see how you could go about translating it:

Amsterdam Fashion Week is inmiddels uitgegroeid tot hét halfjaarlijkse mode-evenement van Nederland.
Amsterdam Fashion Week has now developed into *the* half-yearly fashion event in the Netherlands.

We zijn dé natuurlijke partner in de ontwikkeling en uitvoering van energiebeleid.
We are *the* natural partner for developing and implementing the energy policy of the future.

Kies een scène uit één van je favoriete films en maak daarvan een schilderij.
Select a scene from (just) one of your favourite movies and make a painting of it.

Vakantie betekent vaak een heerlijke tijd: een periode van ontspanning, van tijd voor anderen én onszelf.
Holidays often mean a delightful time: a period of relaxation, of time for others and also for you.

Note that while we have used italics in the first two sentences, in the third we have used the English word 'one', which already carries its own emphasis (compare it with 'a favourite movie'). Depending on the context, you might want to add the word 'just' to stress the point being made still further. In the final example we have slipped in 'also', but could have italicised 'you' instead.

Direct speech

You are most likely to encounter direct speech in fictional prose, although it does also crop up in journalistic writing. It is worth noting that the conventions in English are not always the same as in Dutch, as the following examples demonstrate:

Oma zei tegen haar kleinzoon: 'Vroeger hadden we nog geen computers.'
Grandma said to her grandson, 'In the old days we didn't have any computers.'

Toen vroeg ze: 'Zou jij brandweerman willen worden?'
Then she asked, 'Do you want to become a fireman?'

Ik zei: 'Ik weet het niet meer.'
I said, 'I don't know any more.'

While direct speech in English is always separated from the indication of who is speaking it ('he said', 'she asked') by a comma, in Dutch a colon can also be used, particularly with the verbs *zeggen* and *vragen*. This would not be correct in English. In both Dutch and English, the punctuation mark closing the sentence is inside the speech marks. Depending on the in-house rules regarding style, you may have to use single or double inverted commas to indicate which part of the sentence is marked as direct speech.

Text 2: *Antwerpen, modemetropool*

This text is taken from an edited collection entitled 'Cultuur en/in de stad', which explores culture – in the widest sense of the word – in the city. As the editors stress, city culture influences personal development and emancipation, integration and social cohesion. It is an essential factor in the way that city-dwellers construct their notion of identity and in how the city represents itself to the outside world. Culture also plays an important role in driving the city's economy and sustaining its levels of employment.

Antwerpen, modemetropool

In Antwerpen is de Belgische mode geboren, een begrip in de wereld. Dat bleek ondermeer uit het feit dat maar liefst 17 van de 150 belangrijkste hedendaagse ontwerpers Belg zijn of afgestudeerd zijn in België. In het lijstje van modesteden neemt Antwerpen naast Parijs, Milaan, New York, Londen en nog enkele andere steden een belangrijke plaats in.

In 1963 richtte Mary Prijot aan de Koninklijke Academie voor Schone Kunsten een modeafdeling op. Op het ogenblik dat de eerste studenten daar nog moesten afstuderen, was Ann Saelens, de enige Antwerpse ontwerpster, een eenzaam icoon van de popcultuur. Saelens, gekend door haar meestal gewaagde breiwerkjurken in zijdeglansgaren met heel lange franjes, had haar winkel in de Wolstraat, vlak bij het Conscienceplein, het centrum van de hippies en de provo's in de jaren 1960.

(continued)

144 *Fashion and design*

> *(continued)*
>
> Begin jaren 1980 studeerden aan de Antwerpse Academie zeer talentvolle ontwerpers af. In maart 1986 trokken Ann Demeulemeester, Dries Van Noten, Dirk Van Saene, Dirk Bikkembergs, Walter Van Beirendonck en Marina Yee naar de Londense designerweek met een vrachtwagen die ze samen hadden gehuurd – kwestie van de kosten te drukken. Initiatiefnemer van deze Londense campagne was Geert Bruloot – de vroegere bezieler van 'Louis', de Antwerpse winkel die van bij het begin de kleding van Antwerpse designers verkocht, en zaakvoerder van de vermaarde schoenwinkels Coccodrillo in de Schuttershofstraat.
>
> Alle designers waren op de afspraak in Londen, behalve Ann Demeulemeester, die op dat moment zwanger was. De Britse modepers was laaiend enthousiast maar kon helaas al de Vlaamse namen niet uitspreken, laat staan spellen. Voor het gemak gooiden de Britten hen op een hoopje, *The Antwerp Six* werden een internationaal fenomeen.
>
> Source: Edith Vervliet (2011) Antwerpen: mode en city marketing, in Mattias De Backer and Patrick Stouthuysen (eds) *Cultuur en/in de stad. Stadslucht maakt vrij*, 4. Brussels: VUB Press, pp. 161–170 (extract on pp. 161–162).

1. Translation strategies and techniques

Below are our two key questions to help you make a first analysis. The first concerns background knowledge relevant for understanding the text, while the second involves reflection on your target audience.

i. What are the first things that you notice about the text?

– *It is quite factual and therefore draws on statistics as well as lists of names.*
  It would be important to double-check in your translation that you have accurately transcribed the names of all the designers mentioned. If you were doing this as a commissioned piece for a client, you would probably have been sent the text electronically anyway, which reduces the risk of such typing errors occurring.

– *It lists a number of place names in Europe.*
  The cities listed here are relatively easy to translate on sight without the help of web sources or dictionaries. But they are a useful reminder that city names are often spelled differently in different languages, as we discussed in Chapter 2. Appendix 2 of Donaldson's grammar is particularly useful for familiarising yourself with all sorts of place names that you might not recognise in an exam situation. Where, for example, are Wenen, Keulen and Rijsel, and on which part of the globe would you find the Zuidzee, Paaseiland or the Middellandse Zee (see Donaldson, 1997: 303–315)?

- *It contains a number of references to places in Antwerp.*
    What are you going to do with the *Wolstraat*, the *Conscienceplein* and the *Schuttershofstraat*? Are you going to translate them or leave them in the original? What do English-language guidebooks do with them?

ii. What do you know about the target audience for your translation and how will it affect your translation?

You might be commissioned to translate this passage within the context of the whole book being put into English for those working in the cultural sector or education, who are interested on a more abstract level in the relations between the city and culture. Alternatively, you might be asked to translate this passage within the context of a work promoting culture or fashion in Antwerp. The audience is likely to comprise people who are generally interested in fashion, design and culture, but who are not necessarily specialists.

2. Text and language

This step is crucial since it determines the accuracy of your translation.

i. Words and expressions

Maar liefst: this is an idiomatic expression that has nothing to do with the 'preferably' or 'ideally' that you usually associate with *liefst*. Rather, it is used to convey astonishment and is generally translated by 'no less/fewer than' or 'even/if not'. So *Er zijn gisteren maar liefst zes bomen omgewaaid!* could be translated into English as 'No fewer than six trees were blown down yesterday!', while *De kosten waren vier tot maar liefst zeven maal lager dan men van tevoren had beraamd* would translate as 'The costs were four times, if not seven times, lower than previous estimates.'

Breiwerkjurk: this compound noun is relatively easy to break down into its constituent elements. *Breiwerk* refers to a textile that is made up of knitted (rather than woven) stitches, while a *jurk* is a dress, so 'knitted dress'.

Zijdeglansgaren: this can likewise be divided up into its separate parts *zijde*, *glans* and *garen*, so 'silk(en)', 'glossy' or 'shining' and 'yarn' or 'thread'. Before you consider how to put these elements together, it might be worth taking a quick look on the internet to see what kinds of products are described using this term. Alternatively, you could endeavour to find style books showcasing Saelens' work, which would give you a reasonable idea of the texture you are trying to convey. If neither of these approaches bears fruit then you are going to have to put these words together in a way that best captures all the various aspects of this compound noun.

Provo's: a word that entered the Dutch language in 1965 and was coined by the psychologist Wouter Buikhuisen, who was writing a study on youth culture and violent behaviour. He invented the term 'provo', derived from the verb *provoceren*, to describe the young 'troublemakers' to whom he was referring. The Provo movement was a Dutch counterculture movement that emerged in the mid-1960s and sought to elicit violent responses from authorities by using non-violent forms of provocation. The *provo's* were officially disbanded in 1967. They had been preceded by the 'nozems' – akin to the 'beatniks' in the United States and the 'teddy boys' in Britain – and were followed by the hippie movement.

Londense designerweek: a quick check online will tell you what the correct translation of this is and whether or not it needs capitalisation.

Op een hoopje gooien: literally 'to throw in a heap', but here to 'lump' or 'bundle' something together.

Voor het gemak: literally 'for convenience's sake', although you may want to think about weaving this into your translation in other ways, along the lines of 'to make matters easier'.

ii. Sentences

Dat bleek ondermeer uit het feit dat . . .

In the context of the sentence you are constructing, *ondermeer* is probably best translated by using 'for instance' or 'for example'. It can, however, also have the meaning of 'amongst others/other things', as in the sentence *Hij wees ondermeer op de noodzaak van een nieuwe geest van partnerschap tussen de overheden*, which could be rendered as 'Among other things, he highlighted the necessity for a new partnership spirit between governments.' There are other instances where the verb 'to include' should be considered, as in *Onze markten zijn ondermeer industrieën zoals distributie en logistiek, olie en gas, papier en print en infrastructuur*. A possible translation of this would be 'Our markets include industries such as distribution and logistics, oil and gas, paper and print and infrastructure.'

In het lijstje van modesteden neemt Antwerpen naast Parijs, Milaan, New York, Londen, en nog enkele andere steden een belangrijke plaats in.

The preposition *naast* can, of course, mean 'next to', 'beside' or 'by' when it is referring to spatial proximity, as in a sentence like *hij zat naast het bed van zijn grootvader, met zijn rug naar me toe*, 'he sat by his grandfather's bed with his back towards me'. In the context of our extract a comparison is being made between Antwerp and other capital cities, so 'alongside' could fit well in the sentence you are constructing. The preposition *naast* can sometimes also be translated using 'apart from', as in a sentence like *Helsinki was in de Tweede Wereldoorlog naast Londen en Moskou de enige hoofdstad van een land in oorlog, die niet werd bezet*, which could be rendered as 'Apart from London and Moscow,

Helsinki was the only capital city of a country at war that was not occupied during the Second World War.' Another option in a different context would be to use 'in addition to', so that *Naast bescherming van de arbeidsrechten van onze eigen medewerkers streven wij ernaar een bevredigende en uitdagende werkplek te creëren* could be rendered as 'In addition to protecting the labour rights of our employees, we also seek to create a satisfying and challenging place to work.'

De Britse modepers was laaiend enthousiast maar kon helaas al de Vlaamse namen niet uitspreken, laat staan spellen.

The main rhetorical construction at the heart of this sentence is the construction *niet . . . laat staan*. The pairing of the two verbs *laat staan* might have caused you some problems. It can mean a number of things depending on context. Literally translated, it of course means 'leave standing', and this helps us to understand sentences like *Hij liet zijn eten staan*. A rough translation gives us the sentence 'He left his meal standing', and, put more idiomatically, it would mean something like 'he did not touch/finish his meal'. Similarly *laat dat staan* means 'leave that alone', in the sense of 'don't touch that'. These are very different uses from the sentence we have in the extract on Antwerp. Here *laat staan* is a fixed expression that means 'let alone'. Couple this with the negative in the phrase before the comma, and we see that the British fashion press 'could unfortunately not pronounce the Flemish names, let alone spell them'.

3. Style, register and tone

i. Stylistic analysis of the source text

The text has a high, formal register but also frequently uses idiomatic expressions.

ii. Assessment of the style of writing appropriate to the target text

The formal and literary features of the ST suggest that the translator should ensure that s/he creates a text in English that appeals to a similar audience.

Sample translation of Text 2: *Antwerpen, modemetropool*

Antwerp, fashion metropolis

In Antwerp, Belgian fashion was born, a global concept. That has become clear from the fact that, amongst other things, no fewer than 17 of the 150 most important contemporary designers are Belgian or completed their studies in Belgium. In the list of fashion cities, Antwerp occupies an

(continued)

148 *Fashion and design*

(continued)

important place alongside Paris, Milan, New York, London and several other cities.

In 1963 Mary Prijot launched a department of fashion at the Royal Academy of Fine Arts. At the point where the first students were still finishing their studies, Ann Saelens, the only Antwerp designer, was a lonely icon of pop culture. Saelens, known for her generally rather daring knitted dresses in glossy silk thread with very long fringing, had her shop in the Wolstraat, close to the Conscienceplein, a central point for the hippies and young provocateurs in the 1960s.

At the beginning of the 1980s hugely talented designers completed their studies at the Antwerp Academy. In March 1986 Ann Demeulemeester, Dries Van Noten, Dirk Van Saene, Dirk Bikkembergs, Walter Van Beirendonck and Marina Yee drove to the London Designer Week with a van they had hired together – to keep the costs down. The person who took the initiative for this London campaign was Geert Bruloot – who had already breathed life into 'Louis', the Antwerp store which from the outset sold clothing by the Antwerp designers, and was the manager of the prestigious Coccodrillo shoe shops in the Schuttershofstraat.

All the designers were at the meeting in London except Ann Demeulemeester, who was pregnant at the time. The British fashion press was gushingly enthusiastic but unfortunately unable to pronounce all the Flemish names, let alone spell them. To make things easier, the British press bundled them all together: the *Antwerp Six* became an international phenomenon.

Dutch translation in practice

To round off this chapter, we have selected a passage that is taken from the same text as the previous extract on Antwerp as a global centre for fashion. It explores how fashion developed in Flanders beyond the work of the 'Antwerp Six', and brings the development of the Belgian fashion scene up to the twenty-first century. For a sample translation of this passage, see p. 185.

Text 3: *Antwerpen, modemetropool*

Martin Margiela, die samen met Walter Van Beirendonck afstudeerde en een van de meest revolutionaire modemakers van zijn generatie is, koos voor een andere weg en vestigde zich vrij snel in Parijs als assistant van Jean-Paul Gaultier. In 1988 richtte hij samen met Jenny Meirens het Maison Martin Margiela op dat sinds 2002 deel uitmaakt van de Dieselgroep.

Na Londen gingen de Zes elk hun eigen weg. Maar het begrip 'Antwerpse Zes' blijft hen achtervolgen tot de dag van vandaag, al hebben ze in principe niets met elkaar te maken. Niet qua stijl, want hun universa liggen mijlenver van elkaar. Ze werken evenmin samen, hebben dat ook nooit gedaan. Wel vertonen ze allen veel wilskracht en doorzettingsvermogen, aandacht voor perfectie tot in de details (show, foto's, styling, invitaties, . . .) en – uiteraard – een flinke portie talent. [. . .]

Antwerpen werd een begrip. Een stijllaboratorium. Een kweekvijver voor talent en een paradijs voor modestudenten uit de hele wereld. In de jaren 1990 en begin 2000 zorgde een tweede generatie ontwerpers (o. m. Anna Heylen, Stephan Schneider, A. F. Vandevorst, Kris Van Assche, Bernhard Willhelm, Raf Simons, Veronique Branquinho, Bruno Pieters, Tim Van Steenbergen, Les Hommes, Christian Wijnants) door hun vastberadenheid, sterke en conceptuele collecties, voor een onmiddellijke doorbraak en bestendigden het avant-garde karakter van de Antwerpse mode. In tegenstelling tot de eerste generatie die zich voor een internationale doorbraak aanvankelijk als groep profileerde, treden de ontwerpers van de tweede generatie onmiddellijk naar buiten als individuen met een sterk concept en eigen defilés.

'Les gens du Nord' brachten een avant-garde, 'L'Anvers de la mode' zoals journaliste Elisabeth Paillié het zo goed beschreef. 'L'Anvers de la mode', de achterkant, de recyclage, de wegwerpmode, een underground fenomeen, de underdog: niet zo extravert als Engelse mode, niet zo sexy als Italiaanse mode, niet zo cerebraal als Japanse mode.

Source: Edith Vervliet (2011) Antwerpen: mode en city marketing, in Mattias De Backer and Patrick Stouthuysen (eds) *Cultuur en/in de stad. Stadslucht maakt vrij*, 4. Brussels: VUB Press, pp. 161–170 (extract on pp. 163–164).

9 The Earth, energy and the environment

Introduction: texts and contexts

In this final chapter we will be looking at how governmental, financial and scientific institutions in the Netherlands and Belgium are shaping the future of these countries on an environmental, political and economic level. We shall be exploring some of the measures adopted in the Low Countries to ensure the future sustainability of energy resources, the protection of the existing infrastructure and the preservation of the natural environment. Both Belgium and the Netherlands are countries with high population densities, and rapid population and economic growth over the last few decades have taken their toll on the countryside. Intense pressures from human activity have meant that air and water pollution are significant environmental problems in the Netherlands and Belgium, with air quality affected by air traffic passing through the exceptionally busy international hub of Schiphol and, to a lesser degree, through Belgium's airports in Brussels-Zaventem and Brussels South Charleroi. Modern mechanised agricultural techniques and the needs of a large urban population for recreational areas have led to the destruction or fragmentation of landscapes that used to hold more unusual forms of wildlife, and numerous types of fish and migratory birds that were once common in the Netherlands and Belgium are now on the 'Red List' of endangered species. Increasing efforts to create more protected habitats for wildlife have, however, ensured that more than 20 national parks and conservation areas have been established in the Netherlands and Belgium. These parks reflect the wide range of different habitats that exist in the Low Countries – from the freshwater lakes of the Lauwersmeer in the Dutch coastal province Frisia and the mud flats of the Wadden Sea region, to the extensive heathlands and sandy soil of the Dwingelderveld in Drenthe, the pine forests of the Hoge Kempen National Park in Belgium and the diverse range of biotopes that form the cross-border park of De Zoom-Kalmthoutse Heide, which has large areas of *veen*, or peatland, that support particular forms of wildlife no longer able to survive in more industrially managed landscapes.

While the influence of humans on nature is therefore a problem that is actively being addressed in the Netherlands and Belgium, tackling the pressure that nature is placing on humans has recently begun to acquire greater urgency. The Low

Countries have long been an area in which people have had to confront the challenges of living at, or below, sea level. The history of water management in the Netherlands can be dated back to around the ninth century, although it was not until the thirteenth century that its inhabitants began to make inroads against the sea and protect themselves from floods by living on dwelling mounds, or 'terps'. Reclamation of peatlands in the west of the country also extended the area of land that could be inhabited, even if this resulted in a considerable drop in water levels, which in turn resulted in a sinking of soil levels in land in the polders. While a system of gates and sluices, dykes, polders and windmills (to power drainage activities) enabled people to tame the forces of nature, floods have regularly claimed many victims down the centuries: the St Elizabeth Flood of 1421 caused tens of thousands of fatalities. In the Dutch Golden Age in the seventeenth century, extensive land reclamation took place, including the drainage of the extensive *Haarlemmermeer*, which would later become the home of Amsterdam's Schiphol Airport.

It was really in the early decades of the twentieth century, however, that large-scale engineering projects began to change the shape of the Netherlands more radically. In 1927 construction work began on the *Afsluitdijk* to close off the *Zuiderzee*, formerly a saltwater inlet of the North Sea, making of it the freshwater lake now known as the *IJsselmeer*. Closing this open connection between the North Sea and the heart of the Netherlands greatly reduced the risk of flooding and also created the possibility of direct travel between the provinces of North Holland and Frisia in the form of a road running along the top of this dyke. Despite the successful completion of ambitious projects such as this, the sea defences were not sufficient to save the Netherlands from catastrophe during the *Watersnoodramp* ('flood disaster') that occurred on the night of 31 January 1953. The fatal combination of a north-westerly storm and a high spring tide resulted in water levels rising to more than five metres above sea level: large areas of the provinces of Zeeland and Zuid-Holland were inundated, causing more than 1,800 deaths and enormous damage to houses and property. A series of dams, sluices, locks, dykes and storm surge barriers, known as the 'Delta Works', were built in the southern delta areas in response to this disaster. The feat of engineering that they represent is considered to make the Delta Works one of the 'Seven Wonders of the Modern World'.

In response to the new set of threats posed by climate change, a series of initiatives have been introduced to protect the Dutch coast in other ways against the forces of nature. A key major project, called *Bouwen met natuur* ('Building with Nature') seeks to imitate natural systems and thus build up ways of countering the destruction wrought by the sea. The *Zandmotor* ('Sand Motor', or 'Sand Engine') is an innovative method of coastal protection that no longer places the emphasis on inflexible solid sea defences, such as dams and dykes, but rather on flexible soft structures that are in harmony with the sea, such as dunes and beaches. In 2011 the Dutch Department of Waterways and Public Works, the *Rijkswaterstaat*, worked together with the provincial authority of Zuid-Holland to create a hook-shaped peninsula of sand that will gradually be spread along the shore through tidal action to reinforce the coastline and create new areas for wildlife and recreation (for further details, see http://www.rijkswaterstaat.nl/water/). It is not only the force of the sea that engineers in the Netherlands and Flanders are seeking to harness in innovative ways. Wind turbines, particularly in offshore wind farms, are beginning to make an important contribution to sustainable energy generation. In Flanders there are plans to make artificial islands off the Belgian coast that will provide power storage reservoirs for the energy generated at sea.

This concern with renewable and sustainable energy is the main subject of the first extract in this chapter. It is the first part of the introductory section to the two-volume academic work *Energie voor een Groene Economie. Hernieuwbare energie: hoe en waarom?* (Ghent, 2011). In this book, a number of issues are addressed, including the different forms of renewable energy and the size of their respective CO_2 emissions, issues of energy pricing and tariffs, and national and regional energy policy in Belgium. The employment possibilities offered by the energy sector in this important transition period are also discussed, with the aim of understanding how it can contribute to the labour market in the future. Two of the authors of this book are economists working for *De Sociaal-Economische Raad van Vlaanderen* (SERV). The Social and Economic Council of Flanders is a public agency that acts as an advisory body and think-tank for the Flemish government and parliament, and also functions as the strategic advisory council for energy policy. The third author is a researcher at the University of Antwerp.

Text 1: *Energie voor een Groene Economie*

We hebben *veel meer* hernieuwbare energie nodig. Veel meer hernieuwbare energie is essentieel in de vereiste transitie naar een duurzaam energiesysteem. Die *energietransitie* moet zorgen voor de technologische en maatschappelijke veranderingen om de uitstoot van broeikasgassen drastisch te beperken en om te anticiperen op de schaarste en eindigheid van fossiele energiebronnen. Hernieuwbare energie kan tevens een belangrijke motor zijn in de vergroening van de economie en voor economische groei en nieuwe jobs. Het kan ook zorgen voor een versterking van de energiebevoorradingszekerheid, competitieve prijzen en een meer stabiele en sociale toegang tot energie. De promotie van hernieuwbare energie is daarom een belangrijke peiler van het energie- en klimaatbeleid.

Nog los van de recente kernramp in Japan is er politiek en maatschappelijk een duidelijk *momentum* om de transitie naar een duurzame energievoorziening meer vaart te geven. Bovendien zullen de komende jaren heel wat grote infrastructuurinvesteringen in de elektriciteitsnetten, het

> energieproductiepark en het gebouwenpark gebeuren. Het is nu het moment om daarbij volop rekening te houden met de vereisten die de grootschalige introductie van hernieuwbare energie stelt. Die kans doet zich – gelet op de typisch zeer lange levensduur van veel infrastructuurinvesteringen – weinig voor zoals vandaag.
>
> De geschetste voordelen en kansen benutten, vergt een *expliciete strategie*. Want ze manifesteren zich niet automatisch en niet altijd en overal. Veel hangt af van de vormgeving en uitvoering van het hernieuwbare energiebeleid. Het is onze overtuiging dat vandaag niet alle voordelen en kansen even goed worden benut. Ze kunnen beter worden gerealiseerd: tegen lagere maatschappelijke kosten en met hogere maatschappelijke baten. Bijsturing is dus nodig. Want enkel een vanuit verschillende perspectieven meer doeltreffende, efficiënte, rechtvaardige, gedragen en transparante aanpak zal in staat zijn om ook op langere termijn het noodzakelijke draagvlak voor een heel ambitieus hernieuwbare energiebeleid en substantieel meer hernieuwbare energie te behouden.
>
> Source: Annemie Bollen, Peter Van Humbeeck and Annick Lamote (2011) *Energie voor een Groene Economie. Hernieuwbare energie: hoe en waarom?* Gent: Academia Press, 2 vols, vol. 1, p. 1.

1. Translation strategies and techniques

Drawing on our two standard questions to make a first analysis, we need to think about what kind of background knowledge is relevant for understanding the text and who our target audience is, so that we can make conscious decisions about the kind of readership for whom we are translating.

i. What are the first things that you notice about the text?

- *Although it is an introductory text, it does use terms that are quite specialised.*
  The authors are clearly writing for an audience that is already reasonably well informed about the economics of sustainable energy generation.

- *It uses italicisation and tends to repeat terms from one sentence to the next.*
  The italicisation is printed above as in the original text. There it appears to be used to emphasise the main aspects addressed in each of the three paragraphs given here. The repetition found particularly in the opening sentences is probably used to reinforce the link between concepts and to demonstrate how one sentence feeds in to the next. You will have to decide whether or not your translation sounds inelegantly repetitive and how close you want to stay to the original in this respect.

154   *The Earth, energy and the environment*

ii. What do you know about the target audience for your translation and how will it affect your translation?

If the translation is commissioned within the context of the whole book being put into English, then your target audience could be students or academics working in the field of business, economics, environmental policy or energy management, given the specialised nature of later parts of this two-volume work.

2. Text and language

Thinking about how to tackle some of the words and expressions in this text is crucial since it will determine the accuracy of your translation.

i. Words and expressions

Energietransitie: compound nouns such as this – others include *elektriciteitsnetten*, *energiebronnen* and *energieproductiepark* – might not be immediately familiar to you. Their English equivalent tends to be a relatively literal translation of the Dutch. By doing a web search you can relatively quickly assess whether or not you have come up with the right translation. If your solution appears on only a handful of Anglophone websites – and perhaps also on websites where the texts are obviously not written by native speakers – then you will need to try out other solutions. In your search you will necessarily come across a whole range of English-language texts written by specialists in the area of renewable energy; just spending a few minutes reading these texts will give you a feel for the vocabulary that is used in this area, and may well provide you with some of the terms that you will need later in your translation.

De vereiste transitie: literally 'the required transition', although this may feel awkward in your translation and you should think about putting the participle *vereist* after the noun.

De eindigheid van fossiele energiebronnen: you may discover the translation 'finiteness' for the noun *eindigheid* in your dictionary, but you may find it sits awkwardly in your translation. Using the adjective 'finite' in combination with a suitable noun may give you more flexibility.

Een belangrijke motor: the word *motor* is used metaphorically here and therefore does not necessarily have to be translated by using the word 'motor'. Other possibilities include 'generator', 'driver' or 'driving force'.

De vergroening van de economie: the expression 'greening of the economy' certainly exists, as a web search quickly confirms. However, a fair number of the websites where it crops up are either not written by native speakers of English or the term is put in scare quotes and therefore marked in the text as a non-standard expression. If you are not comfortable with using it in your text, then you need to think about what it means and paraphrase this in your translation – something like 'making the economy environmentally friendly'.

Een meer stabiele en sociale toegang tot energie: the literal translation, 'a more stable and social access to energy', does not really sound natural in English and it is not entirely clear what 'a more social access to energy' could mean. You will have to be more explicit in your translation about what you understand by *een meer... sociale toegang* as you paraphrase this.

peiler: this is not to be confused with a *pijler*. A *pijler* is a 'column' or 'support', whereas the word *peiler* derives from the verb *peilen*, meaning 'to assess', 'to gauge'.

het gebouwenpark: if you have never encountered this word before, then an intelligent guess would be that it is a compound noun composed of the elements *gebouw* and *park*. However, this would generate the rather odd (and not particularly meaningful) translation 'building park'. If we look at its use in practice – and here the website *Linguee* (http://www.linguee.com/english-dutch) is particularly helpful – then we can see that its range of meanings covers 'buildings', 'building stock', 'real estate' (in American English) or, quite simply, 'premises'.

die kans: this does not necessarily have to be translated literally as 'chance'; it can also be 'possibility' or 'opportunity'.

ii. Sentences

Nog los van de recente kernramp in Japan is er politiek en maatschappelijk een duidelijk momentum *om de transitie naar een duurzame energievoorziening meer vaart te geven.*

This sentence requires some unravelling. The first part, *Nog los van de recente kernramp in Japan*, stands apart from the rest of the sentence, which essentially focuses on the momentum *om de transitie naar een duurzame energievoorziening meer vaart te geven*. The authors use *los van* to suggest that 'irrespective of' or 'regardless of' the recent nuclear disaster in Japan, steps have been taken to ensure that the shift to sustainable energy can occur in the Netherlands.

Want ze manifesteren zich niet automatisch en niet altijd en overal.

Again, the literal translation for *ze manifesteren zich* as 'they manifest themselves' may sound odd in the sentence that you are constructing. To solve this problem, you might want to use a passive construction 'are manifested by' or you might decide to find a verb that forms a suitable collocation with the *voordelen en kansen* – the 'advantages and opportunities' – of the previous sentence.

156 *The Earth, energy and the environment*

> *Want enkel een vanuit verschillende perspectieven meer doeltreffende, efficiënte, rechtvaardige, gedragen en transparante aanpak zal in staat zijn . . .*

This sentence also needs some unpacking. Its complexity derives from the fact that so many adjectives are piled up before the noun *aanpak*. Using brackets to see what belongs together, we can break the sentence down this way:

> *Want enkel een ((vanuit verschillende perspectieven) meer doeltreffende, efficiënte, rechtvaardige, gedragen en transparante) aanpak zal in staat zijn . . .*

If we reorder the units then at its core is *Want enkel een aanpak* – 'since only an approach' – which is modified by *vanuit verschillende perspectieven* – from various perspectives – which is itself further qualified by the series of adjectives *meer doeltreffende, efficiënte, rechtvaardige, gedragen en transparante* – 'which are more effective, efficient, equitable . . .'.

3. Style, register and tone

i. Stylistic analysis of the source text

The text has a high, formal register and presupposes a good knowledge of the topic being discussed. It uses complex sentence structures, and sentences are often long.

ii. Assessment of the style of writing appropriate to the target text

The style of the TT will depend upon the audience for whom the translation has been commissioned, although it would be important to produce a text that is accessible by interested non-specialists.

Sample translation of Text 1: *Energie voor een Groene Economie*

Energy for a green economy

We need *far more* renewable energy. Far more renewable energy is essential to ensure that the transition required to achieve a durable energy system can take place. This *energy transition* must bring about the technological and social changes needed to reduce drastically the emission of greenhouse gases and to react in advance to the shortage and finite supplies of fossil energy sources. Renewable energy can also be an important driving force behind making the economy environmentally friendly and promoting economic growth and creating new jobs. It can also ensure that the efforts to secure energy supplies are strengthened, prices are competitive and access to energy is a more stable and socially more equal affair. The promotion of renewable energy is therefore an important gauge of energy and climate policy.

Regardless of the recent nuclear disaster in Japan, considerable *momentum* has developed on a political and social level to accelerate the transition to durable energy provision. Furthermore over the next few years a great deal of large-scale infrastructure investments will be made in the electricity networks, the energy generation parks and the building stock. Now is the time to take full account of the demands made by the large-scale introduction of renewable energy. Given that the typical life of many infrastructure investments is extremely long, today is one of those rare opportunities to act.

An *explicit strategy* is required to make full use of the proposed advantages and opportunities, since they do not arise automatically or indeed at every moment and everywhere. Much depends on how policy on renewable energy is shaped and implemented. It is our conviction that not all advantages and opportunities are currently being used to their full potential. They can be better used to set lower social costs against higher social advantages. Further adjustment is therefore necessary. Since only an approach which is, from various perspectives, more effective, efficient, equitable, commonly shared and transparent will also be capable of maintaining in the long term the necessary support for really ambitious renewable energy policy and substantially more renewable energy.

PRACTICAL TIPS: CONJUNCTIONS

In the previous chapter we looked at the punctuation around conjunctions – words that are used to provide a transition from one sentence to the next. In the text you have just looked at, you will have encountered words like *tevens* and *ook*, *daarbij* and *daarom*, *dus* and *want*. These words might seem minor, relatively insignificant terms in the sentence, yet they play an essential role in holding the various elements in a passage of text together. In some cases they are used to give a sentence internal structure (such as in pairings like 'neither . . . nor' and 'not only . . . but also') and in others they help to give a passage greater cohesion by weaving a particular sentence into the body of text through agreement or disagreement with previous statements made (using terms like 'as a result' and 'consequently', or 'on the contrary' and 'instead'). In this section we will be focusing less on the so-called

(continued)

(continued)

co-ordinating conjunctions – those small words that link parts of sentences together, like 'for', 'and', 'nor', 'but', 'or', 'yet', 'so' – and more on correlative conjunctions and conjunctive adverbs.

Correlative conjunctions

These belong in pairs and are used to join words and groups of words that carry equal weight in a sentence. There are several different pairs of correlative conjunctions that are most commonly used:

of . . . of/ofwel . . . ofwel: 'either . . . or'

This is probably the most common pairing that we use in a sentence affirmatively when referring to a choice between two possibilities:

Passagiers die na annulering van hun vlucht niet vrijwillig afstand doen van hun boekingen, moeten ofwel hun tickets terugbetaald krijgen ofwel hun reis onder bevredigende omstandigheden kunnen voortzetten.
Passengers whose flights are cancelled and who do not volunteer to surrender their reservations should either be able to obtain reimbursement of their tickets or continue their journeys under satisfactory conditions.

niet alleen . . . maar ook: 'not only . . . but also'

Like the previous construction, this is also a pairing used to bring two pieces of information together and to frame parallel sentence parts:

We hechten waarde aan open communicatie met niet alleen onze collega's, maar ook met onze zakenpartners, onder wie klanten, leveranciers en investeerders.
We value open communication not only with fellow employees but also with our other business associates, including customers, vendors and investors.

noch . . . noch: 'neither . . . nor'

This is also a construction used to join two statements negatively:

Bij de betaling via internet of gsm is het mogelijk dat noch de afzender noch de begunstigde van geld zich in een land bevindt waar de operator verplicht is verdachte verrichtingen te melden.

When paying via the internet or mobile phone, it may be that neither the sender nor the beneficiary of the money is located in a country where the operator is required to disclose suspicious transactions.

zowel ... als: 'both ... and'

This is used to bring together two elements that complement each other:

Ik ben ervan overtuigd dat mooi, intelligent design ons leven zowel in psychologisch alsook in fysiek opzicht verbetert.
I am convinced of the fact that beautiful, intelligent design enhances our life psychologically as well as physically.

enerzijds ... anderzijds: 'on the one hand ... on the other'

In English the construction 'on the one hand ... on the other' has to be used to link statements that are strongly contrastive. This is not always the case in Dutch. Take a look at the following sentences and think about whether or not they really set up clear contrasts:

Enerzijds is hij een toegewijde huisvader, maar anderzijds zou hij soms liever buitenshuis werken.

Voedselprijzen zijn op het ogenblik enerzijds één van de belangrijkste oorzaken van de grotere kwetsbaarheid van arme huishoudens, maar anderzijds ook een prikkel om de eigen voedselproductie te verhogen.

Enerzijds zijn we groot genoeg om te kunnen investeren in kwaliteit. Anderzijds zijn we klein genoeg om te kunnen investeren in persoonlijk contact.

The first sentence sets up clear contrasts between the two roles that the male subject of the sentence embodies – that of the stay-at-home father and that of the man who would like to work outside the home. The second example is less clear-cut. The first part of the sentence (*Voedselprijzen zijn op het ogenblik enerzijds één van de belangrijkste oorzaken van de grotere kwetsbaarheid van arme huishoudens*) communicates the fact that the price of food means that poor households are economically vulnerable, since they cannot afford to meet basic needs. The second part of the sentence (*ook een prikkel om de eigen voedselproductie te verhogen*) argues that lack of funds to buy food could give poorer households the incentive to increase their own food production. These two ideas are not contrastive and therefore you need to think about joining these sentences in other ways than by using the English 'on the one hand ... on the other' construction. The third example is

(continued)

(continued)

more straightforward: here a company is advertising the fact that its size can be viewed from two different perspectives. From one perspective it is large enough to be able to offer a good quality of service; from another it is small enough to be able to offer a personal touch to its customers. Here, the 'on the one hand . . . on the other' construction would be appropriate.

Suggested translations are as follows:

He is on the one hand a devoted house-husband, but on the other hand he would sometimes prefer to work outside the home.

The price of food is currently one of the principal causes of greater vulnerability in poor households, but also provides an incentive for these households to increase their own food production.

On the one hand we are large enough to be able to invest in quality. On the other, we are small enough to invest in personal contact.

Conjunctive adverbs

These conjunctions are used to join independent clauses together. There are far more conjunctions in use in Dutch than we can possibly discuss here (for more detail see, for example, Chapter 12 of Donaldson, 1997). We shall therefore look at only a few in terms of the types of functions that characterise them and the connections they make between ideas, statements and sentences.

One way of linking two ideas is by demonstrating the relationship between cause and effect. This is shown rhetorically by using terms such as *daardoor, als gevolg van* or *zodoende* – thus, therefore, as a result, consequently, as a consequence of – which you can see in the sentences below:

Deze projecten zijn bijna afgerond en daardoor zal het bedrijf de dienstverlening aan de klant kunnen verbeteren.
These projects are now almost complete and the company will therefore be in a position to improve its service to customers.

De investeringen in 2014 lagen volgens plan op een relatief hoog niveau als gevolg van de uitbreiding waartoe in 2012 werd besloten.
The investments in 2014 were, according to plan, relatively high as a consequence of the expansion decided on in 2012.

Zij klapte in haar handen en zodoende schrikte zij de vogels op.
She clapped her hands and therefore startled the birds.

Sometimes we use conjunctive adverbs to expand on a point made earlier or explain in greater depth and clarify another statement. Words such as *omdat, daarom* and *aangezien* – because, since, hence, therefore, thus, given that – are used to make this connection, as the following examples demonstrate:

> *Omdat het water door lagen zand, grind en steentjes naar boven komt, wordt het op natuurlijke wijze gefilterd.*
> Since the water passes upwards through layers of sand, stones and gravel, it undergoes a natural filtering process.
>
> *De regelgeving kan van land tot land verschillen; raadpleeg daarom altijd de informatie op de relevante websites.*
> Regulations can differ from country to country: it is therefore always advisable to consult the information on the relevant websites.
>
> *De arbeiders hebben goed gewerkt aangezien de problemen maar van hele korte duur waren.*
> The workers did a good job, given that the problems lasted for only a very short time.

In some cases, we use examples or other terms to explain further what we mean. Constructions like *met andere woorden, namelijk* and *bijvoorbeeld* – in other words, namely, for example, for instance – are used to help the author get his or her message across, as the following sentences show:

> *Hierbij kan er sprake zijn van ernstige leerproblemen bij het lezen en rekenen, met andere woorden; er kan sprake zijn van dyslexie of dyscalculie.*
> This could point to serious learning difficulties in relation to reading and arithmetic, in other words, dyslexia and dyscalculia.
>
> *De emissies van grond- en brandstoffen worden vertaald in een reeks milieu-effecten, namelijk het broeikaseffect, de ozonlaag, en het effect op de menselijke gezondheid.*
> Emissions are translated into a series of environmental impacts, namely global warming, the ozone layer and the effect on human health.
>
> *De werkzaamheden kunnen ook uitgevoerd worden door bijvoorbeeld een daartoe aangestelde ambtenaar.*
> The work may also be carried out by, for example, an official appointed for this purpose.

There are occasions where we want to contrast statements and we would use words like *daarentegen, toch* and *hoewel* – on the contrary, nevertheless/nonetheless, rather/instead – for this purpose, as you can see in these examples:

(continued)

(continued)

> *Het ontbijt en avondmaal, telkens in buffetvorm opgediend, waren ondermaats. De lunch was daarentegen wel smaakvol.*
> Breakfast and dinner, both served as a buffet, were mediocre. Lunch, by contrast, was really tasty.
>
> *De meest toegankelijke en gebruiksvriendelijke toepassingen kunnen toch door gebruikers als onaangenaam worden ervaren.*
> The most accessible and user-friendly applications can nevertheless be experienced by their users as awkward.
>
> *Deze verordening is in werking getreden op de dag nadat zij is vastgesteld, hoewel zij bijna een maand later is bekend gemaakt.*
> This regulation came into force one day after it was adopted, although it was not made public until almost one month later.

Finally, we also use conjunctive adverbs to sum things up and to make concluding statements. Words and expressions such as *kortom, dus, daarom* and *alles bij elkaar genomen* – 'in short', 'then', 'therefore', 'all in all', 'overall' – serve this purpose. Take a look at the sentences below and try to think about the contexts in which they might have been written and on the basis of which terms we can detect that these are concluding or summarising statements or questions:

> *Wat is kortom de rol van een kunstenaar in de huidige maatschappij?*
> What is, then, the role of the artist in today's society?
>
> *De kijker kan dus genieten van een nog duidelijker beeld met een hoger contrast.*
> Viewers can therefore enjoy an even clearer picture with higher contrast.
>
> *Alles bij elkaar genomen is de inspanning die nodig is zeer klein in verhouding tot de verwachte voordelen.*
> Overall/All in all the effort required is tiny in proportion to the benefits anticipated.

Text 2: *Aanpassing van het waterbeheer in Nederland*

This text is taken from an edited collection that investigates the relationship between people and the natural world from a number of different angles. It considers the impact of urbanisation and population growth on the environment and our changing ecological footprint, discusses the growing scarcity of water resources and problems related to world food distribution, and assesses the effects of tourism on the natural world, as well as the importance of sites of world heritage. The political dimensions of climate change are explored in chapters on global and regional environmental policy. In a final section, the contributors look at the threat posed by the changing natural world, as well as the challenges that it presents. The editors of the book are academics and researchers working in the fields of social and political geography, and the book appeared with an academic publisher, Amsterdam University Press. The passage for you to translate below comes from the fourth section of the collection, which focuses on climate and environmental change. This extract is from a chapter written by two authors. The first is a doctoral student at the Institutut voor Milieuvraagstukken, an institute for environmental issues, at the Vrije Universiteit Amsterdam, with a special interest in climate change and flood damage. The second is Professor of Climate Change and Water Safety at the Wageningen Universiteit and the Vrije Universiteit Amsterdam, and is one of the country's experts on climate change. He has worked on a number of high-level projects such as the United Nations Environmental Programme and the Global Environmental Facility.

Aanpassing van het waterbeheer in Nederland

Wat zijn de gevolgen van wateroverlast en overstromingen? De huidige kans dat bijvoorbeeld West-Nederland overstroomt, is weliswaar klein, maar de economische schade die kan optreden en mogelijk ook het aantal dodelijke slachtoffers dat bij een overstroming kan vallen zijn de afgelopen decennia enorm toegenomen (Bouwer & Vellinga, 2007). Dit komt vooral doordat steeds meer mensen in lager gelegen gebieden zijn gaan wonen, en deze mensen steeds meer kapitaalgoederen bezitten. Daarbij komt dat de bodem van West-Nederland steeds verder daalt, door drainage en inklinking van het veen. Juist de laatste decennia is de stedeljke ontwikkeling in Nederland geconcentreerd in deze gebieden.

De geconstateerde klimaatverandering en vermoedens omtrent het verdere verloop van dat proces nopen tot beleidsaanpassingen, in het bijzonder in gebieden die gevoelig zijn voor de hierboven geschetste problemen. Door klimaatverandering zijn ook hier de historische gegevens van extreme weercondities niet meer de juiste referentie voor het ontwerp van dijken, riolen en andere infrastructuur. Voor het Nederlandse waterbeheer betekent dit dat de zogenaamde randvoorwaarden voor de verdediging tegen hoogwater niet meer geldig zijn.

Voor lokale wateroverlast zijn normen vastgesteld die bepalen hoe vaak een stuk land onder water mag staan. Deze normen stammen uit het zogenaamde Nationaal Bestuursakkoord Water dat in 2003 werd gesloten tussen diverse overheidspartijen en de waterschappen. Ze vormen een leidraad voor waterschappen in Nederland om te bepalen welke maatregelen zij moeten

(continued)

> *(continued)*
>
> nemen om te voorkomen dat in graslanden of stedelijke gebieden respectievelijk vaker dan eens per tien jaar of eens per eeuw wateroverlast ontstaat. Indien extreme neerslag vaker voorkomt, betekent dit dat deze normen niet langer gebaseerd kunnen zijn op historisch waargenomen neerslag. Voor lokale wateroverlast kan worden gezocht naar meer waterberging, zowel in boezems als in stedelijke berging.
>
> Source: Laurens Bouwer and Pier Vellinga (2008) Klimaatverandering en overstromingen, met een focus op Nederland, in Ton Dietz, Frank den Hertog and Herman van der Wusten (eds) *Van natuurlandschap tot risicomaatschappij: de geografie van de relatie tussen mens en milieu*. Amsterdam: Amsterdam University Press, pp. 186–190 (extract on pp. 187–188).

1. Translation strategies and techniques

Referring back to our two key questions as a way to make a first analysis, we need to think about the background knowledge relevant for understanding the text, and about who the target audience might be.

i. What are the first things that you notice about the text?

– *It is an academic text, since it refers to related sources – '(Bouwer & Vellinga, 2007)' – and makes use of a number of specialised terms.*

 As with the previous text, the authors are writing about a relatively specialised area of knowledge, although the text is not weighed down with terminology. It is probably aimed at an audience of specialists, given the context in which it was published, but should be accessible by interested non-specialists. If you are to leave these academic references in the text ('Bouwer & Vellinga, 2007'), then it would be wise to check with those commissioning the article that a bibliography is also included in the translation, otherwise such references are meaningless.

– *It refers to specifically Dutch water management policies such as the 'Nationaal Bestuursakkoord Water'.*

 Two different translations for this appear to be in circulation: the 'National Administrative Agreement on Water' and the 'National Administrative Water Agreement'. The former is far more widely in use on the web, and is also to be found both on governmental web pages and in scientific reports on water management, which suggests that it is the better one to take.

ii. What do you know about the target audience for your translation and how will it affect your translation?

While the source text was originally intended for a Dutch academic public, the text could easily be used in its English translation to attract the interest of a wider public by offering a case study specific to the Netherlands of how issues of urbanisation and local flooding can be addressed. The translation therefore needs to be aimed at an audience of non-specialists with an interest in environmental, economic or political issues.

2. Text and language

This step is crucial since it determines the accuracy of your translation.

i. Words and expressions

> *Wateroverlast en overstromingen*: some dictionaries give the translation 'flooding' for both *wateroverlast* and *overstroming*, but the authors clearly wish to differentiate between them, so you will need to find two different terms to describe them.
>
> *Dodelijke slachtoffers*: literally 'dead victims' – although this combination sounds very odd in English. We would simply tend to say 'deaths' in English, given that it is implicit that the people are victims of environmental disasters.
>
> *Dit komt vooral doordat steeds meer mensen in lager gelegen gebieden zijn gaan wonen*: the juxtaposition of three verbs *zijn gaan wonen* may be rather bewildering, but it is not uncommon in Dutch. In cases where you have a form of *gaan* and another verb in the infinitive, this can be translated using the English conjunctional construction with 'and', so 'to go and do something'. *We gingen zitten* therefore translates as 'We went and sat down' and *Ik ging een heel jaar geen nieuwe kleren kopen* would be 'I didn't go and buy any new clothes for a whole year.' In the past tense, these sentences require a double infinitive, so *We zijn gaan zitten* and *Ik ben een heel jaar geen nieuwe kleren gaan kopen* (see Donaldson, 1997: 234, 291). In our extract, the construction *meer mensen ... zijn [in lager gebieden] gaan wonen* would mean 'more people have gone and lived/gone to live [in lower-lying areas]'.
>
> *Kapitaal goederen*: this is a specialist economic term that is relatively straightforward to translate as 'capital goods'.
>
> *De geconstateerde klimaatverandering*: are you able to find an adjective that will neatly sit between the article and the noun you have chosen in English for *de ... klimaatverandering* to represent *geconstateerd*? Translations like 'the determined climate change' will clearly not work. You may need to use a verbal construction working with possible translations of *constateren* (to 'determine', 'identify') that go after the noun *klimaatverandering*, rather than before it.
>
> *De hierboven geschetste problemen*: this presents you with the similar problem of how to deal with *hierboven geschetst* between the article and the noun *de ... problemen*. This can be more easily resolved with adjectives like 'above-mentioned' or 'aforementioned', although you may consider

that these do not suit the register of your translation. Your solution would therefore be, as before, to produce a verbal construction around *schetsen* that would go after the noun.

3. Style, register and tone

i. Stylistic analysis of the source text

The text has a high, formal register but also frequently uses idiomatic expressions. The author clearly varies the style of her writing to produce a text that engages the attention of her readers: the rhetorical questions at the end of this extract are an important feature that you would want to consider reproducing in the TT.

ii. Assessment of the style of writing appropriate to the target text

The formal and literary features of the ST suggest that the translator should ensure that s/he creates a text in English that appeals to a similar audience.

Sample translation of Text 2: *Aanpassing van het waterbeheer in Nederland*

Adaptation of water management in the Netherlands

What are the consequences of damage through excess water and flooding? The current chances are certainly slim that, for example, the western Netherlands should suffer from flooding, but the economic damage and possibly also the number of deaths that can occur due to flooding has grown enormously over the previous decades (Bouwer & Vellinga, 2007). This primarily has to do with the fact that more and more people have chosen to live in lower-lying areas and these people possess increasing amounts of capital goods. Moreover the ground in the west of the Netherlands is continuing to sink, through land drainage and the shrinking of peatland. Over the last few decades the urban development of the Netherlands has been concentrated in these areas.

The climate changes that have been identified and the concerns about the further development of this process mean that policy has to be adapted in particular in those areas which are sensitive to the problems outlined above. As a result of climate change, historical data regarding extreme weather conditions also no longer serve as a correct point of reference for designing dykes, sewers or other infrastructure. For water management in the Netherlands, this means that the so-called boundary conditions for flood defences are no longer valid.

> With regard to local flooding, norms have been established which determine how often a piece of land can be under water. These norms derive from the so-called Nationaal Bestuursakkoord Water ('National Administrative Agreement on Water') that was concluded in 2003 between various governmental bodies and the water boards. They form a steering committee for water boards in the Netherlands which determines which measures need to be taken to avoid grassland or urban areas from being flooded more often than once every decade or once every century respectively. Should extremely heavy rainfalls become more frequent, this would mean that these norms could no longer be based on historically recorded levels of precipitation. More water storage can be found for local flooding, both in polders and in urban storage facilities.

Dutch translation in practice

To round off this chapter, we have selected a passage that is taken from the same collection as we used for Text 2. Where the focus of that text was specifically on the progress made in water management, this extract reflects on the impact that recent events have had on Dutch water management and on the decisions that must be made to avoid catastrophes in the future. The author is a geographer who has also worked as an independent adviser on spatial development and is chairperson of the *Koninklijk Nederlands Aaardrijkskundig Genootschap* (Royal Dutch Geographical Society). For a sample translation of this passage, see p. 186.

> **Text 3:** *De (bijna-)ramp als basis van de ommezwaai*
>
> Het is half september 2006. Op het nieuws zie ik dat vanwege hevige regenval de Rijn onbevaarbaar is in Zwitserland en delen van Duitsland. De scheepvaart ligt stil en het redderen in dorpen en steden begint. Een ziekenhuis in Dillenburg is inmiddels ontruimd. De hoge waterstand bereikt ongetwijfeld een dezer dagen Nederland. De 'Ruimte voor de rivier' is nog niet gerealiseerd. Wel in de hoofden en op papier, maar nog lang niet in de praktijk. De planologische kernbeslissing is door de overheid vastgesteld, de lagere overheden en partijen uit het bedrijfsleven en het maatschappelijk middenveld hebben heel wat vergaderd. Het resultaat bestaat uit vele 'winwinsituaties': ruimte voor de rivier betekent ook ruimte voor een jachthaven, kansen voor grind- en zandwinning, het herinrichten van uiterwaarden, het aanleggen van nieuwe natuurgebieden.
>
> Maar er moet ook bebouwing verdwijnen, bij Elst bijvoorbeeld om de Waal bij Nijmegen meer ruimte te bieden en her en der worden nieuw
>
> *(continued)*

(continued)

dijken aangelegd. Die worden niet zo hoog als in de oorspronkelijke plannen, want door verbreding van het winterbed, door nieuwe strangen (parallelle afvoeren) en door noodoverloopgebieden is de technocratische aanpak die ruim anderhalve eeuw de boventoon voerde, omgebogen. [. . .]

De schrik kwam er goed in toen in 1993 en in 1995 sprake was van reëel overstromingsgevaar. Nederland was in rep en roer. Alle vertrouwen in de beproefde technocratische aanpak van Rijkswaterstaat en de waterschappen kwam onder vuur. De ingezette evacuatie was achteraf gezien wellicht niet nodig geweest, maar feit was dat het water klotste tot aan de rand van de dijken. De beelden van oneindige watervlaktes, van het leger en de bevolking met zandzakken, van gewichtige mannen met geruststellende teksten, het riep sterke herinneringen op – nu in kleur – van de Watersnoodramp van 1953.

Source: Marijke van Schendelen (2008) Het waterbeheer verbindt zich met de ruimtelijke ordening, in Ton Dietz, Frank den Hertog and Herman van der Wusten (eds) *Van natuurlandschap tot risicomaatschappij: de geografie van de relatie tussen mens en milieu*. Amsterdam: Amsterdam University Press, pp. 153–158 (extract on pp. 153–154).

Conclusion
Revising your translation

As we discussed in the introduction, revision is an absolutely essential part of the translation process. But how you go about revising your text does depend on a number of different factors – how much time you can allow yourself to spend on revision, how difficult you found it to put one particular text into English and what you know to be your own weaknesses (e.g. spelling, grammar, omission). As Brian Mossop puts it in his extremely useful work *Revising and Editing for Translators*, the key to finding mistakes lies in working out 'not only *what* to look for, but *how* to look for it' (Mossop, 2014: 165). In short, you can only correct mistakes once you have found them, and identifying where they are is half the battle. Being critical about one's own work is also never easy, although you should gradually acquire a sense of where your own strengths and weaknesses as a translator lie. Some people are able to produce a first draft of a translation very quickly that reads fluently but is not necessarily very accurate, while others may succeed in transferring the content of the ST into the TT with a good eye for detail, but construct a text that does not, at this first stage, read particularly fluently in the target language. In both of these cases, it is clear that some degree of revision is necessary, and how you go about tackling this final, absolutely essential, stage of the translation process forms the focus of this conclusion.

The degree of revision that is possible clearly depends on how much time you have. In the translation industry, clients often leave their translators very little turnaround time, often because they have underestimated just how long it can take to translate a piece of text. To complicate matters further, sometimes they come up with their own revisions to the ST while you are still in the midst of translating it (which can be extremely frustrating and swiftly lead to confusion!) and sometimes they also wish to make their own revisions to your translation once you have finished, thus adding a further post-translation stage to the communication between client and translator, and another step to the editing process. In a classroom context, you will presumably only have one or two deadlines to deal with – dates for the submission of your pre-final and final translations for assessment. Nevertheless, you still need to factor in enough time between receiving the ST and submitting your TT both to avoid the practical problems that frequently cause tight deadlines to be missed (IT issues, illness) and to factor in time *away* from your first draft of the translation to provide yourself with a productive distance from your initial version.

So, if time allows, it makes sense to put the translation to one side for a day or even a couple of hours. When you pick it up again, you are likely to look at it with fresh eyes and you can more easily detect obvious errors related to meaning transfer, as well as passages that read awkwardly, where tense, register or choice of vocabulary might be an issue. When you are working under extreme pressure of time, you are unlikely to be able to check every word, so you are going to have to prioritise. Perhaps you might only revisit the text on a micro-level and address just one particular paragraph that you found very difficult. Or perhaps you want to examine on a macro-level whether you have used vocabulary, tense and spelling consistently throughout. Even if you found the translation easy and are confident that your English version is near perfect, it is worthwhile checking that you have not left anything out.

Whether you read the Dutch text first or start with your English translation as you begin to revise depends, again, on the problems that you sense you encountered. If you are still unsure about the meaning of various parts of the source text, then it makes sense to pick up the Dutch text and see if, by re-reading it, you can clarify these uncertainties. If you feel that you understood the original well but had problems putting it into English, then re-reading your translation *as a piece of English* might be your best course of action. Mossop's 'revision parameters' are helpful in enabling you to think about the error types you could be looking for (Mossop, 2014: 134–149). He has compressed the kinds of questions you could be asking into four main categories: problems of meaning transfer, problems of content, problems of language and style, and problems of physical presentation. He breaks these categories down further into questions regarding accuracy and completeness, logic and factual accuracy, smoothness and idiomatic language usage, as well as grammatical correctness, and issues related to layout, typography and organisation.

Throughout this book we have emphasised the need for accuracy, particularly in the use of appropriate terminology across a series of domains, including finance and economics, the transport and energy industries, telecommunications and art history. In our Practical Tips sections in Chapters 2 and 5 in particular we stressed the need to be accurate in translating names of places and numbers. In Chapter 8 we discussed how the inaccurate use of punctuation either makes sentences unclear or detracts from the hard work that has gone in to making a polished piece of text. In Chapters 3, 6, 7 and 9 we emphasised how important it is to be able to understand the way in which a sentence is constructed and how its constituent parts fit together, as well as how sentences themselves interconnect with one another within a given section. Throughout this book we have stressed the need to tailor language in terms of style and register to the assumed target audience, and we discussed in Chapter 4 how the use of the different pronouns 'you' and 'one' can give a translation a radically different feel. While we only specifically focus on issues of presentation in Chapter 1, where we reflect on the particularities of web translation, throughout this book we have mentioned the need to think about the use of referencing and footnoting, depending on the type of text and audience for which the translation is being prepared. Regardless of context, though, it would clearly be important to check that your translation has similar structuring devices to those in the original and is broken down into separate paragraphs (probably following the form of the ST), that you have used bold and italic type for emphasis in more or less the same way as in the original, and that you have ensured that any footnoted material or headers have also been translated.

Problems of language and style are harder to discuss here without taking a longer passage as material for analysis. However, you need to think about whether connections between sentences are clear, how well the passage flows and if you have made good use of idiomatic expressions. While it is difficult to give specific tips about what to correct in awkward-sounding sentences, look for the uneven use of tenses, word order that follows too closely that of the Dutch, inappropriate register (vocabulary that is too formal or informal for the given context) and un-English collocations (i.e. noun + verb combinations such as 'to make a photo' rather than 'to take a photo' for *een foto maken*). It is probably easiest to home in on problems of grammar, problems of content, i.e. factual and conceptual errors, and problems of meaning transfer, where the message of the source text has not been fully represented in the target text. By comparing your ST and TT carefully, line by line, you should be able to detect where these final problems lie.

Below we have picked out just a few of the problems that regularly recur and can easily be identified and corrected as you troubleshoot in your translation: misuse of apostrophes, spelling of homonyms, names and place names, and omissions.

Apostrophes

We noted in Chapter 8 that it is absolutely essential that you have a good grasp of punctuation in English before you set out to translate anything into it. Look at the Dutch sentences in italics below, think quickly about how you would translate them, and then decide which of the English translations we have given make correct use of the apostrophe and which do not:

> *Voor organisaties is het belangrijk dat zij zich hierop voorbereiden.*
> It's important for organisations to prepare themselves for this.

> *Als we vertrouwelijke informatie van derden ontvangen, respecteren we de vertrouwelijkheid ervan en zorgen we voor de nodige bescherming.*
> When we receive confidential information from a third party, we will respect it's confidentiality and afford it appropriate protection.

> *Maar voor de mensen in ontwikkelingslanden blijft het in de eerste plaats gaan om zeggenschap over hun eigen toekomst.*
> But for the people's in developing countries, the key concern remains the control of their own future.

The apostrophe in the first sentence is correct, since it stands for letters that have been omitted: the opening of the sentence would read in full 'It is important for organisations ...'. The apostrophe in the second sentence is incorrect, as the word before 'confidentiality' needs to be the possessive adjective 'its'. In the third sentence, the apostrophe in 'people's' is also incorrect, since we are not looking at a possessive construction but at a plural. The plural of 'people' (in the sense of a certain racial, social or political group), is simply 'peoples'.

Spelling of homonyms

Words that sound the same (known as 'homonyms') tend to cause confusion and lead to mistakes, particularly when working at speed, although the grammar programs on computers are now very good at picking them up. In the following, we address the problems caused by confusing 'their', 'they're' and 'there'. Look at the Dutch sentences in italics below and have a go at translating them into English yourself. Then compare your solution with the one given below. Which of the sentences are correct and which contain mistakes?

> *Vooral bij de Turkse en Marokkaanse gemeenschappen is sprake van een sterke concentratie op de eigen groep en daar is in de loop der jaren weinig in veranderd.*
> The Turkish and Moroccan communities in particular have associated primarily with members of there own groups and their has been little change over the years.
>
> *Daarom is er dringend behoefte aan meer inzicht om de voordelen en mogelijkheden van migrantenvrijwilligersorganisaties voor de integratie van migrantengemeenschappen in de samenleving te benutten.*
> There is therefore an urgent need to understand better and make use of the benefits and the potential that migrant volunteering holds for the integration of immigrant communities into society.
>
> *Mijn kinderen willen weer bij mij wonen maar krijgen daar geen toestemming voor, ze krijgen zelfs geen toestemming om elkaar te zien.*
> My children want to live with me again but their not allowed to do so, and they don't even let them see each other.

In the first sentence we have transposed 'their' and 'there', so the second half of the sentence should read 'their own groups and there has been little change'. The second sentence is correct. In the third translation 'their' and 'they're' have been confused and the middle of the sentence should read 'they're not allowed to live with me again'.

Names

If you are commissioned to translate a piece of text for a company then you are likely to be sent it electronically as a file in which you can work as you transfer it

Conclusion   173

from Dutch to English. You will probably work around the names of people and places, and typing errors are much less likely to creep in than if you were typing up your translation as a new document. If you do have to produce your translation 'from scratch', however, then you should watch out for the kinds of mistakes that you should be able to identify in the following sentences:

Mode-ontwerper Walter Van Beirendonck spreekt over zijn werk, de dood als inspiratiebron, en het verschil tussen ontwerp en kunst.
Fashion designer Walter Van Beirendonk talks about his work, death as a source of inspiration and the difference between design and art.

Zijne Majesteit Koning Albert II huldigde de D'Ieteren Gallery op 15 maart 2003 in en nam deel aan het colloquium over Belgische ondernemingen in de autobranche.
His Majesty King Albert I inaugurated the new D'Ieteren Gallery on 15 March 2003 and participated in the seminar on Belgian businesses in the automobile industry.

Het Museum Plantin-Moretus werd in 2005 erkend als UNESCO-werelderfgoed en prijkt als enigste museum ter wereld op deze lijst.
The Plantijn-Moretus Museum was recognised as UNESCO World Cultural Heritage in 2005 and is the only museum worldwide on this list.

You should have noticed that the surname of the fashion designer was missing a 'c', that 'King Albert II' had suddenly become 'King Albert I' and that the *Museum Plantin-Moretus* had gained a 'j' in translation.

Place names

As we discussed in Chapter 2, the names of cities, rivers and countries confront us with other difficulties: here it is not simply a question of ensuring that the spelling in the English text matches that of the Dutch. You need to think about whether the names actually need to be translated and/or spelled differently in English. Identify the place names in the following sentences and think about whether they also need translating as you put the sentence into English:

De rijke geschiedenis, de archeologische vondsten, maar ook de kleurrijke winkelstraten lokken dagelijks veel toeristen naar Brugge.

De vliegtuigen bevinden zich in Suixi, de provincie Guangdong, en op het vliegveld van Wuhu, 250 kilometer ten westen van Sjanghai.

Ongeveer 70% van de groei komt voor rekening van de stadsverwarmingsnetten in Rotterdam, Utrecht, Den Haag en Delft.

De constructie biedt een panoramisch uitzicht over de historische stad en de samenvloeiing van de Moezel in de Rijn.

174 *Conclusion*

While translators working between Dutch and English are attuned to the fact that *Brugge* needs to be translated as 'Bruges' and *Den Haag* as 'The Hague' (note the capitalisation), more exotic locations such as *Sjanghai* need to be put into English spelling as 'Shanghai', just as *de Moezel* and *de Rijn* become 'the Mosel' and 'the Rhine' in translation. Suggested translations of these sentences are:

> With its rich history, archaeological finds and also its colourful shopping streets, Bruges attracts many tourists every day.

> The aircraft are based at Suixi, in Guangdong province, and on the airfield at Wuhu, 250 kilometres west of Shanghai.

> Around 70% of the growth can be attributed to the district heating networks in Rotterdam, Utrecht, The Hague and Delft.

> The building offers a panoramic view over the historic town and the confluence of the Mosel and the Rhine.

Omissions

Finally, check that all the information in the original is present in the translation. This is something that you should do by comparing the source and target text sentence for sentence, since simply reading through the English translation will not necessarily alert you to the fact that words have been left out. Compare the following Dutch sentences and their English translations and see if you can spot what is missing:

> *Over twee jaar zullen ongeveer 100 vrijwilligersorganisaties door het bieden van stageplaatsen hun medewerking aan het project hebben verleend en tot nu toe hebben 30 deelnemers de cursus voltooid.*
> In two years' time, 100 volunteer organisations will have contributed to the project by offering a work placement for on-the-job training and up to now 30 trainees have completed the course.

> *Lagere verkopen van ijs en ijsthee waren verantwoordelijk voor bijna tweederde van de daling van de onderliggende verkopen in de regio als geheel.*
> Lower sales of ice cream and iced tea were responsible for two-thirds of the underlying sales decline for the region as a whole.

> *Europol ondersteunde de internationale operatie meer dan een jaar lang met ondermeer analytische verslagen, waaruit de internationale dimensie van de zaak naar voren kwam.*
> Europol supported the international operation for more than a year, by drawing up analytical reports which highlighted the international dimension of the case.

Each of these English sentences reads fluently and makes sense on its own. But you may have seen that what was missing from the first sentence was a translation of the word *ongeveer* in *ongeveer 100 vrijwilligersorganisaties*, so 'approximately 100 volunteer organisations' or 'some 100 volunteer organisations'. In the second sentence the small word *bijna* was missing from *bijna tweederde*, which should have been translated as 'almost two-thirds' or 'practically two-thirds'. The translation of the third sentence lacks a translation for *ondermeer* to indicate that Europol contributed in other ways than just drawing up analytical reports. You would need to add something like 'amongst other things', or use the verb 'include' – for example, 'Europol supported the international operation for more than a year by, amongst other things, drawing up analytical reports . . .' or 'Europol's support of the international operation for more than a year included the drawing up of analytical reports . . .'.

In this book we have sought to give you an impression of how multifaceted the work of a translator can be, the kinds of linguistic challenges with which you will be confronted, and the sorts of questions that you need to think about before, during and after translation. We hope that the texts we have analysed here have offered you a stimulating insight into the various types of textual material that require translation on a daily basis, the different subjects that they cover, and the various communicative purposes they serve. While translation may not be your intended profession, as a linguist working between Dutch and English it is possible that in a number of areas of employment – press officer, administrative assistant, PR adviser, marketing specialist, web page manager, to name but a few – you will be asked to put a piece of Dutch text into good English that is appropriate to the audience for which it is intended. As you become more confident about your skills as a translator, you are less likely to think consciously about the separate steps and points that we have stressed in each chapter. We hope, though, that this book provides a useful platform for discussion and reflection about translation and revision practices, which will serve you well in your unique and immensely valuable role as a mediator between the peoples, cultures and societies of the Dutch- and English-speaking worlds.

List of grammatical terms

adverb	Word that describes the action denoted by a verb, e.g. *Hij deed het goed*. (He did it well.)
adverbial conjunction	Word linking clauses – adverbial conjunctions do not belong to the group of grammatical conjunctions like *maar* and *of*. Examples of adverbial conjunctions are *bovendien* (furthermore) and *trouwens* (indeed).
apostrophe	A punctuation mark that signifies omission of one or more letters or numbers, as in 'can't'. Also in Dutch to signify a long vowel: *paraplu's*.
auxiliary verb	A verb used in conjunction with another verb. The auxiliary is the finite verb in the clause and the other verb, which normally carries the focus of meaning, is in the infinitive form, e.g. *Zij gaat het doen*.
collocation	Words that are said to 'collocate' belong together, i.e. are frequently used in a fixed or predictable combination.
compound adjective	Adjectives consisting of more than one word, frequently a number + adjective, e.g. *driejarig*.
compound noun	Nouns consisting of more than one conjoined noun, e.g. *hotelkamer*.
conditional tense	Used to signify something that may happen, consisting of auxiliary verb *zou(den)* + infinitive, e.g. *Ik zou het doen* . . .
conjunction	Word linking two clauses. For example, *en* and *maar* link two main clauses, while *dat* and *omdat* link a main and subordinate clause.
diminutive suffix	The ending *-je/tje/kje* added to a noun to convey small size.
discontinuous elements	These are components of a word or construction that belong together, but can be placed apart in a sentence, e.g. *Ik droom er vaak van*.
er as indefinite subject	In Dutch a sentence may not begin with an indefinite subject such as *een paar mensen*. *Er* introduces this kind of sentence, while the indefinite noun follows the verb, e.g. *Er komen een paar mensen langs*.
er-construction	Any construction involving the word *er* in any of its functions.

List of grammatical terms

genitive construction	Phrase in which belonging or possession is indicated by a preposition, e.g. *van haar* (hers).
idiomatic phrase	A set phrase used in everyday speech whose meaning cannot be deduced from the components, e.g. *voeten in de aarde hebben* = be difficult to bring about.
indefinite pronoun	Used instead of a noun to denote an unspecified individual or quantity, e.g. *niemand* (no one), *enkele* (some).
infinitive	The neutral form of a verb cited in the dictionary, e.g. *lachen* (to laugh).
inflected adjective	Used with -*e* added to the end of the adjective.
inseparable prefix	An element added to the front of a Dutch verb, e.g. *geloven*, *voorkómen*. An inseparable prefix is never stressed.
locative use of *er*	*Er* in its function as an adverb of place meaning 'there'.
main clause	The clause that contains the main idea or action expressed in a sentence, characterised in Dutch by the position of the finite verb in second place.
modal particle	Small word in Dutch, such as *toch*, *maar*, which helps to convey the speaker's feelings.
modal verb	A group of auxiliary verbs: *kunnen, moeten, mogen, willen, zullen*.
noun phrase	A group of words formed around a noun, e.g. *de mooie witte tulpen*.
partitive use of *er*	Used to denote a part of a whole, e.g. *Ik heb er drie* (I have three (of them)).
passive verb	A form of the verb which denotes that the action is being done to someone. It is formed using the auxiliary verb *worden* and the past participle, e.g. *Hij wordt goed betaald*.
past participle	The form of the verb used in perfect tenses together with the auxiliary *hebben* or *zijn*. The past participle is formed with the prefix *ge*-, which is added to the stem of the verb + -*t/-d/-en*, e.g. *gedrukt, gebaseerd, gelachen*.
past tense	The tense of the verb that indicates an action in the past. Where Dutch has one past tense – *we lachten* – English has two forms: 'we laughed' and 'we were laughing'.
perfect tense	The tense of the verb that indicates a completed action, e.g. *ik heb het boek geschreven* (I wrote/have written the book).
prefix	An element that is attached to the front of a noun or verb, e.g. *doorgang, uitzicht*.
preposition	A word that specifies the position of the noun it precedes, or indicates a relationship in space, e.g. *op de grond, met mijn moeder*.
preposition phrase	The construction preposition + noun, e.g. *op de grond, met mijn moeder*.
present participle	The verb stem + the suffix -*end*, used to signify a continuing action, e.g. *weglopend* (running away).

(continued)

178 *List of grammatical terms*

(continued)

pronominal use of *er*	This is when *er* is used instead of a pronoun to refer back to a noun.
pronoun	A word such as *het* (it) used to refer back to a noun.
reflexive verb	A verb used with the pronoun *zich* where the action denoted refers to the subject, e.g. *zich ontwikkelen* (to develop), *zich wassen* (to wash (oneself)).
relative clause	A subclause introduced by *die* or *dat*, which refers back to a noun in the previous clause.
relative pronoun	The pronoun *die* or *dat*, which introduces a relative clause.
repletive use of *er*	*Er* introduces a sentence with an indefinite subject, which itself follows the verb, e.g. *Er komen een paar mensen langs*.
semantic field	A field of meaning covered by one or more lexical items (words).
separable prefix	A stressed verb prefix that can be separated from the verb.
separable verb	A verb with a separable prefix, e.g. *weggaan – zij gaat morgen weg*.
stressed prefix	A prefix that carries emphasis.
strong verb	A verb that normally undergoes a vowel change in forming the past tense and past participle. The past participle ends in *–en*, e.g. *zwemmen, zwom, gezwommen*.
subclause	A clause that is dependent on a main clause. The main characteristic of a subclause in Dutch is the word order in which the verb is placed at the end of the subclause.
subject	The 'actor' performing the action denoted by the verb, e.g. *Het meisje liep langs het raam*.
two-part preposition	A preposition consisting of two conjoined prepositions, which can be separated by the noun to which they refer, e.g. *op twee studenten na* (except for two students).
uninflected adjective	An adjective with no final *-e* added to it.
unstressed prefix	A prefix that carries no emphasis.

Useful resources for translators

This list simply draws your attention to some of the resources that may be of use to you. We have not listed all the various editions of monolingual Dutch or monolingual English dictionaries that are widely available, nor the bilingual Dutch–English/English–Dutch dictionaries currently on the market. It is not only important that you can check the meaning of a given word within its context and look up possible translations – you also need to think about related synonyms that would best suit the register and style of the text that you are producing as a translator. Before you start, you should therefore also try to ensure that you have a good English-language thesaurus to hand; leading publishing houses offer them in a variety of different editions, sizes and referencing styles.

Reference grammars of Dutch

Donaldson, B. (1997) *Dutch: A Comprehensive Grammar*. London: Routledge.
Fehringer, C. (1999) *A Reference Grammar of Dutch*. Cambridge: Cambridge University Press.
Haeseryn, W., Romijn, K., Geerts, G., de Rooij, J. and van den Toorn, M.C. (1997) *Algemene Nederlandse Spraakkunst*, 2nd edn. Groningen/Deurne: Nijhoff/Wolters Plantyn. Available online as the *Elektronische ANS (E-ANS)* at: http://ans.ruhosting.nl/e-ans/.
Quist, G. and Strik, D. (2010) *Essential Dutch Grammar*. London: Teach Yourself.
Shetter, W.Z. and Ham, E. (2007) *Dutch. An Essential Grammar*, 9th edn. New York and London: Routledge.

Reference works on translation

Baker, M. (1992) *In Other Words: A Coursebook on Translation*. London and New York: Routledge.
European Commission Directorate-General for Translation (2009) *Web Translation as a Genre*. European Commission. Available as a free download at: http://bookshop.europa.eu/en/web-translation-as-a-genre-pbHC8009160/ (accessed 10 January 2014).
Hatim, B. and Munday, J. (2004) *Translation: An Advanced Resource Book*. London: Routledge.
Lemmens, M. and Parr, T. (1995) *Handboek voor de vertaler Nederlands-Engels*. Leuven: Wolters.
Mossop, B. (2014) *Revising and Editing for Translators*, 3rd edn. Abingdon: Routledge.

Reference works on English grammar and language

Peck, J. and Coyle, M. (2012) *The Student's Guide to Writing: Spelling, Punctuation and Grammar*, 3rd edn. Basingstoke: Palgrave Macmillan.

Sinclair, C. (2010) *Grammar: A Friendly Approach*, 2nd edn. Maidenhead: Open University Press.

Online translation resources

British Centre for Literary Translation – http://www.bclt.org.uk/
Dict.cc – http://ennl.dict.cc/
Expertisecentrum Literair Vertalen – http://literairvertalen.org/
IATE (Interactive Terminology for Europe) – http://iate.europa.eu/
Linguee – http://www.linguee.com/dutch-english/
Mijnwoordenboek – http://www.mijnwoordenboek.nl/vertaal/EN/NL/

Sample translations of third texts

Chapter 1: | *Machtsvertoon* | *Over prestige en symbolen*
(See Dutch text on p. 23)

| *Displaying Power* | *About prestige and symbols*

The fourth floor is devoted to the theme of 'Displaying Power' with collections on prestige and its symbols.

Power is seductive, power is everywhere. Important leaders, but also ordinary people in their everyday lives, convince others that they deserve power by seductive and persuasive means.

In all cultures beautiful, sacral status symbols play an important part in displaying power. And if power is disputed, these symbols are the first to be destroyed, violated or stolen.

The MAS collection houses thousands of these status objects from around the world. This should come as no surprise. The exclusivity of this heritage made its objects desirable to the international art trade and museum collections.

Fascinating stories

The theme of Displaying Power confronts visitors with the fascinating stories behind these exclusive objects. Stories about power close to home and far away, past and present.

- From power and images of changing rulers of Antwerp in the age of rebellion (1568–1648) to Japan, where status consciousness is a constant feature throughout history and where relations between those with high and low status are ever-present in education.
- From the prestige of African leaders from the 16th to the 19th century to a collection of Indonesian weapons from the colonial era, and Maori artist George Nuku's view of Polynesian heritage in Western museums.

Chapter 2: *Talige en culturele variatie* (See Dutch text on p. 41)

Linguistic and cultural variation

There is a great deal of variation in language and culture among the different parts of the Dutch language area. This can be experienced as an enrichment, but at the same time as a limitation. At any rate, if the Dutch language is not a dominant factor in a particular culture, this may have all kinds of consequences for the academic study of this language. A great deal more attention should be paid to the area of literature and the promotion of reading. This could be brought about through making annual budgets earmarked for this purpose available in the language area. Probably there are such initiatives, but it is not really known how to tap into them. I notice that in the media too much emphasis is placed on politically engaged topics, and less on the literary dimension (quality) of the contributors. Likewise, often little attention is paid to compositional aspects either. The Dutch language is an effective means of communication in our society, which means that it remains important to continue directing attention towards fundamental aspects such as phonetics and phonology, etymology, grammar, semantics and sentence structure. It is advisable that Dutch Studies specialists and linguists collaborate more in order to optimise the level of Dutch in our country.

Chapter 3: *De Schoonspringer* (See Dutch text on p. 57)

The Highdiver

It is eleven thirty in the morning when the Highdiver phones.

I freeze when I see his name pop up on my mobile. It is exactly four months, six days, eight hours and sixteen minutes since he last rang me. I'm very busy on the set of the photoshoot, on the point of asking the models to assume a different pose, and I've just taken a deep breath because the now-or-never moment has come for this glossy reportage.

The Highdiver.

This is what I have called my father since as a boy of about eight I lay in the bunk bed I shared with my brother and we eavesdropped on the conversations between him and his friends in the living room, which was above our bedroom. His friends visited every other week without fail. We never really saw these friends because they came in when we were already in bed, though I did manage to catch a glimpse of them. Clad in the pyjamas our mother had bundled us into ready for sleep, I would creep carefully out of bed, sneak out of the room, and from the bottom of the stairs look up to where I could see them sitting, if the living room door was open. Not long before, they had entered the hallway where I was sitting and their worn-out shoes were waiting for their return. Our four-room flat had been generously allocated to us by the housing association the year before, so we were able to leave our cramped two-room flat behind. This was the first half of the 1980s. Chernobyl was still intact. Maradona hadn't yet scored against the English assisted by the Hand of God. And if at all possible, my father listened to classical Arabic music every day, humming along with whole passages.

Source: Abdelkader Benali (2014) trans. Jane Fenoulhet, 'The Highdiver'. London: Centre for Low Countries Studies. Online at: https://www.ucl.ac.uk/centre-for-low-countries-studies/texts-and-translations/abdelkader-benali.

Chapter 4: *Immigranten* (See Dutch text on p. 77)

Immigrants

The Netherlands cannot escape the question of how it must behave towards immigrants: firstly because the Netherlands have already had experience of many immigrants and secondly because there will always be immigrants that will continue to come. Just as native Dutch people are attached to their cultural identity, so immigrants in the Netherlands cherish their own culture. As a result of this, the Netherlands is confronted with a number of fundamentally different views which provoke strong emotions, particularly in the area of male-female relations, religious convictions and the freedom of expression. Cultural differences do not, in essence, need to pose insurmountable problems. Society can do something about this. By adopting a pluralistic policy – Canada is a good example of this – it can be made easier for immigrants to identify with that society than if that society forces assimilation upon them. A feasible approach would be to allow immigrants a considerable measure of freedom to express their own culture, but to demand a considerable amount of instrumental adaptation at school and in the workplace. What is meant by 'instrumental adaptation' is the acquisition of culture-related skills required to do the work well. Chief among them is a command of the Dutch language. The importance of this has only increased, since the type of work has changed. In the period when *gastarbeiders* (migrant workers) came to the Netherlands, there was need for a lot of hard manual labour, particularly in the industrial and agrarian sectors. Nowadays the number of jobs in the service sector has, in relative terms, shown a sharp increase. Communication skills are particularly important in that sector. The question is whether that kind of instrumental adaptation must be imposed at work. Most immigrants make this adjustment spontaneously because they themselves see the point of it and want to get into employment.

The problem of cultural diversity should not, for that matter, be exaggerated. The dark side to immigration is emphasised all too often. However, immigrants are in very many cases hard-working, ambitious and successful citizens who make an important contribution to our society.

Chapter 5: *Visserij* (See Dutch text on p. 94)

Fishing

Fishing focuses on production, in particular the catching of fish and the harvesting of shellfish. The sector primarily comprises a cutter fleet and a small number of trawler companies. With the exception of the shipping companies, the fisheries sector is made up in particular of partnerships, which means that most of the people working in cutter fishing have a position as a self-employed person without staff (a so-called 'zzp' in Dutch).

The odds are not good for the fisheries sector, despite the increase in fish consumption and the increase in sale prices. The sector is faced with a series of changes which are negatively influencing its activity. Firstly, there have been developments in the area of laws and regulations, such as catch restrictions, limitations on the effects on non-target species, food safety, etc. An important topic for fisheries in governmental policy over the last few years has been the demand that the sector be sustainable. In view of this, permits were no longer issued for cockle fishing in the Waddenzee from 2005. This form of fishing has therefore since disappeared from the Waddenzee. Mussel fishing does, however, have enough of a future.

Secondly, fisheries are faced with high fuel prices which, considering the narrow profit margins in fishing, place relatively heavy pressure on profits. Finally, the lack of room on land means that people are increasingly looking towards the sea (wind parks, Maasvlakte 2, marine nature reserves). In so doing, the fisheries lose a proportion of their fishing grounds.

As a result of these developments, the number of companies has in recent years fallen from almost 800 in 2001 to 730 in 2005 (see table 2.10). [. . .]

The subsectors within the fishing industry in which the prospects are less bleak, are trawler fishing (larger ships which can fish in distant waters outside Europe) and mussel fishing. In these sectors too, employment has dropped, albeit less steeply (4 and 5% respectively).

Chapter 6: *De virtuele krant* (See Dutch text on p. 111)

The virtual newspaper

Publishers often draw on their own experience for successful strategies. In this way, a number of publishers put forward the idea that for their internet products to have a realistic chance of success, they should be less of an electronic edition or summary of something in print and more of a 'value added feature'. According to them, internet activities are more successful when they function as a stand-alone medium that is in competition with their own printed product. This is possible if optimal use is made of features specific to the internet: interactivity, multimediality and involving hyperlinks.

Other experiences also point to the possibility of success. Online projects should therefore not be regarded and presented purely as experiments within the newspaper industry; rather, electronic products should function as independent operations. Products are only introduced into the market and the internet after production of a full business plan and with careful planning. The aim is not solely to bring out the paper online, but to offer extensive information sites in collaboration with partners inside and outside the world of the press. For example, the *Wall Street Journal* expects success above all from working with other players in the field. The newspaper collaborates via various websites in diverse ways with other enterprises which have different things to offer. These *alliances* can jointly promote a product or service, create or deliver site content, distribute specific editorial content for third parties, and offer e-commerce services. According to the *Wall Street Journal* even collaboration with a major competitor can prove lucrative for both parties when they can profit from each other's brand recognition. But for such alliances to be successful, it is crucial that well-considered aims are kept in mind and to accept that *both* parties must be able to gain advantage from the collaboration.

Chapter 7: *Een schilderswerkplaats* (See Dutch text on p. 129)
An artist's studio

A painter's studio generally had high north-facing windows, the bottom half of which were closed off with shutters. Painters positioned their models here so that as they were sitting light fell on them diagonally from the front left with short shadows disappearing behind them to the right. A composition of figures pictured in this way gives the impression that the light falls diagonally from in front through the frame of the painting. This 'studio light' was sometimes combined with a light source in the painting, as the painter Dou had done, although de Hooch put an end to that practice. This shows how much more important lighting effects were for him than for his predecessors.

Johannes Vermeer dealt in art but his main profession was that of an innkeeper. He did some painting on the side, but he only produced on average one painting per year. A few early historical scenes by him are known and in 1656 he painted a genre study that reminds us as much of a Van Honthorst as of a piece by a pupil of Rembrandt. Vermeer probably knew indirectly of both these examples, without being in close contact with a teacher. That would also have been contrary to expectations, since his training in historical painting had been completed years earlier. A second proof of the ease with which he retrained to become a genre painter reminds us in terms of light and colour even more strongly of the Rembrandt pupil Nicolaes Maes. In both compositions an Eastern carpet serves to hide the poor perspective of a table. Only with de Hooch's help could Vermeer succeed in overcoming his initial problems as an artist.

Two of Vermeer's genre pieces owe so much to de Hooch's work from 1658 that the one appears to have been the pupil of the other, but in reality this was a meeting between two novices who were not yet thirty; after this brief experiment they went their separate ways.

Chapter 8: *Antwerpen, modemetropool* (See Dutch text on p. 148)
Antwerp, fashion metropolis

Martin Margiela, who graduated with Walter Van Beirendonck and is one of the most revolutionary fashion designers of his generation, chose to take a different path and settled reasonably quickly in Paris as an assistant to Jean-Paul Gaultier. In 1988 he established the Maison Martin Margiela together with Jenny Meirens, which has been part of the Diesel group since 2002.

The Six went their different ways after London. But the term 'Antwerp Six' continues to pursue them to this very day, even if in principle they have nothing to do with each other. Not in terms of style, since their universes are miles apart. Nor do they work together, and have never done so. But they do all demonstrate great strong-mindedness and perseverance, perfectionism in an attention to detail (show, photos, styling, invitations, . . .) and – naturally – a good portion of talent. [. . .]

Antwerp became a concept. A laboratory of style. A breeding place for talent and a paradise for fashion students from around the world. In the 1990s and at the start of 2000, a second generation of designers (including Anna Heylen, Stephan Schneider, A.F. Vandevorst, Kris Van Assche, Bernhard Willhelm, Raf Simons, Veronique Branquinho, Bruno Pieters, Tim Van Steenbergen, Les Hommes, Christian Wijnants) were able due to their determination, strength and conceptual collections, to break into the fashion industry immediately and perpetuate the avant-garde character of Antwerp fashion. Unlike the first generation which originally presented itself as a group to make an international break, the second generation of designers took the stage directly as individuals with a firm plan and their own catwalk shows.

The 'people of the North' ushered in an avant-garde, the 'Antwerp of fashion' as the journalist Elisabeth Paillié described it so neatly. The 'Antwerp of fashion', the reverse side, recycling, disposable fashion, an underground phenomenon, the underdog: not as extrovert as English fashion, not as sexy as Italian fashion, not as cerebral as Japanese fashion.

Chapter 9: *De (bijna-)ramp als basis van de ommezwaai*
(See Dutch text on p. 167)

The (near)catastrophe as basis for the change of direction

It is mid-September 2006. On the news I see that due to heavy rainfall the Rhine is not navigable in Switzerland and in parts of Germany. The ships are at a standstill and the rescue of people from villages and towns is beginning. A hospital in Dillenburg has in the meantime been evacuated. The high water level will undoubtedly reach the Netherlands in the next few days. The 'space for the river' has not yet been found. It has in people's minds and on paper, but in practice not by a long chalk. The key planning decision has been made by the government, and local authorities and business groups, as well as third sector partners, have held many meetings. The result comprises many 'win-win-situations': more space for the river also means room for a yacht marina, opportunities for gravel and sand extraction, the provision of a floodplain and the establishment of new nature reserves.

But buildings have to be removed, at Elst, for example, to give the River Waal more room at Nijmegen and construct new dykes here and there. These will not need to be as high as in the original plans, since due to the widening of the winterbed level of the river, and the creation of new arms to the river (parallel drainage channels) and emergency flooding areas, the technocratic approach which prevailed for around one-and-a-half centuries has lost ground. [. . .]

The shock really came in 1993 and 1995 when there was talk of the real danger of flooding. The Netherlands was in turmoil. All the trust that had been placed in the tried and tested technocratic approach adopted by the Ministry of Waterways and Public Works and the water boards came under attack. The evacuation plans that had been implemented were considered with hindsight to have probably been unnecessary, but the reality was that the water was splashing against the walls of the dykes. The pictures of endless stretches of water, the army and civilians with sandbags, of important men with reassuring texts, evoked powerful memories – now in colour – of the flood disaster of 1953.

Index

accents 141–2
acronyms 32, 73, 92–3
apostrophes 140–1, 171, 176
approaches to translation 1–3
art and art institutions 112–14

Belgium: art and art institutions in 112–13, 123–4, 128–9; energy and the environment in 150–3; fashion and design in 131–3, 147–9; finance and economics of 78–9, 89–91; languages in 24–7, 45; societal/cultural change in 59–60, 71–6, and federalisation of 96; *see also* Brussels; *see also* translating: place names
Brussels 79, 89–91, 93–4, 113, 128, 132–3, 150; bilingual 25, 26, 31; *see also* translating: place names

commas 139–40
Common European Framework of Reference for Languages 3
complex sentences 12–13, 21, 29, 84, 108–9, 146–7, 155–6
compound adjectives 88–9
conjunctions 157–62
cultural practices 27
currencies 87–8
decimals, dots and commas 86–8
design and fashion 131–3
dictionaries 6, 179; monolingual Dutch 12, 28, 54, 104; translation 12, 20, 28, 116; using 28, 55, 100, 165; *see also* resources for translation
direct speech 142–3

Dutch language area 24, 34–5, 40–2, 49, 181–2
Dutch Language Union *see* Nederlandse Taalunie

employment 59–60
energy and the environment 150–5
'er' 50–2, 176
'er'-constructions 29, 37, 48, 109, 127
European Commission 1, 16, 17
Expertisecentrum Literair Vertalen 1, 180

fashion and design 131–3
finance and economics 78–9, 89–91
formal register 13, 39, 65, 75, 85, 93, 115, 118, 124, 128, 137, 147, 156

gender in translation 59–60; gender-neutral approach 74, 134–5, 137
grammars 6, 24, 179–80; use of 12, 28, 38, 50, 109, 144; reference grammars *see* resources

idiomatic expressions 37, 47, 70–1, 83–4, 136–7, 145–7, 166, 176
indefinite pronouns 65, 66–71, 177
infinitive constructions 109, 118, 122
Interactive Terminology for Europe database (IATE) 27, 32–3, 36–7, 180; using 20, 100

literature 5–6, 13–14, 43–55, 147, 166
long sentences 38–9, 101–2

maritime trade 79–80, 82–3, 85
'*men*' 66–71
migration 61–4

names of organisations 26, 31, 34, 60, 132, 173
Nederlandse Taalunie (NTU) 1, 24, 32, 34, 35–6, 38, 40
Netherlands, the: art and art institutions in 112–14; energy, engineering and the environment in 150–5, 162–5, 166–8, 186;

fashion and design in 131–3; finance and economics of 78–9; literary tradition of 43; maritime sector in 94–5; migration and 61–4, 66, 183; seaports in 79–80, 82–3, 85; societal/cultural change in 59–60, 96–8; *see also* new approaches to translation; *see also* translating: names of organisations, personal names, place names
neutral register 49, 56, 109
numbers 64, 86–8

omissions 174

particles 28, 48, 117–18
passive constructions 38–9, 51, 68–9, 119–22, 177
percentages 86–7
personal names 19, 32, 107, 118, 172–3
place names 31–34, 124, 144, 173–4
punctuation in translation 138; accents 141–2; apostrophes 140–1, 171, 176; commas 139–40; compound adjectives 88–9; currencies 87–8; decimals, dots and commas 86–8; direct speech 142–3

register 5; formal 13, 39, 65, 75, 85, 93, 115, 118, 124, 128, 137, 147, 156; in revision 170–71; mixing of 49, 102; neutral 49, 56, 109; web 21; *see also* punctuation in translation; *see also* translating
resources for translation 6, 24, 179–80; other internet-based 8, 16, 43, 63, 154, *see also* IATE; maps 6, 8
revising a translation 6, 14, 30, 40, 144, 169; of literature 47; parameters for 170
revision regarding: apostrophes 171; names 172–3; place names 173; omissions 174; spelling of homonyms 172

separable verbs 101–2, 103–5, 109, 178
style 5, 21, 30, 39–40, 47–9, 115, 124, 137; web 16; *see also* register

target audience 1–2, 6; assessment of 11, 14, 16, 19, 27, 30, 63, 73–5, 99–100, 102, 107, 128; *see also* translation orientation
tourism texts 8, 33, 112–130
translating: acronyms 32, 73, 92–3; cultural practices 27; currencies 87–8; for websites 6, 8, 15–17; idiomatic expressions 37, 47, 70–1, 83–4, 136–7, 145–7, 166, 176; literature 5–6, 13–14, 43–55, 147, 166; names of organisations 26, 31, 34, 60, 132, 173; numbers 64, 86–8; percentages 86–7; personal names 19, 32, 107, 118,172–3; place names 31–34, 124, 144, 173–4; register 51, 62, 67, 100, 165–6, 179; tourism texts 8, 33, 112–130
translation of: complex sentences 12–13, 21, 29, 84, 108–9, 146–7, 155–6; '*er*' 50–2, 176; '*er*'-constructions 29, 37, 48, 109, 127; indefinite pronouns 65, 66–71, 177; infinitive constructions 109, 118, 122; long sentences 38–9, 101–2; '*men*' *see* translation of: indefinite pronouns; particles 28, 48, 117–18; passive constructions 38–9, 51, 68–9, 119–22, 177; separable verbs 101–2, 103–5, 109, 178
translation orientation 14, 36, 40, 81–2; towards target audience 27, 62, 65, 135, 137, 164–5; dependent on translation brief 47, 54, 73, 107, 115–16, 135, 145, 154; *see also* websites
troubleshooting and revising 169–75

websites 6, 8, 15–17

eBooks
from Taylor & Francis

Helping you to choose the right eBooks for your Library

Add to your library's digital collection today with Taylor & Francis eBooks. We have over 50,000 eBooks in the Humanities, Social Sciences, Behavioural Sciences, Built Environment and Law, from leading imprints, including Routledge, Focal Press and Psychology Press.

Choose from a range of subject packages or create your own!

Benefits for you
- Free MARC records
- COUNTER-compliant usage statistics
- Flexible purchase and pricing options
- 70% approx of our eBooks are now DRM-free.

Benefits for your user
- Off-site, anytime access via Athens or referring URL
- Print or copy pages or chapters
- Full content search
- Bookmark, highlight and annotate text
- Access to thousands of pages of quality research at the click of a button.

ORDER YOUR FREE INSTITUTIONAL TRIAL TODAY

Free Trials Available

We offer free trials to qualifying academic, corporate and government customers.

eCollections

Choose from 20 different subject eCollections, including:
- Asian Studies
- Economics
- Health Studies
- Law
- Middle East Studies

eFocus

We have 16 cutting-edge interdisciplinary collections, including:
- Development Studies
- The Environment
- Islam
- Korea
- Urban Studies

For more information, pricing enquiries or to order a free trial, please contact your local sales team:

UK/Rest of World: **online.sales@tandf.co.uk**
USA/Canada/Latin America: **e-reference@taylorandfrancis.com**
East/Southeast Asia: **martin.jack@tandf.com.sg**
India: **journalsales@tandfindia.com**

www.tandfebooks.com